BORIS GODUNOF

PUBLISHED ON THE FUND ESTABLISHED
IN MEMORY OF GANSON GOODYEAR DEPEW

BORIS GODUNOF

BY STEPHEN GRAHAM

WITH A PREFACE BY GEORGE VERNADSKY

RESEARCH ASSOCIATE IN HISTORY IN YALE UNIVERSITY

1933

NEW HAVEN · YALE UNIVERSITY PRESS

Copyright 1933 by Yale University Press

Printed in the United States of America

All rights reserved. This book may not be reproduced, in whole or in part, in any form (except by reviewers for the public press), without written permission from the publishers.

PREFACE

THE first American appearance of Boris Godunof off the operatic stage is to be welcomed. Stephen Graham has chosen an enigmatical character for the subject of his biography, and one also that has been too long concealed from readers other than Russians. He is a sympathetic and skilful chronicler. Whether or not the "true" Boris emerges from these pages would have to be decided not by historians but by metaphysicians. Even an autobiography sometimes produces a portrait different from those of other observers who in their turn have prejudices of their own. Mr. Graham has often been confronted with conflicting and sometimes nebulous evidence. In such cases no forthright portrait could be entirely accepted without reservations. For example, there is the question of Boris' illiteracy. There are left a few samples of Boris' signature and some of the contemporary statements infer that he was illiterate. Mr. Graham takes this view. On the other hand, an eminent Russian historian, the late Professor Platonof, took the view that what Boris' contemporaries meant was that he was not a reader of books and was not acquainted with theological literature.

In any event, the sixteenth century in Russia was a confused time. The social organization was somewhat shapeless. To begin with, there were no closed castes in Russia, nor was there a definite boundary between the nobles and the common people. All strata of society were overshadowed by the authority of the Moscow

Grand Dukes, and this was more than ever true after Ivan the Terrible was formally crowned Tsar in 1547. Under Ivan's rule, descendants of those who had been feudal rulers (princes) and of those who had been their "servitors" (boyars) alike became "servitors" of the Tsar. Men outside of these circles might also be taken into the royal service but they had to start in the lower ranks.

A peculiar co-ordination was gradually established between the desire of the old families to keep their prominence and the tendency of royal service to subordinate everyone to the Tsar. This was the so-called *miestnichestvo* system, that is, the principle of co-ordination between the place (*miesto*) of a man in the Moscow social register and the place of the office to which he was about to be appointed in the royal service. If, for example, Prince A had been a commander-in-chief of a Moscow army, and Prince B his subordinate, Prince A's eldest son would not accept an appointment under the command of any of Prince B's sons. But Prince A's fourth or fifth son would perhaps not mind accepting such a position under the eldest son of Prince B, provided that the families A and B were socially on about the same level. However, none of Prince A's family would accept a command under a member of, let us say, Prince Z's family. The *miestnichestvo* system was a check on the absolute power of the Moscow Tsar. The Tsar could execute a man but could not induce him to accept a position that would impugn his family honor. A vivid reconstruction of these *miestnichestvo* arguments among the boyars has been given by Count Alexey Tolstoy in the first act of his tragedy, *The Death of Ivan the Terrible*.

In the same way the Tsar was then limited as to his power of promotion. Ivan could appoint a man boyar, that is, a member of the Royal Council (Duma), but on the other hand up to the eighteenth century he could not invest a man with the title of prince. This was strictly hereditary. The *Opritchina* of Ivan the Terrible, which Mr. Graham pictured in his previous book, was an attempt of Ivan to break the *miestnichestvo* system. But the system proved stronger than the Tsar.

Gradually, three strata were established among the prominent families in Moscow society. First, there were the descendants of the senior branches of the feudal princely families; second, the descendants of the old Muscovite boyars; third, the junior branches of princely families and the new boyar families. It was to the second group in the social hierarchy that the Godunof family belonged, together with others like the Zakharins, who became better known under the name of Romanof. In 1578 Boris won a *miestnichestvo* case against a certain prince on the ground that his grandfather had held a higher office than the grandfather of the prince.

The story of Boris and the Pretender Dimitry is as fantastic as the social background is complicated. Mr. Graham has presented both these personages and their time in their vigor and paradox.

GEORGE VERNADSKY.

New Haven, Connecticut
  August 15, 1933

CONTENTS

	Preface by George Vernadsky	vii
I.	The Rise of Boris	1
II.	The Council of Five	17
III.	The Polish Armistice	31
IV.	The Queen of Livonia	37
V.	The Institution of the Patriarchate	47
VI.	Peace with Poland and Sweden	54
VII.	The Murder of the Tsarevitch Dimitry	60
VIII.	Vasilly Shuisky	65
IX.	The Moslem at the Gates	75
X.	Power and Influence	85
XI.	Persia Asks for Friendship	94
XII.	The Death of Fedor	104
XIII.	Interregnum	109
XIV.	Boris Is Crowned Tsar	119
XV.	The New Era	124
XVI.	The Betrothal of Xenia	130
XVII.	The Famine of 1601–1602	145
XVIII.	Bielsky Loses His Beard	152
XIX.	The Dispersal of the Romanofs	161
XX.	First Insurrection	168
XXI.	Dimitry Rises from the Dead	175
XXII.	Conversion to Rome	183
XXIII.	The Mother of Dimitry	199
XXIV.	The Standard of Revolt	206
XXV.	The Patriarch Pronounces Anathema	217
XXVI.	Civil War	225
XXVII.	Twelfth Hour of the Night	239
XXVIII.	Death of Boris Godunof	244
XXIX.	The Destruction of the Godunofs	252
XXX.	Dimitry Crowned, Married, Murdered	261
	Appendix	279
	Bibliographical Notes	281
	Index	285

ILLUSTRATIONS

Moscow in the Sixteenth Century . .	*End papers*
Boris Godunof	*Frontispiece*
Stephen Batory, King of Poland . . .	32
The Patriarch Job	110
Fedor Romanof, Father Philaret, afterward Patriarch of Russia	166
The Dimitry, by some supposed to be the forsworn monk Grishka Otrepief . . .	176
Marina Mniszech	186
Sigizmund III, King of Poland	192
Sir Thomas Smith, ambassador of James I to the court of Boris Godunof	218

BORIS GODUNOF

I.

THE RISE OF BORIS

BORIS GODUNOF was thirty-three years of age at the death of Ivan the Terrible, handsome, sagacious, profoundly ambitious. He had been made boyar; his sister had married the heir to the throne; he had been nominated by the dying Tsar one of a Council of State to safeguard the throne. The way of a usurper was clear before him and all the power of Russia within his grasp.

He had been the most lasting favourite of Ivan the Terrible and survived fifteen years of intimacy without having been in danger of execution or of being put to the question. The worst that befell him was a blow on the head when he intervened between father and son. One must surmise a man of parts, wary, circumspect. He was playing chess with Ivan when the latter fell dead—a chess player in life, not a characteristic, ebullient, impulsive Russian, but then not an aristocrat nor a fighting man, a man of the people, of Tartar extraction, wily, subservient, cool-headed.

What had seemed the surest way to gain Ivan's favour had been to condone his cruelty, share his bloodthirstiness, take pleasure in the torture-shows, ape the ferocity of the master. Most of those who ventured to reprove the Tsar, came, like the Metropolitan Philip, to a violent end. Yet on the other hand most of the favourites and cronies of the Tsar's table, the men who bettered his example in vice and cruelty, did not escape a dreadful death at their master's hands.

Those who watch the spectacle of fearful suffering in a fellow man and gloat over it are always in some danger from malignant Fate. Ivan liked to have onlookers for his great torture scenes and *autos da fé*, his favourites in the first rows, the boyars and gentry in the second rows, the common people behind them. He was as watchful of the demeanour of his subjects as of the torments his executioners were inflicting. His favourites, taunting the victims and yelling curses at them, pleased him. Their behaviour was what he required. And yet it must have occurred to him cynically that certain of those who were exulting in the show would be themselves quite interesting, roasting over a slow fire. Or it occurred to him that some recompense might be made to God by applying to them the test of the Golden Rule to see whether they liked having done to them what they enjoyed seeing done to others. For the Tsar remained in a sense religious, though barbarous. In his consciousness he was too near to God to be afflicted constantly by a sense of sin. God had wronged the Tsar by taking from him his beloved consort Anastasia. He was not a God of justice: Ivan accepted that. God visited the sins of the unjust upon the just: Ivan accepted that also. Ivan the pious and saintly put God to the torture by plunging into a life of vice and hideous sin. But neither lightning nor plague was sent to make him pay for his apostasy. Then he allowed his subjects to barter their eternal salvation for a glance of favour from himself. But relenting toward God in certain moods he determined to send not a few of his servants to hell betimes.

Boris Godunof took a middle path. He did not rebuke the Tsar like Philip, nor did he encourage the Tsar's cruelty like Viasemsky. At the time when the adolescents of Russia were given the power to ride roughshod over their fathers and their elders the young Boris kept his hands unstained by blood. A stripling at court, he caught the Tsar's eye because he was handsome. Educated and gifted in conversation, he caught also the Tsar's ear. But although he was young he did not moralise about the dreadful things happening in Russia. He held himself dispassionate and aloof. It could not be said that he appeared disgusted by the spectacle of torture, nor did he take pleasure in it, but looked on much as some king of Siam might at a football match. He began at once to tread the borderland between the Tsar's two moods.

Boris Godunof was born in or about the year 1550. He is supposed to have been descended from a certain Tartar prince who came to serve the Russian Prince Ivan Kalita two centuries before. Hence Shuisky's speech in Pushkin's drama:

"He'll jump the throne. Boris is not so timid.
But what an honour for us and for all Russia!
Yesterday's slave, Tartar, son-in-law of Maliuta,
Son-in-law of the executioner, in soul an executioner,
Will seize the diadem and mantle of Monomakh.
. . ."

But actually it could hardly be said that the family of Godunof had emerged from serfdom. They prided themselves for generations on having been free servants of the Grand Dukes of Moscow. They belonged to that meagre class which provided the executive for a turbulent military state. They were subservient without being servile, bred to listen and not gainsay, to avoid the axe and the thumbscrew and yet to get their own way, fulfilling the function of those who cannot afford to have honour and risk life and position for principle.

Ivan, owing to the ill-treatment he received in his childhood at the hands of bearded men, the princes and boyars of the realm, had an undying prejudice against older men. The inauguration of the *Opritchina* was the handing over of the older people to the children for revenge. The Tsar's minions were lads and he was surrounded at his court with young men. A hobbledehoy of fifteen or sixteen might well have responsibilities equal to those of a minister of state. Then the Tsar was a talker. He was no hunter and despite his wars he was no soldier. He had an interest in dialectics and a gift for flowery speech, not to say rodomontade; he must have a listener. Despite his cruelty and distrust he was not aloof. He could be social, engaging, witty. He had a way of engaging unlikely people in converse. Thus it was that the young Boris found favour. The Tsar found a lad in whose company he could show off, the best recipient of his thoughts since he had had Alexey Adashef.

The young Boris could neither read nor write. It was a disturbed time for youth. Schooling was thought of by few parents, for Ivan had set the children against the fathers. Few occupied themselves with teaching. Boys of twelve boasted of murders; boys of fourteen boasted of rapes. Boris had no taste for murders or rape and yet had not learned his letters. It is unlikely that he learned to do more than sign his name and during his whole life he never read a book. Yet Ivan for his time was a learned man. He had probably read all the hand-written tomes available in Russian and Church Slavonic. It is curious that the erudition of the Tsar found a counterpart in the natural wit and intelligence of Boris Godunof. Ivan had found a handsome youth who was so far out of fashion as to dislike bloodshed, who had not yet drunk and was virginal in his relationship toward women, but was possessed of a certain natural genius for listening and for conversation.

The pure young man was brought to the table of the roisterers and introduced to the prime favourite, Maliuta Skuratof, he who in anticipation of the Tsar's desire had murdered the Metropolitan Philip in his cell at Tver. What the wine bibbers and debauchees thought of Boris is not recorded, but the probability is that Boris said the right thing to each of them and though he could not attack the drink and viands as heroically, he made himself the friend of favourites who in any case could not have seen in him a person to be feared.

Skuratof had endeared himself to the Tsar by murdering the holy Metropolitan Philip, a man who was obviously a saint and sure of an exalted position in heaven. It was no small merit on Maliuta's part to have taken upon himself eternal damnation for the sake of the Tsar. This young Boris, with the looks and wisdom and discourse of a St. John, was the antithesis of Skuratof, and yet the two somehow became friends.

It is in the realm of surmise, which is always risky for the biographer, but it would seem that Boris' advice was asked regarding Ivan's matrimonial tangle. But Boris first comes to the notice of the chronicler about the time when the Tsar and the Tsarevitch Ivan jointly chose for themselves wives from the daughters of commoners. The Tsar, in a benevolent mood, said that a bride must be found for Boris also, and a daughter of Maliuta Skuratof was given him. The alliance was as strong a one as could have been found at the time, and meant a continuance of his influence at court as long as the influence of Skuratof endured. There was not likely to be an immediate quarrel with the favourites. Boris had a surer foothold and could work to make a much greater alliance, and that was of his sister Irene to the Tsar's second son Fedor. It must remain uncertain at what stage in a usurper's career he meets the witches on the heath and they discover to him his secret mind, and so we cannot say whether at this early date of his marriage—he was only twenty—he was consciously feeling his way toward the highest position in the state. But Destiny, even if not implicit in the stars or in the runes of the palm of the hand, is written in the consciousness, and what a man has the supreme capacity to do in his maturity germinates through his early years.

When the Tsar's third wife died a fortnight after the wedding, he at once bethought him of a fourth, although it is contrary to the law of the Orthodox Church for a man to marry for the fourth time. He circumvented the authority of the Church and it was Boris Godunof who advised the way in which he might obtain indulgence. Another favourite in the same age, Thomas Cromwell, had risen to power by giving the desired advice about a new marriage and a difference with Mother Church.

It was a propitious moment for the rise of a new favourite in the reign of Ivan the Terrible. Long-suffering God had at last seemed to answer the Tsar's infamous behaviour and had allowed holy Moscow to be burned to the last stick by the Moslem. Ivan acknowledged that the Khan of Tartary was the instrument of God's anger. If not repentant, he was at least impressed. The Almighty had undoubtedly taken notice of Ivan's devilry. It occurred to the monarch, as in fact it did repeatedly throughout his reign, that it might be better to renounce the throne and all earthly vanities and become a saint instead. But the flesh was weak. He postponed and kept postponing the day of renunciation. He continued with dual nature to reign over Russia, making the sign of the cross with the right hand and torturing with the left, blessing with one and cursing with the other. But with the cross-signing hand he advanced Boris Godunof.

Another circumstance caused a further modification in the Tsar's behaviour. He wished to be elected King of Poland, but the dread of his name was a great obstacle to obtaining the suffrage of the Polish people. The Tsar indignantly repudiated the stories that were current abroad. He believed that his repute as a conqueror in the field and as a strong character whom everyone in his realm obeyed should outweigh all scandals in the foreign mind. But at the same time he thought it politic, and Boris advised him to that end, that he put on a milder mien and thus try to improve his moral standing as a candidate for the throne. Upon the suggestion of Boris Godunof, he abolished his murderous bodyguard, the *Opritchina*, who, many thousand strong, had ravished the country in his name for nigh on seven years. And the titled gentry whose functions the *Opritchina* had usurped were brought back to power at court. Obviously, the proud aristocracy of Poland would not vote for a man who seemed to have a lasting feud with the chief lords of his lands.

When, in 1572, Sigizmund Augustus, King of Poland, died, the subject of the election of a new king was rife in Moscow. It is testimony to the megalomania of Ivan that he thought he stood a fair chance in a ballot. The Tsar's brain was rank with over-eating, over-drinking, and nervous excess. The young blood and cool head of Boris Godunof must normally have produced an opinion greatly at variance with that of Ivan. But he was not such a fool as to advise his master to banish the foolish dream from his mind. On the contrary, he would use the dream for his own ends. The *Opritchina*, in whose gross doings he had no part or lot, he would have abolished as a step toward rehabilitating Ivan's name in Europe. The Tsar had in any case become a little tired of the men with the masks and brooms. He consented to get rid of them. The idea seemed a stroke of genius. He pathetically believed that it would at once convince the Poles that he was the "father of his people." The titled gentry were allowed to come back and petition to resume their positions at the Tsar's festal board where he sat down to dinner several hundred strong. There would be a clash between military and feudal rank, for many men had risen to power and position in the new Russian army. Boris Godunof became in practice the arbiter as to precedence at court, a position which yielded increasing power into his hands.

The long and bloody struggle for place and precedence at Ivan's court commenced. Boris, quiet, tactful, astute, not himself of noble birth, but something between a court usher and a prime minister, was clever enough to avoid picking quarrels on his own account. He acted always in the dreaded monarch's name with the menace of torture or execution just beyond his shadow. He deferred angry petitioners to the Tsar's personal judgment of their claims, and that generally silenced them. He stage-managed his potential enemies into fighting one another or incurring the Tsar's murderous wrath. And yet he successfully avoided attracting great enmity to himself. The boyars and princes and generals must have thought of him merely as a creature of the Tsar, a nobody, neither a soldier nor a gentleman, a runner and go-between. For he had not the position which the upstart Alexey Adashef had held. Adashef had been practically chancellor of the realm. Boris was merely the Tsar's secular adviser, one of the queer outsiders and young men of no family he chose to converse with in preference to his peers of noble blood. He would pass.

Eight years of court intrigue dragged on. Boris did not fall out of favour. He became in fact the chief intimate of the Tsar and of the Tsarevitch Ivan. The monarch grew older and feebler. Boris, if his influence was to continue, must remain as close a friend of the heir as he was of the Tsar. Hence in the disputes which occurred at times between father and son we find Boris mildly espousing the cause of the son. This did cause the Tsar's displeasure, and yet in a subtle way also his esteem. He never forgot for long that his son was flesh of his flesh, and that one who stood up for his heir was a friend of the dynasty and of himself. Even through petty quarrels Boris grew closer to the throne, as if almost Ivan had adopted him as a third son. He was free to enter all palace doors at any time, and his presence with the Tsar's consorts, mistresses, or children was never misconstrued. It is likely that the Tsar consulted him greatly concerning his women, and the needs of the flesh. The chaste have often an attraction for the unchaste, and sexual perverts have often an obscene desire to discuss their incontinency with ascetics. That is not to say that Boris was a saint. He was merely content with his wife and his ambition had crowded out the desires of the flesh. Neither is it to be thought that he reproved Ivan. On the contrary, he condoned uxoriousness and adultery, and the Tsar, when he had found some new luscious morsel of femininity, brought the news to his favourite, that they might share the pleasure of the idea of taking her to bed.

Thus it was when Ivan picked his seventh wife, Marya Nagy. It was not merely a matter of mutual congratulation. The Tsar loved double and treble weddings and Boris had advanced so far in intimacy that he told Fedor, his second son, to marry Boris' sister. They would have the two weddings at the same time.

Such an alliance with the royal blood was *ipso facto* ennobling to Boris, but that the latter should not be wanting, Ivan took the opportunity to make him a boyar.

The feeble-minded Fedor was no match physically for Irina Godunof; he was a weakling without likelihood of issue, but that did not weigh in the balance with the catastrophic honour of being united to the Tsar's house.

The double marriage of September, 1580, at Ivan's pleasaunce of Alexandrov, is a key event in this history. The mysteries of Fate met thereat. The one marriage raised Boris near the level of the throne, made it possible for him to foresee a chance of his becoming one day Tsar. But the other marriage was to produce a third son for Ivan the Terrible, the Dimitry, who, though seemingly murdered by order of Boris in 1591, must rise again and bring ruin upon Boris Godunof and all his family.

It must be said, however, that at the time of the double wedding there was not any obvious probability of the untimely death of Ivan Ivanovitch, the vigorous elder brother of the puny Fedor. The Tsarevitch Ivan possessed robust health and barring accident must have survived his father. And even should Ivan the heir die prematurely, it was not thought that Fedor was fit to succeed him. "Better suited to be a monastery bell-ringer than to be Tsar," was his father's comment on him. But the sagacious Boris must have reflected even then, that as chance offered, after the decease of Ivan and his elder son, he would be able to step into the place for which Fedor was so manifestly unfitted. Boris was even in 1580 "the man behind the throne."

Fate, perhaps aided by Boris himself, was to play into his hands. Next year, in 1581, the Tsar murdered his son and heir. It was the result of one of those altercations which had taken place frequently between father and son in the later years of the Tsar's rule. What part Boris Godunof had in the conversation is unknown, but the fact that he was present is suggestive. It must have occurred to him that the chief danger in which the heir stood was from the mad impulsive choler of his father, who did not brook contradiction. The Tsarevitch was probably the only person who crossed the Tsar with impunity. It was far from Boris to permit himself the liberties to which the Tsarevitch was privileged. One blow from the Tsar's steel-pointed staff was enough to snatch away the life of the person struck. Ivan, the son, was not prudent. His father would never murder him in cold blood, but in a moment of sudden ungovernable rage he might strike down anyone, even the heir.

That Boris Godunof was entirely silent during the altercation between father and son is improbable. Eventually, when it was too late, he interposed to shield the Tsarevitch from the rain of blows from Ivan's staff. But it had been a better rôle to intervene in the conversation betimes, to pour oil on troubled waters. A man of his coolness, tact, sagacity cannot be entirely exonerated. And it was to his advantage that the Tsarevitch Ivan should die, making way for the heir presumptive Fedor, now the brother-in-law of Boris.

However, at the actual moment of the murderous attack of Ivan upon his son it was impossible for Boris

Godunof to remain a passive spectator. The Tsar would not have forgiven that. Boris would have lost his head for not preventing the murder. On the other hand, in placing himself between the Tsarevitch and the inflamed Tsar he risked being killed there and then. Actually he was wounded and that was the best that could have happened for Boris Godunof's career. He was struck down trying to shelter the beloved heir.

But Boris Godunof had interposed too late. The Tsarevitch was dying and all the murderous father's rage was changed instantly to calamitous grief. For the time, Boris Godunof, if in disgrace, was forgotten. The terror of the Terrible had turned upon itself and destroyed the dynasty.

Boris was in disgrace, but those were mistaken who thought the disgrace would be lasting. Ivan had no grievance against his dead son. His repentance for his dire act was profound. He was plunged in melancholia. In his dreams he sought his slaughtered child. He became a somnambulist and went seeking the dead Tsarevitch through the palace halls. All that could be said about Boris Godunof was that he had tried to stop Ivan and that he had himself been wounded trying to save the Tsar from himself. It was not long before Ivan was solicitous regarding Boris' health, ready to reinstate him, even to give him the place left empty by the murdered heir.

Ivan pronounced Fedor unfit to succeed to the throne and seemed voluntarily to propose the extinction of his dynasty. He asked the Council of Boyars to search their hearts and confer among themselves as to which man among them was best fitted to govern Russia in the case of his death or his renunciation of the throne for monastic retreat. They must elect the best man in Russia to be Tsar in his place. This revolutionary idea of election instead of inheritance remained a seed in Godunof's intelligence. At a later date he did use the expedient of election to obtain the throne. It seems probable that in 1582 the only man the boyars would have dared to nominate was Boris Godunof and that at the moment it was also Boris whom the Tsar had in his mind. But the proposal was too dangerous. The Tsar's psychology was inscrutable. He was capable of turning upon the nominee as the most dangerous man in his realm, a potential revolutionary and usurper, and having him tormented to death in ribald triumph. Neither Boris Godunof nor anyone else would risk a nomination.

In any case the position of Boris Godunof was sufficiently favourable without any premature nomination to the throne. In the event of Ivan's death he could reckon confidently upon becoming Regent. That was enough for his cautious calculating nature. He would mount step by step and jump over none in his haste to the top of affairs.

The Tsar was told that he was irreplaceable and that he must continue to be the father of his country, putting the well-being of Russia before the well-being of his soul. And the boyars were so attached to himself and his house that they could not contemplate with equanimity the setting aside of Fedor. The Tsar was still capable of being flattered and he resigned himself to carry on his nefarious rule for the good of mankind, and he appeared to be touched by the love for his house and relented toward Fedor. It should be as the lords wished. Fedor should be accounted the heir to the throne. But for the good of Russia he would appoint a committee of safety to take over when he died, to advise Fedor and to protect him.

This appointment Ivan made simply by word of mouth. Neither the Church nor the boyars as a whole had any part in the transaction. It was not ratified by them, not confirmed in writing by the monarch, not solemnised by oath. On a previous occasion when binding the boyars to protect and support the heir Ivan had called upon each to swear "on the Cross," but this was not repeated. The Tsar was senilely preoccupied with the idea of procuring an English bride and other more important matters lapsed. Nevertheless the arrangement had some binding quality, for the five chosen were the most important men at court.

The most famous of the five was Prince Ivan Shuisky, the heroic defender of Pskof, the man who had checked the victorious march of Stephen of Poland. He was the head of a powerful family of lineage second only to that of the Tsar. After Shuisky, Prince Ivan Mstislavsky was at the time the most famous, also a great soldier and of high lineage. Yurief, the Tsar's uncle was an old boyar, popular and reputed wise. Bogdan Bielsky was a drinking companion and great favourite of Ivan the Terrible. He was not a noble but had been a leading spirit in the Tsar's infamous bodyguard, the *Opritchina*. But of the five, Boris Godunof was by far the strongest, both in talents and in position at court.

The Tsar was a broken man after the death of his eldest son, and it must have been evident that his days were numbered. But dynastic fortune smiled on him capriciously for on top of the great disaster his seventh wife Marya Nagy bore him another son and his hope began to be centred upon the future of the infant, Dimitry. But he did not see in Boris Godunof an enemy of his new progeny. He was as intimate with Boris during his last months as he had been with the Tsarevitch Ivan. Even at the moment of his death he was with Boris. He was playing chess with him. In life he had been playing chess with him for some time. But Boris had been playing the deeper game.

II.

THE COUNCIL OF FIVE

FEDOR, kindhearted, pious, puny, stupid, was crowned Tsar with all the pomp and ceremony attendant upon a Russian coronation. The Council of Five gave orders to the Russian people to pray for the soul of the departed Ivan and for the long life of his son, Fedor. As a sign of the inauguration of a happier rule many executioners and adepts of the torture chamber were dismissed from their positions and the more notorious banished or sent to prison. The wizards from the North who had predicted the death of Ivan and were to have been burned at the stake had the prophecy remained unfulfilled were allowed to go their own ways in freedom. The English ambassador, Sir James Bowes, who had been under arrest, was sent back to Queen Elizabeth with a gift of inferior sables. Fedor meekly assented to all that the five official "uncles" advised.

Boris Godunof comported himself with dignity but without exalted pride. He was not the haughty upstart bursting to use his power, but the benign counsellor of Fedor whom he influenced more through Irina than in direct converse. There is no reason to imagine that Boris' love of his sister was feigned. But Irina's interest was his interest and interest helped Nature to keep brother and sister in the fondest intimacy. Both were devoted to the helpless Fedor.

It was important to the career of Boris that he do the

right thing at the right time and the right thing first. It seemed to him most prudent to have Marya Nagy, the widow of Ivan the Terrible, together with her infant son, Dimitry, and the more ambitious of her kindred, removed at once from the immediate scene of action. Of the Council of Five, the contumacious Bogdan Bielsky alone objected to the banishment of Marya and her child. He said that Ivan the Terrible had bequeathed to him the care and protection of Marya and Dimitry. He said the banishment was contrary to Ivan's will. Having been a greatly indulged favourite of Ivan he was accustomed to think only of himself and the Tsar. It was a shock to him to see others disposing of the liberty of the Tsar's widow. He wished Fedor would be as terrible as his father had been. He had himself been one of the most ruthless of the *Opritchina* and he believed the greatest safeguard for the Tsar Fedor would be for him to resurrect and re-establish that wild bodyguard, governing the country with their aid but without the co-operation of the boyars. He plied the dull Tsar with this idea and according to one witness* had even the foolhardiness to close the Kremlin gates and attempt a *coup d'état*.

Bielsky was presumptuous and over-estimated his own strength and following. It is possible he was buoyed up by a false hope of support from Boris Godunof. Boris had taken care not to thwart him during Ivan's reign and with infinite tact flattered him after Ivan's death, letting him assume that his position at court was at least as strong as it had been while he was

* L. Sapieha, the Lithuanian envoy.

assured of Ivan's favour. The contumacy of Bielsky was therefore more menacing to Ivan Mstislavsky, Ivan Shuisky and Yurief than to Boris Godunof. But although Bielsky was opposed to the banishment of Marya Nagy and the infant Dimitry, there is no reason to believe that he wished to set aside Fedor in favour of Dimitry with himself as Regent.

The other four had their way. Dimitry, with mother, kindred and adherents, was arrested and banished to the city of Uglitch. Fedor was loath to agree because he loved his baby step-brother as it had been his own child, and it is said he wept copiously when he kissed him good-bye, but Irina had said there was danger of faction and murder, and the child must go.

The arrest and banishment were achieved without much commotion or disturbance. Marya was submissive; her kindred had no great influence or following. The banishment might seem cruel but it was not accompanied by acts of unnecessary violence. The ex-Tsaritsa was placed in honourable exile at Uglitch, held court there and was allowed to live in semi-royal grandeur.

But the moment was dangerous for Godunof. Had he been over subtle in feigning friendship for Bielsky? Shuisky saw in it an opportunity to compromise him and possibly obtain his death or banishment. The rumour was spread abroad that Bielsky had poisoned Ivan the Terrible and was plotting to murder Fedor and the leading boyars in order to place his friend and confidant Boris on the throne. That he would have done all these things for Boris' sake is palpably absurd. Possibly few believed that Boris was privy to such a plot, but the rage against Bielsky was so great that any story was good enough to use against him. Insurrection flared up like a dry forest fire. Thousands of armed men led by aristocrats rose against Bielsky and were reinforced in the city of Moscow itself by the offscourings of the population. There was a constant element in the city, called "rabble" by the historians, always ready to throw themselves into any disturbance where there was a chance of rapine and pillage. It is remarkable that in this century of condign mass punishment there was always in Moscow a revolutionary mob, an uncowed proletarian element ready to lend hand and voice to an assault upon the Kremlin as occasion offered.

For three days there was civil war in Moscow. The Kremlin was besieged. Cannon from the market place of the Kitai-gorod fired their bolts among the palaces and cathedrals. It was a strange way to try to save Tsar Fedor from the supposed conspirators. The Tsar did not recognise the besiegers as his friends but sent Mstislavsky and others out to them to arrange terms of peace. It was fortunate for Boris Godunof that the voices crying for the head of Bielsky greatly outnumbered those crying for his. The besieged were so close to the besiegers that it was easy to know the answer to Mstislavsky—the one vociferated name "Bielsky!" There was consternation within the citadel. Only one person was in a good humour, the fat pudgy little Fedor with his unfading silly smile. Godunof was grave. As for Bielsky, he fled to the Tsar's bedroom and hid under the bedclothes, pretending to be the Tsar, prostrated by fear and hoping desperately that if his enemies broke in they might be afraid to pull the sheet from his head. But it was not Godunof's intention that Bielsky should be torn to bits by the mob, nor even that he should be publicly executed to appease the wrath of the insurrectionaries. In the popular mind, he, Godunof, was privy to the conspiracy. A capital sentence upon Bielsky might seem equivalent to pronouncing them both guilty and lead to a demand for the punishment of himself. He encouraged the Tsar to be sorry for Bielsky and to declare that he was innocent, and yet, to avert bloodshed, to promise to banish him from Moscow.

Bielsky was conveyed under escort to Nijni Novgorod. The insurrectionaries shouted "Long live the Tsar!" and dispersed. The Council of Five had become the Council of Four and Boris Godunof had cause for satisfaction in having extricated himself from a dangerous tangle and stepped at the same time one rung higher on the ladder.

His next task was to punish the ringleaders of the insurrection, and those who had linked his name with that of Bielsky—not Shuisky, who was as yet too powerful to be touched or to be openly suspected, but the lesser lights, the Kikin family, the Liapunofs—banish some to the distant North, throw others into dungeons from which they would hardly again see light of day.

The Tsar heaped great honours on Boris. He made him Master of the Horse which was apparently a great distinction in those days. He was made vice-Tsar of Kazan and Astrakhan and was given precedence of all others at court. Vast revenues were also diverted to his treasury and he became by far the richest man, after the Tsar, in all Russia. He had the means to place an army of a hundred thousand men in the field. He took a large graft from the city of Moscow, as, for example, fifteen hundred roubles from the bathstoves and bathing houses outside the city walls.*

In messages of English envoys he soon began to be described as the "Lord Protector" and was evidently regarded as having a position similar to that of Somerset in the reign of Edward VI.

As was to be expected, his aggrandisement attracted deepest enmity and resentment from the nobility of Russia. But it was difficult to oppose him openly because Fedor was popular and Godunof acted cautiously, obtaining everything in the Tsar's name and snatching nothing for himself without that sanction. The Council of Safety ceased to sit as a council. Boris himself was the guarantee of the security of the throne. Shuisky, Mstislavsky and Yurief were engaged purely in administrative work, and in fact guided by Godunof in making many much needed reforms. There was a period of wise and mild government. Fedor prayed and went on pilgrimage while Boris Godunof demonstrated how much better it was for Russia to be governed by a wise and merciful protector than by a tyrant like the late Ivan. He removed from their posts corrupt and brutal governors and substituted better men. He made peace with the mutinous tribesmen on the Volga steppes. He sent a second expedition into Siberia to renew the claim of Russia upon vast territories. He discounted the commercial pretensions of Queen Elizabeth and the English merchants. He bluffed the menacing emissaries of

* Fletcher: *Of the Russe Commonwealth*, ix.

King Stephen of Poland who asked a great war indemnity as the price of peace.

But the even tenour of this sway was destined to be rudely disturbed. Nikita Yurief, another of the five deputed by Ivan to safeguard the realm, died suddenly, some said of poison. The Five were reduced to three. A process of elimination had set in and it was at least far from the mind of Shuisky that he should be the next to go or that Boris Godunof should be left unique among the inheritors of power. Whisper grew to intrigue and intrigue grew again to baleful conspiracy. Even Mstislavsky, seeming friend and loyal fellow worker of Godunof, was drawn into it.

In the second year of the reign of Fedor, 1585, Godunof and Mstislavsky had actually made a pact of eternal friendship. Mstislavsky, by his achievements in the field (he had been a great soldier under Ivan) and by his birth was in truth the greatest of the boyars. In a sense Boris usurped his place at court ceremonies, and this irked him somewhat. He felt self-conscious taking the precedence which Mstislavsky should have had. But it was for the good of Russia. He took pains to convince Mstislavsky of that. They drank together and kissed as Russians do, and in fact got rather maudlin in forgiving one another and protesting their eternal devotion to one another. Boris called himself Mstislavsky's son and knelt to him to ask for a father's blessing. Yes, and Mstislavsky accepted the rôle of father to the Lord Protector.

But in his cups Mstislavsky was weak. The swaggerers who told him of his exalted birth and theirs convinced him. It was certainly true, it seemed to Mstislavsky drunk, that Boris had taken a position in Russia which was never envisaged by Ivan the Terrible. In short, almost against his will Prince Ivan Mstislavsky was brought into the great conspiracy and his adherence seemed to guarantee success. The principals were Golovin, treasurer of the late Tsar, Vorotinsky and Shuisky. As usual the unruly "children of the boyars"* and the rabble of Moscow were made cognisant of the plot, it being evidently intended to seize the Kremlin by force of arms after Godunof had been murdered. Godunof was invited to a feast outside the Kremlin walls and had he accepted was to have been murdered at the festal board.

One cannot but feel that the enemies were of poor mettle. The way to succeed was for one man to take it upon himself to assassinate Boris. Not one of the conspirators dared do that. Their plot was cowardly. And too many were privy to it. Some had been brought in passively like Mstislavsky and others quite against their will. It is not surprising that apprehensive conspirators stole secretly to Boris to warn him of the danger threatening his person.

It suited Boris well. He took the intelligence to the Tsar and brought the informers to the Tsar's presence. He refused the invitation and placed his would-be hosts and murderers under arrest. Whether he was astonished by the defection of Mstislavsky is not recounted, but he knew the others were his enemies and the time and opportunity had come when he could be quit of some of

* These were not the actual children of the boyars. The phrase was used to designate a group of minor officers.

them. Mstislavsky was forcibly shorn as a monk and sent to end his days in enforced asceticism at the distant Northern shrine of St. Cyril. The Vorotinsky princes—there was a band of them—were dispersed, some banished, some thrown into dungeons, others were imprisoned. Again, however, Shuisky and his kindred got off free. It is said that the Metropolitan interceded for them, but Boris Godunof must still have felt that it was not safe for him to have their blood upon his hands. And he still showed that dislike of capital punishment and torture which had distinguished his character throughout the reign of Ivan. Golovin had also remained unpunished but unable to endure Boris' mercy he fled to Lithuania to King Stephen and was a traitor to his country. The Council of Five was now reduced to merely two: Shuisky and Boris Godunof.

Ivan Petrovitch Shuisky, head of the house of Shuisky, was a national hero. It was he who, in the reign of Ivan the Terrible, had checked the invasion of Russia by the victorious King of Poland, Stephen Batory. He had successfully defended the ancient city of Pskof from Poles and Lithuanians. As part reward, Tsar Fedor had made him a grant of the revenue of Pskof as a coronation gift. His position at court was one that could not be gainsaid. He was popular: the people of the city would always shout for him. That the family had once been very tyrannical and then deservedly chastised and disgraced by Ivan was forgotten. The family was too great, it had too many branches for all its members to disappear from Russian history at the frown of a Tsar. It was also a family which exploited commercially the great natural resources of its estates, and had a strong bond with the merchant class. Ivan Petrovitch Shuisky was as safely established in greatness as any prince could be said to be in the reign of Ivan the Terrible. And his power was carried over undiminished into the reign of Fedor. It is undoubted that but for the crafty Boris he would have dominated affairs.

It is probable that he was personally a wiser man than the page of history suggests. He was a good soldier, he was elderly, he was tried. One must surmise that he was no fool. But he was the head of a clan. He was a prince of many princes and was obliged to plot, not for himself alone but for all the Shuiskies. Those others had not his military glory nor his revenues, and they were greedy for the patronage of the realm. Shuisky knew with whom he had to deal in Godunof and was commendably cautious, but the other hotheads saw in the mild Protector an upstart and poltroon, the choice of adviser of a half-witted Tsar.

Boris, fully aware of the enmity raging against him in the Shuisky camp, yet believed he could liquidate it by seeming humility and soft words. He took a seat below Shuisky in the state councils as if recognising that the other was greater than he. He caused the Tsar to invite the leading Shuiskies to dinner and deliberately omit his name from the list of guests as if he, Godunof, were held in less honour than they. He himself would have another dinner party at his own house, but so great was his position that the Tsar's guests would wish they had been invited to the smaller dinner.

"The devil he laughed, for his darling sin was the pride that aped humility." It was rather devilish, and the Shuiskies were not deceived. They were not content to mistake the shadow for the substance. The mercy which Godunof had shown them they despised and took it as a sign of weakness or of cowardice. The barbaric primitive Russian seldom understands or appreciates magnanimity. But it may be admitted at once that the Shuiskies were right in branding Boris as a tyrant, even before he had shown himself tyrannical.

Mstislavsky, monk against his will, did not long survive the rigours of the shrine of St. Cyril. In a few months he was reported dead and could not be brought back to taste revenge. But the Shuiskies hit on a mad idea of posthumous revenge, and that was to get Fedor to divorce his wife Irina, Boris' sister and take the Princess Mstislavsky, Mstislavsky's sister instead. It could be done, they urged, because Irina had no issue and it was believed Fedor could be persuaded that he would have posterity by the other.

They were aided in this conceit by the Church, which was heartily on the side of the Shuiskies and by the Metropolitan Dionysy, who had found that Boris Godunof, while always polite, was yet unwilling to accept his advice as a mandate direct from God. Boris played his game of state-craft without the aid of prayer. The Metropolitan therefore favoured the plan to have Irina put away, although in fact the Orthodox Church had never lightly countenanced divorce. Boris, however, met the plot with the reasonableness of a Socrates. It was unfortunate that Irina had no issue, but first the fault might not be hers and second she was not past the age of child-bearing, and the happy event might still be vouchsafed. But even if the union proved to be finally barren, had the Metropolitan forgotten the existence of the baby, Dimitry, heir presumptive to the throne? There was no good reason to say that the dynasty would become extinct because of the childlessness of Fedor and Irina.

Dionysy was abashed and withdrew his support from the project of the Shuiskies. The plot was frustrated. Boris had the Princess Mstislavsky seized and forcibly vowed to eternal chastity, shorn and sent to a cloister—his answer to Irina's rival.

But Fedor and Irina were greatly perturbed by this conspiracy against their peace. The Tsar was fondly devoted to his consort. But he might not have been strong enough to withstand the wishes of the Metropolitan. He was too weak and godly and prayerful; his soul was mortgaged to the Church. The divorce might have come about without his will. The idea bred terror in his dull mind and that terror was increased by the natural resentment in the breast of Irina at the affront which was to have been offered her. There could be no peace for Irina while the Shuiskies remained at large. For Boris was not slow to inform her that the whole matter had been engineered by them and that the Metropolitan was merely their instrument. It seemed the time had come when Boris must show his hand. In the summer of 1587 the chief members of the Shuisky family were arrested.

It is said that Boris suborned witnesses to the effect that the Shuiskies were conspiring against the life of Fedor. If he had to buy evidence, it could not have cost him much. For Moscow, though honouring Shuisky, the defender of Pskof, was now alive with rumours against the Shuisky family, and the rash words of some of them were constantly brought by eavesdroppers to Boris Godunof. They were hatching treason and they were capable of treason all the while. Their immunity from arrest was as much due to the strength of their adherents as to the forbearance of the Protector. At length, however, the hour of their chastisement had arrived. Armed bands were dispatched in the Tsar's name and all the leading members of the family were put in chains as were also many of their supporters in other families. Some of the kindred of Marya Nagy were beheaded—that to show that they had had in mind to proclaim her child, Dimitry, Tsar after they had murdered Fedor. The Metropolitan Dionysy was removed to a monastery and Job of Rostof took his place. The lesser lights of the Shuisky family were loaded with irons and flung into dungeons, or banished to very distant regions. The two principal members of the family, Ivan Petrovitch and Andrey Ivanovitch, were destroyed.

Sir Jerome Horsey recounts the death of one of the Shuiskies, Ivan Vasilowich, which is probably a mistake for Ivan Petrovitch:

"Prince Ivan Vasilowich Suscoie, prime prince of the blood royal, of great esteem, power and command, chief competitor in commission for the government, his discontentment and greatness was much feared: some colour of offence conceived; the Emperor's displeasure cast upon him, was suddenly commanded to depart the Musco to his own repose; surprised with a corronelle guard, and not far off was smothered in a cottage with wet hay and stubble set on fire, lamented of all men. Here was the chief stumbling block of fear removed away from that house and family of Goddanoves."*

The Council of Five nominated by Ivan the Terrible was reduced to a Council of One, and that one was Boris Godunof.

* *Travels of Sir Jerome Horsey.*

III.

THE POLISH ARMISTICE

ALL the conquests which Ivan the Terrible had made in Livonia, Esthonia and Lithuania had been lost in his latter years, owing to his lost grip on affairs and the military capacity of that soldier of fortune, the Hungarian Stephen, elected King of Poland after Sigizmund Augustus. The Pope took credit in Europe for having made peace between Ivan and Stephen, and when Ivan's ambassador to Queen Elizabeth sought military aid against the Poles, she exclaimed: "But there is already peace, as we have heard the Pope has intervened." But actually there was only an armistice. No terms of peace had been signed and Ivan, having gained one victory over his adversary on Russian soil, sought the means of continuing the struggle and wresting his lost territories from Poland and Lithuania. Envoys from King Stephen had arrived in Moscow with a view to concluding a treaty of peace, but Ivan had been too ill to receive them. He died, and they were not received. Had he lived, it is doubtful whether he would have acceded to their terms.

The pretensions of Poland were great and included the restoration of cities and territory which the Russians had held for a long while, and besides that a considerable war indemnity. Actually, the indemnity was expressed as "ransom for prisoners held" but it was a lump sum, not a price list. The amount the Poles wanted was a matter of conjecture. Possibly the chief envoy, Sapieha, was not quite sure how much he should ask. It seeemed probable, upon the death of Ivan the Terrible, that he might be able to get much more from his successors. Accordingly, Sapieha notified the boyars that he had no authority to treat with Fedor; he must first get into communication with King Stephen to discover what modifications, if any, would be made in his instructions.

Boris Godunof took advantage of the opportunity to show an example of generosity by setting free without ransom a large number of notable Polish and Lithuanian prisoners, part of the graciousness of Fedor at his coronation. By the time Sapieha had heard again from Stephen, three months had slipped by and Boris had firmly established himself as the man with whom the envoys had to deal. Sapieha was presented to the Tsar on the 22nd of June, 1584. Fedor, with crown and sceptre stood alone, but at the foot of the throne, like a grand vizier, stood Boris Godunof. The rest of the court was considerably in the background. The dominant position of Boris Godunof was unmistakable.

Sapieha was talkative. He informed the Tsar in confidence and as a friendly gesture that he had it on the best authority that the Sultan of Turkey was preparing an invasion of Russia. The object of giving this false information was to put the Tsar in a flurry, that he might be more ready to accept King Stephen's proposals. But in this he did not succeed, for Fedor cast a hopeful glance toward Godunof, whose face betrayed no panic. Fedor took his cue from Boris, treated Sapieha with great politeness, was coolly interested in

STEPHEN BATORY, KING OF POLAND

THE POLISH ARMISTICE

what he had to say, but did not invite him to dinner. For an ambassador to succeed at the Russian court, he must, upon presentation, be invited to sup afterward with the Tsar.

Sapieha demanded that the Tsar drop the title of Prince of Livonia, as the Russians had all been driven out of the Livonian lands and in any case the title was meaningless. But Fedor objected that he had inherited the title along with his crown and sceptre, and saw no reason why anyone should wish to take it away from him.

Then 120,000 gold crowns were demanded as ransom for Russian prisoners held by the King of Poland. This must be paid and at the same time all Polish and Lithuanian prisoners held by Russia must be freely repatriated. Fedor said he thought that the King of Poland might well have followed his gracious example, by setting the Russian prisoners free without parley, thus inaugurating a new era of goodwill among brother Slavs. He offered little hope of the payment of ransom.

Sapieha's mission failed, but it was, however, promised that the Russians would send accredited representatives to King Stephen to treat for peace, and for that end the armistice was prolonged. But when Prince Fedor Troekurof and his party reached Warsaw in February, 1585, they found the King in a bellicose mood, threatening to teach the new Tsar of Russia the same lesson he had taught his father. King Stephen, if he could persuade the Diet, intended a great war of invasion. He offered Russia a ten years' peace, but on conditions which he knew in advance must be rejected.

He demanded the cession of Novgorod the Great, of Pskof, of Luki, of Smolensk and extensive territory bordering on the Baltic and the Gulf of Finland.

The traitor Golovin, fleeing from the revenge of Boris Godunof, had provided King Stephen with useful evidence to bring before the Polish Diet. According to him the Russian army had become completely demoralised owing to lack of leadership. Russia was divided against itself and on the brink of civil war, and the Tsar was incapable of wise rulership, being in fact a half-wit. There was much truth in what Golovin said, though he exaggerated the possibilities of civil strife. Undoubtedly, the army was in a poor state, and Stephen, could he have persuaded the pacific Parliament, must have gained victories and over-run a large area of Russia. The task of Troekurof became to persuade the Diet that Golovin lied, that he had been suborned to tell his story and was not worth listening to. An intrigue commenced in which Stephen was worsted. The Russians found sympathetic spirits among the Polish gentry and they made shrewd use of the prevailing jealousies. Instead of the failure of their mission, an ultimatum and war, they achieved a surprising diplomatic success. The armistice was prolonged for two years, and the Poles sent Michael Garaburda to propose to the Russians eternal peace and friendship on the basis of a territorial *status quo*. We shall ask no further cession of cities and lands of you, nor shall you lay claim at any time to any territory over which we now hold sway.

This was a generous proposal, but it was accompanied by a proposed gamble on the life of the two monarchs. A pan-Slavic fervour was in the air. Garaburda insisted: "We are brother Slavs, there is no good reason why we should remain disunited and in enmity. Let us make a pact of union. If King Stephen dies first we will agree to unite Poland and Lithuania and come together under the rule of the Tsar Fedor, granting, however, to Cracow the status of Moscow and to Vilna that of Novgorod. But if Fedor dies first Russia will agree to come under the rule of King Stephen in one united realm."

But the Council of Boyars indignantly refused to gamble on the death of God's annointed. Ivan's passion to rule over Poland as well as Russia had died with him. The dynastic megalomania had faded. Boris Godunof was a man of peace, and Russia was enough for him to handle. The prospect of lording it over Poland was not alluring. On the other hand, it was impossible in any circumstances that Russia would agree to be annexed to the Polish crown. Even if Fedor and Godunof agreed, their successors would certainly revolt against such a treaty as unnatural and impious.

The Poles were not pleased to have their proposals rejected. King Stephen was ready at a word to carry fire and sword into Russia and possibly still believed he could persuade the Diet to vote him money and supplies. But he was an elected monarch, and though he had obtained for himself and Poland great military glory, he was incapable of over-riding the constitution. He was not a national leader, being a Hungarian, and his army was one of mercenaries drawn from several nationalities. He could not get his way. The negotiations with Russia degenerated into a wrangle over the amount to be paid as ransom for prisoners. Both Poles and Russians are gifted procrastinators. There was no further war and in the following year Fate extinguished the menace to Russian peace. On the 12th December, 1586, King Stephen died.

IV.

THE QUEEN OF LIVONIA

WHEN in the Kremlin palace the health of the Tsar and Tsaritsa was drunk by the assembled boyars, the name of Boris Godunof was always included. "Long live their majesties, Fedor and Irina and the great lord Boris Godunof!" At court functions he stood between the bodyguard and the Tsar and sometimes held in his hand, as a sign of his high office, a golden apple. At his own house within the Kremlin he held his own court which vied in pomp and ceremony with that of the Tsar. An ambassador being received at Boris' court had as much significance as being received at that of the Tsar. Foreign envoys received food from his table sent to their lodgings and that was equal to a royal favour.

It is characteristic of his greatness that having the substance of power he did not grasp at the shadow. There was nothing of the characteristic Shakespearean villain of tragedy of history about him. He was no Macbeth or Richard III. But he was rather like a Wolsey with his character re-arranged, a Wolsey with purely secular ambitions. Wolsey wished to be Pope; Godunof to be the autocrat of Russia. And Wolsey cheated himself when he said to Cromwell:

> "Had I but serv'd my God with half the zeal
> I serv'd my king, he would not in mine age
> Have left me naked to mine enemies."

The butcher boy of Ipswich was not content to be the greatest man in England but wished to be the holy father of Christendom. Boris knew what he could safely achieve, achieved that and kept a mind at peace. He never grudged to Fedor the show of Tsardom nor planned to remove him and have himself proclaimed Tsar.

At the same time Boris was well aware of dangers ahead. Fedor would not live forever. The presumption was that with his ill-health he would not live very long. In the unhealthy Moscow of those days one needed a strong constitution to survive past middle age. The majority of the male population died before the age of fifty, taken off either by disease or violence. Boris was a strong man of sober habits and physical well-being. It was natural for him to assume that he would survive the Tsar by many years. But the period of his survival would be the period of his greatest danger. It well might happen that with the death of the Tsar he and his kindred would lose all they had attained. The child, Dimitry, would be brought forward and made Tsar, and Dimitry and his mother and the Nagy family had no cause to be grateful to him.

Logically considered Boris would have to make himself Tsar if he wished to retain his position as autocrat of Russia. But logically also he would have to remove the heir and any other possible claimant of the throne. In his characteristic way he proceeded to do what was more easy before accomplishing what was more difficult. There was another possible claimant to the throne besides Dimitry. Marya of Holstein, the cousin of

THE QUEEN OF LIVONIA 39

Ivan the Terrible, might be championed by a powerful body of gentry, both at home and abroad. It seemed important to Boris that he destroy her pretensions whatever they might be.

Prince Vladimir Andreyevitch, whom Ivan had poisoned, had been the heir to the throne in the case of Ivan dying without male issue. His sons were murdered but his daughters had been spared. The elder died a natural death; the other, Marya, had been married to Magnus, Duke of Holstein, brother of King Frederick of Denmark. Magnus, self-styled King of Livonia, was a soldier of fortune, but too simple minded to cope with his patron Ivan and too profligate to make and keep a fortune. He died in poverty at Pilten on the Baltic, leaving the Duchess Marya and her daughter, Evdokia, in abject poverty. Marya was the possible pretender to the throne whom Boris had envisaged. Someone of her kindred was bound to invite her back to Russia where she was heiress to lands and slaves. Boris anticipated the action of any other Russian and invited her back himself, promising to find her a new husband and to re-establish her in her family domains.

Marya, with the empty title of "Queen of Livonia," was living without servants or attendants in two rooms in the fortress of Riga. Livonia was controlled by the Polish government and yielded no revenue to its queen. The Poles on this occasion, despite their reputation for gallantry, were not liberal. Not that they were embarrassed by her presence in Livonia as Elizabeth was at the same time by Mary Queen of Scots. Marya was a *quantité négligeable*. The Poles placed no obstacle in the way of her repatriation. But the lady herself distrusted Boris Godunof and his invitation.

Boris was at pains to give her assurance of his good faith and must have entrusted various envoys with the business of persuading her back to Russia. Anyone passing through Livonia on affairs of state was likely to be asked in an informal way to do what he could in the matter. Thus, curiously enough, we find the English ambassador, Sir Jerome Horsey, returning to London from Moscow, to straighten out the commercial relationship of England and Russia, entrusted with a message to the Livonian queen. Probably little depended on his personal success or failure in this mission, but his account is picturesque.

"My journey was overland from the Moscow, the 20th of August, 1585, six hundred miles to Vobsco, and thence to Dorp in Livonia, Perno, Wenden, Libau and to Riga . . . where my commission was to treat with Queen Magnus, the next heir of the imperial crown of Moscow; she being left in great distress and kept upon small allowance, issuing out of the treasury of the crown of Poland, in the castle of Riga."

He found her to be virtually a prisoner and that no one could have access to her without first obtaining a permit from the governor of Livonia, Cardinal Georgius Radzivil, "a bouncing princely prelate, loving the company of the Livonian ladies, the fairest women of the known world."

The cardinal proved to be a jolly fellow whose face, when he espied Horsey, lit up with a broad grin, even as he walked in stately procession in the cathedral. The necessary permission was granted. Sir Jerome was conducted to the Queen's apartments. He found the little Evdokia to be "a proper gerrell of nine years of age" and he was evidently greatly affected by the condition of the forlorn queen. This was his speech to her as reported by himself:

"The Emperor, Fedor Ivanovitch . . . takes notice of your necessity you and your daughter live in, desires your return into your native country, to hold your state and well-being, according to your royal birth and place; and the Lord Protector, Boris Fedorovitch, doth, with due remembrance of his service vow the performance of the same."

But the distrustful Marya interrupted him. "Sir," says she, "they neither know me nor I them." She added that Horsey's gallant demeanour almost persuaded her against her judgment. The interview took place in the presence of a Polish official who thereupon hurried Horsey out of the room. Marya shed tears but thanked him and he promised to seek her presence again. Horsey returned to the cardinal, indignant that his interview had been cut so short. The merry prelate made little difficulty and Horsey was soon granted another permit. Then Queen Marya told him that she had little hope "to be dealt otherwise than they use to do with their queens' widows there, to be shut up in a hellish cloister, before which I choose death."

Horsey at least was generous. He could not persuade her that Boris meant her well but he handed her from his own purse a hundred gold ducats and at parting he pressed twenty more pieces into the little daughter's hands. Cardinal Radzivil was greatly amused and was convinced that the Englishman had fallen in love. "He is a suing youth, and fine," said he. "I wish he had her, so I had the charge she hath cost me."

But Horsey continued his way to England, being unwilling to dally further with the Livonian queen. As he was leaving Riga a young girl pressed up to his stirrup and handed him a curiously wrought white kerchief embroidered with rubies. When he learned later that Marya had returned to Russia he believed he had been largely instrumental in persuading her, and hearing of the fate that overtook her and her daughter there he reproached himself considerably. When he returned to Russia he sought to obtain access to her in the nunnery where she was immured but was refused.

With the co-operation of the Poles, who were not unwilling to be relieved of her, Marya and her daughter were escorted over the frontier and brought to Moscow. But no warm welcome awaited her. A kiss and a smile from the Tsar meant nothing. She was brought before the master of Russia who gave her the choice of dungeon or cell. The Queen was shorn and became Sister Martha. She was allowed to have her daughter with her and they were confined in a nunnery near Troitsa. Soon the child was put to death. The mother languished under the black veil for eight more years before she also died. She had disappeared from the page of history and from the way of ambition of Boris Godunof.

Sir Jerome Horsey greatly enjoyed his visits to Russia and his various adventures prancing across Europe on mysterious missions. He was a characteristic English traveller with much the same attitude toward the Russians as a business man in the twentieth century. He was impressed by the wealth, amused by the customs, scornful of the "superstitions," hail fellow well met at the festive board, and delighted to receive the confidences of exalted persons. The Russians liked him but did not understand his personality; he tolerated them and gathered ornamental anecdotes concerning them. It pleased him to carry across Europe an overture of marriage to Queen Elizabeth from Ivan the Terrible and to carry the secret missive in a vodka bottle in his saddle bag. And Queen Elizabeth, sniffing the letter and saying "This smells of spirits," absolutely delighted him. But his quaintest job was to search out a "wise woman" in England capable of putting things right in the nuptial bed of the Tsar Fedor.

When Boris had seemed in danger from the machinations of the Shuiskies, Sir Jerome Horsey came forward and offered himself "men, powder and pistols, to attend the Prince Protector." This was much appreciated by Boris, who enrolled him in his own household, and he became unofficial ambassador to the court of Godunof. To what extent he was in the confidence of Boris may be judged by his being entrusted with the mission to the unfortunate Marya. But that he was asked to procure a "wise woman" and doctors to assist the Tsaritsa Irene shows an even greater intimacy.

Boris Godunof was devoted to his sister and for many years her interests were one with his. It is even possible that had she borne a son and heir he would have adjured his personal dream of royalty and served them faithfully. And Irene was of the same metal as Boris. She was neither weakling nor fool. She comported herself with great dignity and was not the mere instrument of her brother's designs.

"The Empress that now is, being a woman of great clemency and withal delighting to deal in public affairs of the realm (the rather to supply the defect of her husband) doth behave herself after an absolute manner." (Fletcher)

To a proud woman childlessness is an open or secret humiliation. One thing was necessary to complete the felicity of the Tsaritsa and that was a child, and whether an heir suited or not the plans of Boris Godunof he must be consulted. Boris probably was in two minds about it. But his sister's continued sterility was in any case a menace. There were not wanting instances when a consort had been put away merely on the ground of barrenness. Some set-back in Godunof's affairs, some temporary indisposition or sickness might be seized upon by faction to impose another bride upon Fedor. She herself must ardently have desired a child.

The Tsar Fedor, it may be surmised, was not an ardent lover. "The Empress lieth apart from him," wrote Fletcher. She kept one bed and he another, except on certain festival occasions when they were seen in bed together. There were no children, but upon occasion it was given out that the Tsaritsa had had a miscarriage. The hope of progeny was kept alive by Boris. Horsey however misunderstood what was required. He had been led to think that the Tsaritsa was with child when she was not. What was wanted was assistance in conception rather than assistance in delivery. And he made the bad blunder of bringing a midwife to Russia. He had interested Queen Elizabeth herself in obtaining a tried midwife and he bore Irene a letter couched in these terms:

"Elizabeth, by the grace of God, Queen of England, to the most serene Irene, Empress of Russia, Grand Duchess of Moscow. . . . Most serene and potent Princess, our very dear friend and sister! The singular fame of your eminent prudence, most rare virtues and manners truly becoming so great a princess—confirmed moreover by the repeated mention of them by Doctor Jacob, our physician—causes us to love your Serenity with true affection, and most ardently to desire for you all prosperity and happiness. We cannot fail therefore to be anxious for your health and safety; we have accordingly sent, not only what you affectionately requested, an expert and tried midwife to soothe by her skill the pains of childbirth, but also our physician, who has the care of our own health, the aforesaid Doctor Jacob, a trustworthy man already known to you, to direct the conduct of the midwife, by the medical science he excells in, and faithfully to watch over your safety. And we fervently desire most fully to gratify your sisterly affection not only in this matter but in whatsoever else your serenity may wish. Given at Greenwich, the 24th day of March, in the year of our Lord (1586), and the 27th of our reign."

Horsey with the letter reached Moscow ahead of the medical party. The Queen's letter was read by Boris before being presented to the Tsaritsa and was found to be embarrassing as Irene was not *enceinte*. A special version, omitting reference to a midwife and the pains of childbirth was made for her. And a messenger was sent to turn the midwife back.

Horsey's *faux pas* was overlooked in the light of the charming presents he brought with him, musical instruments the like of which had not been seen in Russia before, "organs and vergenals, all gilt and enamelled. . . . Thousands of people resorted and stayed about the palace to hear the same. My man that played upon them much made of and admitted into such presence often where I myself could not come."

In what terms the real difficulties of producing an heir were explained to Dr. Jacob we do not know, or whether in fact he was consulted in that matter. When God was unwilling it might seem that a physician could do little. Every year Irene made pilgrimage on foot to the shrine of St. Sergey at Troitsky Monastery, followed by six thousand other women, all ardently praying that she might have a child.* But St. Sergey who had a reputation for performing miracles in sexual life was apparently inattentive.

Something however did happen six years after the arrival of Dr. Jacob: Irene gave birth to a daughter who was christened Theodosia. But in a few months the baby died and that chapter was closed.

* Fletcher: *Of the Russe Commonwealth.*

V.

THE INSTITUTION OF THE PATRIARCHATE

THE TSAR FEDOR has no doubt suffered in reputation through foreign comment. The West dislikes religiosity in monarchs, and even King David had he been only a psalmist would have suffered in reputation. Kings should be worldly, and Charles II and Henry of Navarre are the approved types. "A mental deficient from birth, finding pleasure only in the things of the spirit," wrote the Swedish envoy, and the puritan Fletcher and the mocking Horsey could not interpret his piety other than as mental incapacity. But the view of the educated foreigner was not one with that of the Russian people of the time. The people, despite its sins and manifold moral obliquity, was intensely devoted to religious practice. Fedor was representative and popular, a holy man on the throne. The gentle type of religious maniac has always been held in high esteem in Russia. It is true his father Ivan referred to him scoffingly as a bell-ringer. And Ivan did not believe that a Tsar who spent more time at prayer than in the torture chamber could survive long in turbulent Russia. He was sincerely apprehensive as to Fedor's fate, and with good reason. While the people as a whole might adore a holy Tsar, faction would have little scruple in putting him to death. Boris Godunof became the bulwark of the throne, and but for him it is unlikely that Fedor would have reigned in peace for the span of his natural life.

Godunof himself was a man of the world, a believer but not a man of visions. He was not a man who would impose on himself an arduous penance or spend the time which belonged to affairs of state on long pilgrimages. While he respected the Church, he was not subservient to it. His master Ivan had thwarted the Church and done what he wished in Russia, despite all ecclesiastical opposition. When the head of the Church, the Metropolitan, had been difficult, Ivan had had him removed and had appointed another in his place. The Tsar refused to accept the voice of any Metropolitan as the voice of God. God's anointed was nearer to God than any priest. Godunof was without books and learned from men. And he had learned from Ivan that the Church, despite its pretensions, was merely an instrument in state-craft. When he found himself opposed by the Metropolitan Dionysy he removed him and put Job in his seat. The Shuiskies had been cultivating the Church and when he had dispersed the Shuisky family, Godunof showed that he could learn from his enemies and he in turn began to build up for himself Church support.

Naturally, he did not interfere with the religious preoccupation of the monarch. The deeper Fedor was engrossed with miracle and prayer, the more worldly and civil responsibility fell upon Boris Godunof. But he was wise enough to use his power in a way acceptable to the Church. He let the Tsar's gold go to the building of new churches and the embellishment of the old. He improved the civic buildings of Moscow. New

THE INSTITUTION OF THE PATRIARCHATE 49

stone houses began to arise in the city. He did without forced labour and the workmen were paid good wages. He improved the local administration throughout Russia and was at pains to safeguard justice in the courts of law. It became easier to obtain redress of grievances than it ever had been before. And he allowed petitioners, all and sundry, to his person, as Ivan had done under the beneficent influence of Alexey Adashef. He might lack somewhat in the spirit of pilgrimage, but he shone as a man of virtue. Russia under the joint rule of Fedor and Boris was happily governed.

After the religiosity of Ivan, combined with cruelty and debauch, the Church was relieved to have a rule of piety combined with virtue, and it gave to Boris its approbation and prayed for him together with the Tsar. But possibly this approbation was not enough. Boris decided on a master stroke; he would do more for the Church than any of the pious Tsars. He would raise the see of the Metropolitan to the dignity of a patriarchate. Some historians have thought that he instituted the patriarchate of Moscow to glorify himself, but that seems out of keeping with his character. He was a realist in politics and if he started the patriarchate he did so, not that it might be said "Boris Godunof made the first Patriarch of Russia," but to suit his own ends and ambitions.

The project pleased Tsar Fedor greatly. Electing and consecrating a Patriarch was something into which he could enter fully. That would provide an illuminated page in the chronicle of his reign. That was of more immediate interest than being elected to the throne of Poland. But if the Poles wished religious unity, Fedor thought the institution of a patriarchate a step toward it. The Catholics had their Pope; Russia would have her holy father, too. Eastern and Western Slavs might more easily unite under a Russian Patriarch than under the sway of Rome. There was a hubbub of ecclesiastical controversy in court and cloister. Russia was proclaimed the Third Rome, the spiritual successor of Byzantium.

Boris Godunof had made Job of Rostof head of the Russian Church, Metropolitan of the Moscow see, and Job was both grateful and loyal. He was well beloved of the people, a good man, traditional, no innovator. He believed as strongly in devils, evil spirits, sorcery, as he did in the power of the ikons and relics, and that was popular. He was stupid, but that was no handicap to holiness. He was a simple soul possessed of an innocent vanity which showed itself as zeal. For conscience' sake he must convince himself that Boris was God's instrument. It was natural for him to regard Boris Godunof as a paragon of virtue, one incapable of ignoble action, God's gift to Russia. Godunof saw great advantage to himself in having this man made Patriarch. He could thereby rescue the Church from the ignominy of the humiliation it had suffered under Ivan the Terrible. He could raise its authority to such a point that in the event of Fedor's dying childless and the absence of an obvious heir to the throne, the Patriarch's voice in the affairs of state must be supreme. Time might come when Boris Godunof might need such a voice of authority to pronounce for himself. Therefore, he suggested Job as Patriarch to Tsar Fedor. The Tsar had no objections; he was eager for it.

THE INSTITUTION OF THE PATRIARCHATE 51

When in 1586 the Patriarch of Antioch was visiting Russia, the project had already been mooted and Fedor asked his good services in sounding the Greek Church in the matter. Russia was by far the richest community in the Eastern Church, and probably the most pious. She was even then the most powerful, and was growing steadily in dominion and influence. She began to be out of the range of petty jealousy, and the Orthodox East saw that it must in time owe more to her than to any other power in Christendom. And still it was difficult to persuade the Greeks of the expediency of raising Russia to a patriarchate.

In the summer of 1587, Father Nicholas, a Greek emissary, arrived in Moscow with the intelligence that the Eastern Church was sending the Patriarchs of Jerusalem and Alexandria to treat in the matter. They did not hasten to Russia and so were forestalled by the Patriarch of Constantinople, Jeremiah, who was nominally the senior Patriarch of the Orthodox Church. He was not explicitly the voice of the Church as a whole. Russia, however, seized the opportunity of obtaining from him early sanction for her design.

Jeremiah arrived in Moscow in July, 1588, bringing ostensibly the blessing of the rest of the Church. He brought with him relics and holy gifts, and he magnificently looked the part of a man who had been sent by God. He had a marvellous reception, as of a whole nation on its knees. The religious splendour of Russia dramatised itself in the churches and streets. All the thousands of the bells of the city, in diverse tones and clangor, rang for him, the dissonances of the free individualism of the little bells, the sombre uniting resounding tolling of the great bells. Jeremiah of Constantinople, greatly moved, appeared before the kneeling populace and gave his benediction.

The Tsar granted him a state reception. Boris Godunof received him in private. Jeremiah told the story of his life, and how the Turks affronted Christendom in the holy city of Constantinople, how the glorious cathedral of St. Sophia had been converted to Mahometan use and prayers to Allah. Even then, at that early date, the suggestion may have been made that Russian arms revenge the sacrilege.

At first, as a matter of form, the patriarchate of Russia was offered to Jeremiah himself, and he made some show of being willing to accept it, although he did not speak the language (services were conducted in Slavonic, not in Greek) and at least nominally he had his own see of Constantinople. The offer pleased him; but when the Moscow Government notified him that the see would be not in Moscow but in the small provincial town of Vladimir, he was unenthusiastic at the prospect of spending his life there. He declined the appointment but pronounced himself willing to give his blessing to whomsoever the Tsar should name.

There was never any doubt in Boris' mind who would be Patriarch of Russia, none other than his nominee the Metropolitan Job, but as a formality three names were placed before the Tsar, those of the archbishops of Novgorod and Pskof and of the Metropolitan. Fedor chose the last, and Job became the first Patriarch of Russia. On the 26th January, 1589, the solemn consecration took place and the mitre with cross and crown was placed upon his head, and he faced a

THE INSTITUTION OF THE PATRIARCHATE

white carven double-headed eagle behind which on an eminence were twelve lighted lamps, symbol of Russia before the Lord.

Thus began the patriarchate destined to last 110 years, to be abolished by Peter the Great, and to be resuscitated for a short spell after the downfall of Tsardom in the year 1917. Although the church in Russia proved itself grateful to Boris Godunof, the institution of the patriarchate was an aggrandisement which greatly increased the authority of religion. It proved more difficult to remove patriarchs than it had been to remove metropolitans. The authority of the Patriarch complicated the functioning of complete autocracy.

VI.

PEACE WITH POLAND AND SWEDEN

IF Fedor had any personal desire in foreign policy, it was for universal peace and the brotherhood of man, the Byzantine dream of human unity. In this he was at one with Godunof, who was also by nature pacific. And Boris believed that peace suited Russia better than war. In internal affairs the policy was "peace between man and man"; in external, "peace between nation and nation." The monarch and his vizier put their heads together to alleviate human suffering and to relieve the poor. Both bestowed great alms upon beggars, and Boris upon occasion would stroke his jewelled mantle and profess his willingness to fulfil the behest of Christ and sell what he had and give it to the poor. In that, of course, there was some exaggeration and parade. Applied logically, there would soon have been no treasure in the Kremlin, and Fedor and Boris would have been walking barefooted to Jerusalem. On Godunof's part, it was policy rather than creed, but even so, it is surprising he did not achieve great popularity.

When the bellicose King Stephen died there seemed to be an opportunity to unite Poland and Russia in eternal peace. Poland preferred to have a foreign king rather than be ruled by a Pole; why should she not accept the peace-loving holy rule of Fedor of Russia? Ivan had wanted to be King, but Ivan was a tyrant. What he had done in his own country showed what he might do in Poland. The security he offered could not set off the cruelty he might introduce into internal government. The Polish aristocracy liked a somewhat colourless king, one who would do their will rather than initiate schemes of his own. The hero Stephen had not been entirely popular. He wished to use Poland for his own aggrandisement and was constantly in conflict with the wishes of Parliament. The meekness of Fedor was a primary recommendation. Fedor himself was greatly pleased with the prospect and sincerely believed that the common Slavonic origin of the two nations was a bond of unity. Boris may have been shrewd enough to realise the deep-seated racial antagonism in Poles and Russians, and the vanity of the Polish nation, which would never submit to Russian domination. There was culture in Poland, music and poetry. There was a high standard of domestic comfort and personal hygiene. It was natural for Poles to consider Russians barbarous and for them to assume superiority in civilisation. In horsemanship the Poles definitely excelled the Russians and they did not in the least fear them as a military force. The obstinate refusal of the kings of Poland to regard the monarchs of Russia as anything more than grand dukes sprang more from a conviction of Russian inferiority than from jealousy.

But curiously enough there was at the time a Russophile faction among the Polish nobles, and on this faction the Russian envoys built their hopes. Godunof used this, rightly surmising that only good could come out of an assiduous propaganda for Tsar Fedor. He desired primarily peace with Poland. He was no soldier himself and did not wish to have to enter the field against them, or to entrust one of the boyars with a large army to continue the old war.

There were several candidates in the field: Maximilian of Austria, Sigizmund of Sweden, Semigradsky, brother of the late King Stephen, Fedor. The armed partisans frequently attacked one another. Warsaw was in such a state of tumult that it was dangerous for the Russian envoys to appear there. Outside the capital there were repeated affrays between mounted men. In an informal way, in a field some twelve miles from the city, a kind of election was made. A Russian cap was placed on a stake at one point; an Austrian hat at another; a Swedish emblem at a third, and the horsemen were invited to range themselves behind the token of their choice. By far the greatest number were found to be for a Russian king. Apparently Fedor was elected. But the Diet did not ratify this informal choice. It proposed granting the throne to Fedor on certain terms which must first be agreed. There was to be a payment of a large sum of money. Russia must put part of the Polish army on her pay-roll. She must build fortresses in Lithuania. Fedor would be allowed to retain his Byzantine faith, but he must seek the blessing of the Pope at Rome and must hold out some hope of uniting Russian Orthodoxy and Roman Catholicism. The financial and military provisions could have been met, but the religious requirement was an insuperable difficulty. Fedor's notion of the union of Christendom was not a union under the Pope, and Russia would never have allowed him to seek a blessing at Rome. So after having taken many rich gifts the Polish nobles did what was likely to be most distasteful to Russia. They chose

Sigizmund, the eldest son and heir of the King of Sweden.

Apparently this was the worst that could have happened. The Russian armistice with Sweden was petering out and a resumption of hostilities with that country was almost inevitable. Sweden held Ivangorod and certain small towns on the Gulf of Finland which Russia considered her inalienable property. Now it appeared that Sweden might have Poland and Lithuania as allies against Russia. But the emissaries of Godunof had seized the opportunity afforded by the seeming choice of Fedor as King to obtain from the Polish Diet a treaty of fifteen years' peace. The Russians had spent much treasure buying support in Poland. They failed in their ostensible mission, but they had obtained something which was perhaps more valuable, the assured neutrality of Poland in any further dispute they might have with Sweden.

Sweden, under King John III, was implacably hostile to Russia. Fedor wrote to King John that he had allies in the Archduke of Austria and the Shah of Persia, and John replied that he could tell how impotent Russia was by her friends. As a military power, Russia had fallen into disrepute. The failures of Ivan in his latter years, the loss of Livonia, Polotsk, the Baltic seaboard, the invasion of Russian territory by King Stephen, the abject quest of peace by the Russian Tsar, had given Sweden an erroneous impression of weakness. King John saw the puny Fedor on the throne, but he did not realise the power of the figure behind him, or he misinterpreted the pacifism of Godunof. Swedish bands raided Solovetsky Monastery, Petschenga, the shores of Lake Ladoga, and were a menace to the whole of the North. The Russians sought peace on terms, but war was inevitable. Boris told the astonished Tsar that he must quit his prayers and take the field. His presence would be necessary to the spirit of the army he was mobilising.

A great force gathered from all over Russia and from the confines of Asia, moving against Sweden and the North. Fedor and the Tsaritsa Irene went with the army, as did also Boris Godunof. Almost the principal command was held by the son of the unfortunate Ivan Mstislavsky, Prince Fedor Mstislavsky. The most capable general was Prince Dimitry Khvorostinin. The Swedes were outnumbered five or six to one on each occasion when they fought. They were good soldiers, well equipped and well led, but they could not withstand the elemental force opposed to them. They fought well, especially in the defence of Narva, but Russia took back all the disputed ports and over-ran Swedish territory with fire and sword. King John was soon moved to grant an armistice and Fedor went back to Moscow to celebrate a great victory and be hailed as a soldier-saint.

Sigizmund made some small diversion, but could not persuade the Diet to allow him to rush to the assistance of his father. He then strove to explain away his hostility, but his envoys to Moscow were coldly received. It was grasped that the Poles were by no means contented with their choice of king, and that he had little influence with his subjects. The war with Sweden had begun in January, 1590. The petty armistices, the renewed hostilities need not concern us here. King John was not successful in the war. In 1595 a conclusive treaty of peace was signed. Russia got her towns on the Gulf of Finland with Kexholm thrown in. And there was general peace in the West.

VII.

THE MURDER OF THE TSAREVITCH DIMITRY

MARYA NAGY and her child Dimitry lived in honourable banishment at Uglitch, some two hundred miles from Moscow. The medieval holy city of Uglitch was not wanting in pomp and circumstance. It had three cathedrals, a hundred and fifty churches and twelve monasteries. It had its castle, fortifications, retainers. Godunof had his spies and agents there but there was no interference in the family life of the ex-Tsaritsa and her son. There is no reason to think that Marya was ambitious either for herself or for the Tsarevitch. By no word or action did she ever show that she was other than completely submissive to the power of Moscow. The menace to her peace did not arise from her own temper nor from Moscow where her passivity must have been understood and appreciated. Her court and bodyguard, composed of headstrong brothers and kindred were the sources of danger. They were not content to exchange the patronage and favour of Ivan the Terrible for a provincial life, and they would not forget that they had in their keeping the heir to the throne. Dimitry was the star of their hopes, following which, it seemed to them, they must sooner or later return to power within the Kremlin walls.

The Nagy brothers and cousins hunted together outside Uglitch, farmed the revenues, made the laws of the principality, got drunk, pledged the health of the Tsarevitch and his mother, breathed dangerous words in plenty. The spies and agents kept Boris Godunof informed of all that was said and done. Boris, in complete security in Moscow, waited a time when he could deal with potential rebels. He was a long-headed, crafty Slav, not given to impulsive action. To what extent he considered the child Dimitry an obstacle in his career is only surmised. He was mistrustful and secretive, a misanthropist with a deceptive urbanity, a cunning egotist masking himself as an altruist and the humble servant of the state. His champions in History declare that he could not have wished the death of Dimitry because the Tsarevitch was not a menace to his presumed ambitions. The union of Ivan the Terrible and Marya Nagy had not been recognised by the Church and there is no doubt that if necessary the Patriarch would have made a formal pronouncement against the legitimacy of Dimitry. But it is not certain that the Church's ban would have been effective. The child had one intrepid champion in Bogdan Bielsky and, apart from the support of that stormy character, must have become in the process of time the hope of all the enemies of Godunof. Bielsky had declared that Ivan in his last days had made him swear to be the faithful protector and guardian of the infant Dimitry. It could well be claimed that Ivan regarded Dimitry as legitimate. Even Boris himself, when the Shuiskies deplored the barrenness of Irene, pointed out that there was an heir presumptive living—Dimitry of Uglitch. Legitimacy had no great weight. In the event of the dynasty becoming otherwise extinct, the illegitimacy of

Dimitry would have been waived by most Russians. Should Fedor die without heir there was bound to be a strong movement in favour of the Tsarevitch Dimitry, probably an armed rising.

Boris Godunof was preoccupied with soothsayers and sorcerers, who, like the weird sisters to Macbeth, said to him: "All hail, thou shalt be king hereafter!" His was a curious mind. He believed that the Future was written in the Book of Fate, but he must at the same time co-operate to obtain that part of the Future which was acceptable to him.

Spies foster suspicion and indeed cause it to be magnified. It was difficult to have daily conclave with spies and not become apprehensive. In his secret mind the Nagy family seemed to Boris a very great menace to his security. But he could not meet that apprehension as Ivan would have done. He was no executioner and had a distaste for murder. He was an anæmic intellectual who sought to achieve his ends by ordinances rather than by force. He shrank from bloodshed and torture and was only compelled to these things later by the logic of events.

It is improbable that he actually ordered the murder of the Tsarevitch Dimitry. He wished the death but did not wish to have the death upon his conscience. But if he breathed his irritation against the Nagy, if he exclaimed to some henchman "throw thine eye on yon young boy, he is a very serpent in my way," might not that henchman without explicit warrant or command do what was in his mind?

The suggestion fell on the ears of Andrew Kleshnin, an ardent supporter of Godunof. Kleshnin advanced

MURDER OF THE TSAREVITCH DIMITRY

the *dyak*, Michael Bitiagovsky, as a man likely to organise an efficient control of the court at Uglitch. He and his son Daniel, together with Kachalof, Tretiakof and Volokhof, obtained full powers to repair to Uglitch and deal with the Nagy family. They had no orders to kill the Tsarevitch but they believed they could earn the lasting gratitude of Boris Godunof.

Upon his arrival at Uglitch, Bitiagovsky at once made himself obnoxious to the ex-Tsaritsa Marya and to her brother Michael Nagy, reduced their authority, cut their revenues. It may have been suspected by the Nagy that he intended to murder or kidnap the Tsarevitch. Attempts had been previously made to poison the child and it had become clear to them that Boris Godunof would not have been grieved to have received the report of his death. Bitiagovsky caused alarm by his attentions to Dimitry. Boris' agents and their children made themselves into a bodyguard of the young prince and seldom allowed him out of their sight.

On the 15th of May, 1591, the whole of this unofficial bodyguard was murdered. At an alarm given by the great bell of the cathedral, the Nagy and their followers raised the cry that Dimitry had been killed by young Daniel Bitiagovsky and Osip Volokhof, and Boris' agents were lynched by the infuriated crowd.

Apparently the Tsarevitch Dimitry was dead. Either the body of Dimitry or of another dead child in Dimitry's robes, lay in blood before the altar of the cathedral. The justification of the mass murder of Godunof's agents lay in their supposed murder of Dimitry. If Bitiagovsky had not murdered the child there was no justification.

This is the Nagy story: Dimitry after Mass on Sunday morning, the 15th of May, was playing with other boys, mostly Nagy children, but among them Daniel, son of Michael Bitiagovsky, and Osip, son of the nurse Volokhova. They were throwing knives at a target. In the garden where this was going on there were no grown-ups. The nurse Volokhova was supposed to have been in the plot. She led the child into the garden and left him there to play with the others. Osip Volokhof picked a quarrel with Dimitry as to whether the necklet he was wearing was new or old and being contradicted, stabbed him in the neck and fled. Dimitry fell to the ground and lay there screaming. Daniel Bitiagovsky and young Kachalof came up and finished him off by cutting his throat. The mother ran out, crying alarm. Someone sounded the tocsin, and out rushed the Nagy followers and townsmen and lynched Daniel and Osip and the rest of Boris' agents to the number of twelve. The Tsaritsa herself took a leading part in accusing the supposed murderers and rousing the mob to tear them to bits.

VIII.

VASILLY SHUISKY

THE murder of his agents seemed at first to Boris Godunof a more serious event than the death of the Tsarevitch Dimitry. He was inclined to think that Moscow was beginning to forget the heir presumptive. His own greatness had become so manifest that men looked from the Tsar Fedor to him and looked no further. He had long since caused the name of Dimitry to be omitted from the prayers for the royal family. Fedor wept bitterly when he heard of the death of his little brother. He even wished to go at once to Uglitch but Boris said no; there was plague raging there. The Tsar and even the Tsaritsa Irene took the death greatly to heart, but Boris did not think that the news would make a stir in Moscow. The murder of Bitiagovsky and the rest was more important; the Nagy had dared to do that, they might dare more if not at once chastised.

Actually, Moscow, the boyars, the people as a whole, were much more shocked by the supposed murder of the young Dimitry than by the destruction of Boris' agents. Suddenly universal odium attached to the name of Boris Godunof and he lost in a day all the popularity he had achieved in a lifetime. Such a scandal was raised as brooked no delay on the Protector's part. The accusing voices must at once be silenced. In such cases direct action is generally more effective than clever devices. There was so much that was mysterious in the happenings at Uglitch that it demanded the personal presence of Boris Godunof. But he was a man who seldom chose to meet danger face to face. He thought it would be better to have his name cleared by someone who should seem altogether impartial. He did not go himself to Uglitch: he sent a man who had good cause to hate him —Vasilly Shuisky.

Vasilly Shuisky was a close kinsman of the Ivan Shuisky banished and done to death by Boris Godunof four years previously. The greater part of the Shuisky estates had been sequestered and the survivors of this immensely wealthy family were impoverished. Despite their exalted position, which they had held by virtue of their lineage, their influence in Moscow had been reduced to that of petty nobles. But there was a circumstance which helped Vasilly Shuisky; his brother Dimitry was married to a Skuratof, a sister of Godunof's wife. It is possible that the pardon to the brothers was granted at the intercession of Marya Godunof. But it may also be that Boris Godunof considered them safer in Moscow under his personal supervision than nursing their grudges in banishment. Banished nobles, if not put in dungeons, or summarily despatched, or placed under the control of monks, were capable of returning to Moscow at some critical moment at the head of an army.

But the marriage connection furnished a plausible motive for pardoning the Shuisky brothers and restoring them to court favour. Boris Godunof welcomed them back with considerable show of regret for their relative's death. He paraded sympathy and the brothers were content to forget the past and live in new-

VASILLY SHUISKY

found favour. Dimitry Shuisky was a quiet fellow without ambition. He accepted his pardon and became a loyal supporter of Boris Godunof. But Vasilly was ambitious, shrewd and cunning, a courtier withal whose face did not reflect his secret thoughts. He was potentially one of Godunof's greatest enemies. That Boris recognised him as dangerous is proved by the ban which he placed on any project of marriage which Vasilly might have had. The boyar must remain a bachelor. Boris would not allow his importance in the realm to be increased by alliance with some other exalted family.

Vasilly Shuisky was a short fat man with pudgy hands, gross, prematurely bald. He had flickering eyes which never looked a man in the face. He was a coolheaded liar, tactful and resourceful, very mean, entirely devoid of any nobility of character. In cunning he was entirely outmatched by Boris Godunof.

Nevertheless by sending Vasilly Shuisky to Uglitch to report on the murders Boris Godunof risked more than he fully understood at the time. It was assumed in Moscow that the Tsarevitch Dimitry was dead. Shuisky was not sent to identify the body but to give a verdict as to the cause of death and adequate justification for the chastisement of those who had put Boris' agents to death.

Kleshnin, who knew more of the plot to kill the Tsarevitch than Boris did, was sent with Shuisky to watch him. It would appear that the verdict was prearranged and that Shuisky knew approximately what he had to report. Boris had managed to falsify the first news of the death of the Tsarevitch received in Moscow from Uglitch and had already decided that the child had stabbed himself in a fit. Shuisky must confirm this. There was no possibility that he would confirm the Nagy story of the happenings. That would merely have been construed as treachery on Shuisky's part.

The commission was composed of Shuisky, Kleshnin, the Metropolitan Helasy and the *dyak* Vyluzgin. Their first task when they arrived at Uglitch was to bury the dead body of the Tsarevitch. This provincial funeral was another mistake. The body ought to have been conveyed to Moscow and buried in the cathedral of the Archangel Michael with Ivan the Terrible's other children. But Boris wished to hush up the circumstances of the death. A state funeral would concentrate the attention of Moscow upon the question: had Boris murdered the child.

The investigation at Uglitch proceeded according to plan. The townsfolk of Uglitch were asked how it was that the Nagy family had been so negligent as to allow the young prince to cut his throat. They answered one and all that it was neither suicide nor accident and that Boris' agents had done the deed. Nevertheless Shuisky found some of the Nagy who were willing to confirm Boris' own version. The child while playing with a knife had had a seizure. It was granted that he was subject to epilepsy and had had fits. While playing thus, he fell to the ground in a convulsion and accidentally pierced his throat with the weapon in his hand.

Shuisky discovered that there was a conspiracy to destroy Bitiagovsky, Kachalof, Tretiakof and the rest, but he did not clearly establish whether the conspiracy was entered into before the sudden mortal accident to Dimitry or after it. In justice to the Nagy it ought to have been admitted that the epileptic seizure could not have entered into their plan. But in questioning a great number of people Shuisky must have obtained more information than he vouchsafed to Boris Godunof upon his return to Moscow. There was a plot the details of which have never been made clear. There was much contradictory evidence, but Shuisky did not proceed by way of written question and answer. The results of the cross-examination of the ex-Tsaritsa Marya do not appear to have been reported, though her version of the happenings ought to have been considered the most important of all. At a much later date we have her confessing that her son did not die but was removed into safe hiding.

Vasilly Shuisky had no passion for truth. He did not have a legal mind; he was no intellectual. But he was crafty and secretive; he was capable of hiding what he knew if he thought he might profit later by the secret knowledge. On the whole, however, it would not seem that he had the mental capacity to elucidate the Uglitch mystery. At a much later date, when it suited his purpose, he declared that Dimitry did not die in 1591 and that the boy they buried was a priest's child. We cannot tell whether that was an improvisation on his part or was there some counterpart to that statement in what he found out for himself at Uglitch. In any case he went back on it again in order to further his own ambition to be Tsar.

Whatever did actually happen at Uglitch, the story that the Tsarevitch in a fit fell on a knife and accidentally cut his throat is unlikely and unsatisfactory. Nevertheless it was accepted by the court, and the Patriarch relieved Boris of making a public statement in his own defence. Job was very glad to clear the honour of his friend and benefactor and at once gave to Shuisky's findings the sanction of the Church. He declared the Nagy family to be manifestly guilty of treason. The Tsarevitch Dimitry had died at God's hand and must be accounted blessed. Bitiagovsky and his son Daniel, Osip Volokhof and his mother, Kachalof, Tretiakof and others had been murdered for maintaining the truth. Michael Nagy, with the aid of sorcerers had been plotting against the peace of Russia. Let us pray God for the Tsar and Tsaritsa for health and peace of soul!

The Council of Boyars also condemned the Nagy family for the massacre it had started. But the common people of Moscow still believed that Boris Godunof had instigated the murder of the Tsarevitch. Probably many of the nobility shared that belief in secret. But there is no record of anyone having said in 1591 that the Tsarevitch was not dead.

When, eleven years later, a young man laid claim to be the Tsarevitch Dimitry, he gave a different version of events at Uglitch. He said that Boris' agents had made an attempt to murder him in his bed at night but he had been saved by one of his teachers. Bitiagovsky murdered the wrong child. The Tsarevitch had at once been removed to a place of safety.

The mother, Marya, when questioned by Boris Godunof face to face in 1604, said that the child had been taken abroad.

Jerome Horsey at Yaroslavl was wakened in the dead of night, presumably the 15–16th May, by a party of horsemen led by Afanasy Nagy who reported: "The Tsarevitch is dead. His throat was cut about the sixth hour. . . . Some of his pages confessed upon the rack by Boris his setting on."

The Englishman was undoubtedly scared, roused his servants and came to the postern fully armed. He did not even see his visitor but discoursed with him through the iron work of the gates. He understood Nagy to say that the cause of his visit was not so much to give the information which hardly concerned the Englishman, but to crave from him an emetic for the ex-Tsaritsa Marya who had been poisoned and was at the point of death.

"I ran up, fetched a little bottle of pure sallett oil (that little vial of balsam that the queen gave me), and a box of Vienna treacle. 'Here is what I have! I pray God it may do her good.' Gave it over the wall; who hied him post away. Immediately the watchmen in the streets raised the town, and told how the Prince Dimitry was slain."

But there was no question of Marya's having been poisoned. Horsey without an interpreter understood little of what Nagy said to him, but it may be that he was in quest of a certain elixir which he believed the Englishman possessed and that he wanted it to restore the Tsarevitch who had been attacked but was not actually dead.

In 1606 the tomb where the child's body had been buried was re-opened. As was expected the corpse was in a marvellous state of preservation. Miracles had for some time been vouchsafed at the tomb, showing the saintly quality of the remains. The bodies of saints are supposed to decay much less rapidly than the bodies of sinners. Supposing it was actually the body of the Tsarevitch Dimitry one can find little reason why it should have been regarded as holy, or for the canonisation which followed. But officially, Dimitry had died in an epileptic fit, and Russians long regarded epileptics as persons near to God and subject to unbearable visions. Epileptics were holy.

The disinterment was not ordered with a view to identification. But if that had been the object it could not have served the purpose of Vasilly Shuisky. It was clearly not the child they had buried in 1591, for it bore in its fingers a cluster of hazel nuts which showed a late summer or early autumn burial. Nothing is recorded as to the likeness of features and limbs. Was the wart on the cheek there? Was one arm slightly longer than the other? It was greatly to the interest of Tsar Vasilly Shuisky to prove that the Tsarevitch Dimitry had died in 1591. The fact that he made no use of the proof of identification would seem to show that the likeness of the body did not satisfy.

· · · · ·

But in May and June, 1591, the question as to whether the Tsarevitch was in fact dead did not arise. There is nevertheless a further element of mystery in what happened. The revenge which Boris Godunof took on the people of Uglitch is out of keeping with his pacific character and greatly disproportionate to their offence. A mob of provincials might have been forgiven for lynching the supposed murderers of a Tsar's son. But instead Godunof smote the inhabitants of the city root and branch and such a chastisement of a city had not occurred since Ivan the Terrible decimated Novgorod the Great. It is generally explained as due to the rage of Godunof at losing his good name: he wished to stop the story that he had had the young prince murdered. Many hundreds of babblers had their tongues cut out to ensure that they should never repeat the libel. And the cathedral bell which had sounded the alarm was taken down and melted, as if it had been guilty of accusing Boris Godunof.* Many members of the Nagy family were executed. Thousands of townsfolk were banished to distant regions. The town was dismantled. For a space of time it was dead. Indeed it never recovered entirely from this chastisement.

This was not merely a punishment for killing Bitiagovsky and his friends. It is evident that Boris Godunof desired to find something out, something which he failed to understand in the happenings. Shuisky had not satisfied his curiosity or allayed his suspicion. Many hundreds of people were put to the torture. That seems to imply an inquisition, an endless questioning. Unfortunately questions and answers of inquisitioners are seldom transcribed. And it was never in Boris' nature to proclaim his doubts and suspicions. He was secretive to the point of mania. But something was desired to be known from the kinsmen of the Nagy and the people of Uglitch under the torture. It is just possible that the plot to hide the Tsarevitch, substitute another body

* There is also a legend that the bell was sent into exile in Siberia.

and provoke a mutiny was in some way hinted by some of the prisoners on the rack. As a result we see Boris profoundly disquieted, continuing to arrest, torture, banish or execute people, not only in Uglitch but in other parts of Russia, even in Moscow itself.

But the mother of Dimitry was not brought to the torture. She was sent to the distant Vyksa Lake Convent, forcibly made a nun and kept in strict confinement. Henceforth she was Sister Martha. Many years were to pass and Boris would be forced to bring her back to Moscow to ask her certain questions face to face. Hers was not a very clear personality. We shall yet see her, after the death of Boris Godunof, closed in a weeping embrace of the man who called himself her long lost son, Dimitry of Uglitch, then Tsar of Russia.

IX.

THE MOSLEM AT THE GATES

THE credulous have said that Boris Godunof set fire to Moscow to divert public attention from the Uglitch scandal. They have also averred that for the same reason he invited the Tartars to come and sack the city. Both these suppositions may be dismissed. There was a fire; the Tartars threatened; public attention was diverted first by one mortal danger and then another, but it was absurd to think that Boris had arranged these calamities in advance. "Did Godunof murder the Tsarevitch?" was not a vital question when catastrophic fire was sweeping the capital. Nor did the question rank as important when the Tartar horde was discovered to be on the warpath and threatening the destruction of the city. But after the dangers were past it was probably realised how useful they had been to Godunof in stopping the rising tide of indignation, in stopping intrigue and in countermanding all men's energies for protection and defence.

The fire broke out on Whitsun Eve. Fedor, Boris and the court had gone to Troitsky Monastery for the festival. The French soldier, Margeret, says that on the Saturday night Boris had the principal shops and merchant houses set on fire. According to most of the chroniclers of the time, the fire was started by Godunof's agents about the time when the long Whitsun services would be beginning, late in the afternoon, when most people would be in church. In a few hours the Arbat, the Nikitskaya, the Tverskaya and the Petrovka were burnt to ashes. Happily the fire stopped short at the white stone houses, many of which Boris himself had caused to be built. But the alarm was great and some thousands of Muscovites were suddenly homeless and filled the air with clamour. The homeless went out of Moscow on the Troitsky road to meet the Tsar on his return. But Boris would not admit them to the Tsar's presence, fearing more accusations against himself. Instead he received the leading spirits among the victims, expressed his sympathy, promised help, new homes, made himself in fact the hope of those who might otherwise have charged him with causing their ruin.

The fire was a reminder of earlier catastrophies and especially of the disaster of 1571 when the Tartar had been successful in destroying almost the whole of the city by fire and a hundred thousand people had perished. Thus the thought of the fire begot the thought of the Tartar. Since Vorotinsky routed the Tartar in 1572 there had been little real menace from that quarter. There had been twenty years of peace. The Tartars had not taken advantage of the incompetency of Ivan in his last years, nor had they gained inspiration from the resounding victories of Stephen of Poland over the Russians. But it was not a peace in which the Russians had been without fear. Almost every inhabitant of Moscow had lost relatives in the invasion of 1571. It had taken long for the city to be rebuilt and a great swath of waste land south of the river still bore witness to the catastrophe. The rumour that the Tartar was coming again was recurrent. It was aggravated by the further rumour that the Poles were paying the Tartars to make another great inroad into Russia. Behind the Khan of Crimean Tartary was the Sultan in Constantinople. It was the heydey of the power of the Sultans and even Western Europe trembled because of the Turk.

During the reign of Fedor, Russia was conscious of military weakness. Neither Fedor nor Boris liked war. Fighting was unfashionable and the army was out of training. It is true the Swedes had been dealt with effectually, but the nation had not outlived the sense of inferiority, caused by the evacuation of all the western territories conquered by Ivan the Terrible. And although it counted the holiness of Tsar Fedor a great asset it had a sneaking belief that it was better to be governed by a terrible monarch than by a saint. Moreover the villainy of Boris Godunof seemed to set off the piety of Fedor in the account books of the angels. Some punishment from God was expected as a result of the murder of the Tsarevitch at Uglitch.

It may have occurred to Godunof that it was expedient to announce the danger of Tartar invasion. It was a device of his in later years to do this in order to rally all the forces of the nation for the defence of the country and himself. If he did so in 1591, that would account for the legend that he had invited the Tartars to the attack.

Although the Tartars had confined themselves to small raids and forays during the previous twenty years, it could not be said that they had given up the idea of subjugating Muscovy. Tartar warfare might conceivably have petered out in banditry, but the Khan was the Sultan's vassal. The ambition to re-impose the

Moslem yoke on Russia was kept alive by the Sultans. But the idea which was fanatically religious in Constantinople was merely commercial in Tartary. The Tartars respected Orthodoxy and to some extent believed in the miracles wrought by its saints. They had no notion of converting Russia. The religions had been at peace during the time when Russia was under the Tartar yoke. What grieved the Khan was that the paying of tribute had entirely lapsed. Russia moreover grew richer. Its treasure of gold and precious stones were coveted. The objects of the inroads were the reimposition of the yearly tribute, the spoliation of palaces and altars, the gathering of slaves and of girls for the harems. The slave trade was their chief commerce. The main impedimenta of a raiding army were the thousands of empty baskets for packing boys and girls. Great care was taken of the young marketable captives, though when one got sick he was generally taken by the leg and had his head bashed in on a tree or stone.

About the same time as the Whitsuntide fire in Moscow, Boris announced the Tartar danger. His spies reported great activity in the south and southwest. The Khan, pretending he was going to make a raid on Polish and Lithuanian territory, was planning to descend upon Russia. He believed that the Russians were at war with Sweden and that the army was embroiled in a territory far from Moscow and the coveted riches of the south. The Russian voivodes awaited the advance guard of the Tartars at the fringe of the forested lands. It was never their plan to meet the furious onset of the Mahometan horsemen on the open treeless spaces of the Steppes. In June it was seen that the Khan had mustered an army as numerous, or even more numerous, than that which had laid waste Moscow in 1571.

There was a panic in Moscow. The inhabitants dug holes in the ground and buried their valuables. Some looked malevolently on Boris Godunof: "It is you who have brought this curse on us" . . . "You who set fire to the city have brought the Tartars too." Boris explained that it was the Nagy who had started the fire but he could not say it was the Nagy who had inflamed the Tartar. But the guilt or innocence of Godunof was soon forgotten in the frenzied preparations for defence. The best Russian troops were concentrated in the region of Novgorod and Pskof and there was no time to bring them home. Fedor Mstislavsky and Dimitry Khvorostinin were set to improvise a new young army outside the gates of Moscow.

By the end of June the Tartars were besieging Tula, but leaving Tula invested, the main body, some 150,000 strong were hastening toward Moscow, riding night and day. The Russians seem to have been devoid of strategy, or possibly there was some conflict between the orders of Boris Godunof and those of Mstislavsky. Boris comported himself as commander-in-chief and all orders were supposed to be given in his name or to be invalid. But it is improbable that he could convince Mstislavsky that he was a soldier. The Russians were too late to fight a delaying action and separate forces which should have united were placed out of communication by the advancing Tartar. Godunof may well have reasoned: if a battle is fought thirty or forty miles from Moscow and our army is routed nothing will stop the Tartars. Moscow and ourselves will be at their mercy. He preferred to concentrate all forces available at the actual gates of Moscow itself. Moscow was declared in a state of siege. The inhabitants were diverted from prayer to defence, to the building of ditches and ramparts. To each of the leading princes was assigned a district for defence. The lately pardoned Dimitry Shuisky took over the defence of the Kremlin itself. It was evidently intended to defend the capital street by street.

The Russian armies and advance guards fell back and the Tartars met with no opposition till the towers and cupolas of Moscow were in their view. The chief danger, as in 1571, was fire, but the fire which on that occasion had destroyed Moscow had also robbed the Tartars of the fruits of victory and it was not thought that they would have recourse to firing the city again unless they began to lose in the struggle. Nevertheless as a precaution the new barricades had been set up a furlong beyond the first houses of the clustering wooden suburbs. The army of defence was concentrated at a distance of a mile in advance of these barricades. Various monasteries just outside Moscow were converted into fortresses and manned by soldiers. Probably not a few of the monks were enlisted for the defence. Regiments were posted at intervals all around the city and Boris Godunof on a war-horse went from commander to commander, rallying their spirits for the ordeal of battle. Fedor in the Kremlin prayed or laughed and was light-hearted, being unable to realise the danger in which he and his capital city were standing. But he allowed the whole of his personal bodyguard to go and fight in the army.

THE MOSLEM AT THE GATES 81

The night of the 3rd–4th July, 1591, was remembered for many a year by the people of Moscow. The defenders could hear the thunder of the horses' hoofs, coming as a murmur out of the forests, and with it, the hubbub of the yelling and shouting of the Tartars. All night long the boyars and their sons, and their retainers, the German mercenaries, the Scotch mercenaries, the Russian peasant soldiers, stood to arms. Mobilised with them as a spiritual force were thousands of banners and crosses, all motionless in the breathless summer night. No one slept, but all were silent in expectation. And few moved from the places where they were posted except the restless Godunof, who all night long verified the dispositions of the army and made personally sure that no commander was in doubt as to what he had to do on the morrow. As in a modern battle, zero hour proved to be dawn.

The Russian cannon thundered over the wooded plain, and the big cannon balls, visible in the air, sailed in long curves from the ramparts to the array of Tartar horsemen. The thunder was answered with rain, a thick rain of arrows as every horseman drew his bow upon the Russians. It was a great battle piece in the heroic style. The Tartars were shooting their arrows as they cantered toward the Russians. Then, slinging their bows on their shoulders, they drew their scimitars and galloped. Russian horse, to right and to left, attacked them in flank, but the centre was left open, defended by a long line of musketeers who fired their arquebuses from behind barricades. Every tower and high building on that side of Moscow was crowded with people watching the fight, even from the battlements of the

Kremlin itself. It was the first time in the history of the city that a battle had been fought in full view of the inhabitants. Out of the confusion of the *mêlée* Tartar bands were seen advancing to the outskirts of the city, but they were met and dispersed by reserve forces kept back by Godunof. He had not staked the whole of his army against the first onrush of the Tartars. He had rightly judged that the first encounter was a skirmish. The main force of the Tartars was still three miles distant, with the Khan himself at Sparrow Hills. The advance guard did not expect to take the city but only to make confusion in the Russian camp.

But all day the skirmishing party was reinforced and the battle went on. Obviously, the Khan showed some incapacity in adventuring his forces piecemeal and not staking everything on the shock of the impact of his vast army put simultaneously into action. From a Tartar point of view, the first day of battle was wasted. They had many dead; they achieved nothing, and the riderless horses caused much confusion. The Muscovites were still in a state of great trepidation and at midnight, long after the open fighting had ceased for the day, they began firing all the cannon in the city. There is no suggestion that there was any shortage of powder, but they wasted a good deal. It is explained that they fired in order to keep the enemy scared. Tartars had never taken to gunpowder like modern men, and it was thought that even the sound of cannon frightened them somewhat. But it is likely that the Russians were in an extremely nervous state, expecting a night attack at any moment. The Khan took some prisoners on the morning of the 4th July and asked them to explain the meaning of the continuous cannonade. They lied. They said the army of the northwest had just arrived from Novgorod and Pskof and the salvos were part of the welcome accorded to a new army of deliverance.

It seems the Khan believed this tale and at once commenced to retreat. As soon as the Russians were aware of this happy and unforeseen change of front, they moved out in force to harry the rearguard. Godunof and Mstislavsky, with almost the whole of the men at their disposal, hurried forward to attack the Khan. Had not the latter been craven in the extreme, he might yet have turned and beaten the Russians. But his portentous stupidity communicated itself to his followers, who became panic-stricken, fleeing ever faster and fouling one another in their haste to get away. The retreat became a rout.

The Russians took a thousand or so prisoners, and they seized some valuable booty, but they were not strong enough to destroy the Tartar host, at least half of which must have got safely home. Orders were sent to Mstislavsky to consummate the defeat, but he used his discretion and halted his army at Serpukhof. He and Godunof returned to Moscow to celebrate the victory, to bell-ringing, incense, parade and reward. The praise for the victory was accorded to Godunof, though he and Mstislavsky were honoured equally by the Tsar. Much was due to his organising ability, though he was not a soldier and had no experience in military strategy. But much also was due to chance. Moscow was lucky in that the catastrophe of 1571 was not repeated in 1591.

Before they returned to Moscow, the Tsar Fedor had ridden out to headquarters to congratulate the army in person. To both the commanders he made presents of fur coats with golden buttons, seemingly strange presents to be made in the month of July, but the coats were very valuable. Godunof and Mstislavsky did not mind wearing them in the heat. No doubt they wore them at the great feast at the Granovity Palace in the Kremlin when Fedor and his boyars made carouse and triumphed in wine and song over the Tartars, as they had done in the field by force of arms.

Boris Godunof felt much more secure in power as a result of the victory. Incipient intrigue must have lost its attraction in the excitement of national mobilisation and defence. After the celebrations there were more tortures and executions of the followers of the Nagy. The persecution was resumed at the point where it had been interrupted. Boris could not overlook the saying that despite his glory he was a murderer. The will to impose silence regarding his part in the tragedy of Uglitch was strong, and it grew till it became an obsession.

X.

POWER AND INFLUENCE

THE Tsar gave to Godunof in part reward for his services against the Tartars the revenues of three more towns, and he gave him the title of *Sluga* or servant, which does not sound like an honour, though it was one of the greatest distinctions in the power of the Tsar to award. The Tsar also parted with some of the crown jewels. Between the Tsar's estate and that of Boris there was not much differentiation of *mine* and *thine*. "The Empress and her kindred, especially Boris Fedorovitch Godunof, account it all their own that runneth into the Emperor's treasure. . . ."*

Gregory Godunof, the chief steward of the Tsar's revenues, was an unremitting tax-gatherer and collected from Russia about four times as much as the most diligent of his predecessors had done. So despite the great alms paid out to beggars and religious establishments, the court under the control of the Godunofs grew much richer than it had been under the rule of Ivan the Terrible. Actually, Godunof was liberal, and later as Tsar became prodigal, but in the years in which he was building up his power, he often seemed avaricious. He must have regarded his own increasing wealth as in the nature of a political war chest. Every addition to his personal treasure helped to guarantee his future and his ambition. To him in 1592 needless expense was a squandering of personal power. Thus the largess

* Fletcher: *Of the Russe Commonwealth.*

which he bestowed was mostly out of the Tsar's purse, and he never refused gifts nor omitted an opportunity of personal enrichment.

The state treasures, always heretofore held under the seal of the monarch himself, came under the seal of Boris Godunof, who made himself personally responsible for their safe keeping. It had been one of Ivan's nightly hobbies to bring out his gold and precious stones and gloat over them, saying to himself or his son: "What a rich man am I! Surely there is not a richer sovereign than I in all the world!" But this was not continued by the simple Fedor. Boris saw to it that the treasures were kept locked away and only brought forth when required for state occasions.

When entertainment was to be given for foreign ambassadors, it was provided lavishly at the Tsar's expense. Boris received the ambassadors in great pomp, but it was the Tsar who paid. Boris received the presents which the ambassadors brought from their sovereign. It was soon understood throughout Europe that the person to be honoured with gifts was not the Tsar of Russia but Boris Godunof, and so the most desirable international bribes came his way.

Boris was an affable host, in no sense forbidding. He was an example of the Russian who can talkatively say nothing and say it for a long while. Had he lived in a later century it seems he would have been well fitted for a parliamentary career. Besides the gift of easy talk, he had tact. He had the soft answer which turneth away wrath. He conveyed to most individuals whom he wished to use the impression that he was their particular friend. He made himself appear humble that others might consider themselves great. He bought support with a look, with a wink, with flattery, with pardon. He went so far as to pardon the traitor Golovin, who had fled to Poland to betray Russia. He would welcome Golovin back to Moscow as a supporter, knowing that he would hold the life of the traitor in the palm of his hand and could hand him over to the executioners at the slightest suggestion of treachery to himself. The astrologers had warned him against the Nagy; they had not warned him against Golovin. He seldom took a step in politics now without the advice of wizards. But he could justify most of these steps on religious grounds. In converse with the Patriarch, he was unwaveringly pious. Job was very violently opposed to necromancy, so it may be assumed that Boris was able to conceal his dealings with magicians.

The practice of sorcery may be ridiculed, but it implies the taking of the Devil as guide. Boris, as a young man, was initiated into the black arts by Ivan the Terrible, who in his later years took a pleasure in exploring wickedness. That first dabbling in sorcery by Boris Godunof did not have much significance. But as his ambition grew, sorcery made him promises and became more serious. Wizards read his mind and told him his darkest thoughts, and it seemed as if these thoughts had obtained supernatural confirmation. "To be king stands not within the prospect of belief," said Macbeth, and so might Boris say, but he had thought of it before the wizards spoke of it. His virtue had already crumpled because of his ambition. In his secret mind he rejoiced at the supposed death of the Tsarevitch Dimitry because it meant that another obstacle was down.

Still the way was not quite clear. In 1593, to the surprise and joy of the court, Irene grew large with child. Prayers were ordered for her happy delivery of a son and heir. The birth of a healthy son would have dashed the ambitions of Godunof. But the child born was a daughter. Even a daughter was embarrassing, though the right of inheritance of the throne passed through the male line, not the female. It was said of Boris that the Tsaritsa had actually given birth to a son but he had at once substituted a baby girl brought from some lying-in establishment. This legend was the basis of the claim of another pretender to the throne at a later period. Secondly, it was said that when the baby Theodosia died Boris had secretly administered poison. But both stories may be dismissed. Boris was selfish but his mind was tribal. What the Godunofs did was right, and if his sister bore a child it was quite as much a matter for rejoicing for him as for her husband.

Theodosia was christened at the Chudof Monastery. There was great rejoicing both throughout Russia and at court. Fedor was pleased to have a daughter and perhaps even more pleased at the hope granted him of having other children. In sign of his gratitude to God and his happiness, he released all prisoners in the realm, even those under sentence of death. The irons were taken off the bodies of those suffering slow torture; men on the rack were suddenly released. Men who had been chained to walls in dark dungeons for years were suddenly unpadlocked and restored to freedom. Every prison in Russia was emptied and the shadow of disgrace was taken off hundreds of men living in banishment. And to this great liberation Boris must have been privy. The Tsar Fedor had no power to be clement without his sanction.

Great alms were bestowed on monasteries throughout Russia as thanks to God. Monks set forth from Russia bearing gifts to the shrines of the East, even to the Church of the Sepulchre in Jerusalem. They should start eternal prayer for the soul of Theodosia in Constantinople, in Antioch, in Jerusalem. Alas, before they ever reached these distant places, the baby was dead and the soul had returned to God.

The death of the little child took place on the 25th of January, 1594, and the grief in the palace and in Russia was as great as the joy had been a few months before. Fedor and Irene were beloved and the emotion was genuine, but it was more than an emotion of personal sympathy. Russia was agitated by the prospect of the dynasty becoming extinct. The dynasty was holy. Moscow had risen from nothing under this line of grand dukes and tsars and with difficulty imagined itself being governed by any other family. And Irene had dramatised her need of a child by those yearly pilgrimages to Troitsky Monastery accompanied by praying women. The birth of Theodosia had been hailed as a miracle. God had listened to Russia's prayers and had shown her favour. But when the baby died God had turned His face away from Russia. Perhaps it was God's will that the line of Rurik should rule no more in the land.

When Theodosia was born it may have been assumed by Fedor and Irene that they might have more children following, perhaps a son and heir. But after the death of the baby it seems to have been tacitly assumed that there would be no further offspring. Probably her physicians told the Tsaritsa that the chapter was ended and that she could have no more children. One may surmise that from that moment Irene turned away from the world and its vanities and decided that if she should survive her husband she would enter a convent and leave the throne to Boris. In her intimate talks with her brother she must have said: "You will be Tsar, but I, as is fitting, will end my days in the peace of a convent."

Boris' own little son, Fedor, began to have the aureole of a Tsarevitch. He was being looked upon even then as the heir presumptive and Boris with some paternal vanity referred to him in his dealings with ambassadors of foreign powers as the likely inheritor of the Russian throne.

It became increasingly clear to the boyars that the upstart Godunof intended to make himself Tsar and at this critical time, almost in a state of panic, they began to whisper among themselves would it not be better to invite some foreign prince betimes to come and be Tsar when Fedor died. Overtures were made secretly to the Emperor, Rudolph II, that either he or some Austrian prince should take over the throne of Russia. The *dyak*, Andrew Shchelkalof, had a series of secret conversations with Warkotch, the ambassador of the Emperor, and instructed him to convey the invitation of the boyars to Rudolph II. It seems a mad project to offer Russia to a Catholic prince. Andrew Shchelkalof was a man of parts, considered second only to Boris in capacity. Much had been entrusted to him and he was one of the most important men in Russia at the time. It is surprising that he lent himself to this conspiracy. Boris was soon informed of it by his spies. Andrew Shchelkalof was disgraced in May, 1594, and the administrative posts which he held were given to his brother Vasilly. Boris, however, took no measures against the aristocrats sheltering behind Andrew Shchelkalof. Possibly he saw in the invitation to the Emperor the despair of the boyars. They were jealous of one another. They had no leader. They could not unite to support the claim of the Romanofs, nor could they unite to support either Shuisky or Mstislavsky. So they were reduced to asking the Catholic Emperor to come and rule over them. Boris with the aid of the Church would never have had difficulty in rebutting the claim of the Emperor.

Boris, however, scanned the horizon for possible rivals. The boyars could not agree among themselves but they had shown a tendency to unite to support some neutral candidate. He sifted daily the reports of overheard conversations brought him by his spies. Boris may have been a man of genius but he had one characteristic which is not commonly associated with sagacity, and that was suspicion, which is commonly linked to credulity. He was more suspicious and relied more on spies than Ivan the Terrible had done.

Another neutral personality that might provide a rallying ground for the jealous boyars seemed to be the Tartar ex-Tsar, ex-Grand-Duke of Tver, Simeon. The name of Simeon must have been mentioned by the boyars in their whispered plans for the succession. That would account for the legend that about this time Boris had Simeon made blind. Simeon had never been invited to court by Fedor and Boris Godunof, and it would seem that from the first Boris regarded him with some antipathy. This Simeon was the baptised Tartar to whom Ivan the Terrible relinquished the throne for a year during one of his freakish periods of self-renunciation. Simeon wore the crown, but Ivan played at being his subject though in fact he ruled through him. Boris had been a spectator of this strange episode and like the rest of the court had been forced to recognise and obey the mock Tsar. But he saw clearly enough that Ivan was using Simeon as a cover to plunder the Church and to baffle the envoys of foreign powers. He must have seen the possibilities of a subject being the actual Tsar while the crown-bearer was only Tsar in name. Yet possibly it had given him little pleasure to humble himself before the Tartar to humour Ivan's caprice.

When Ivan had resumed the throne, Simeon was made Duke of Tver. After a campaign against Stephen of Poland he retired to his estates to finish his days in quietness. He was an old man and very simple, not to say stupid. Yet some thought that failing a male issue from Fedor it was not inconceivable that the boyars might invite Simeon to return to the throne as his successor. In fact they did do so, even though Simeon had become blind. On St. Simeon's day, 1593, Boris is supposed to have sent to the ex-Tsar a goblet of Spanish wine containing a poison which would render him blind. Certainly he became blind and the unfortunate old man put it down to the effects of the wine. The historiographer of the time accepted the story which, nevertheless, does sound improbable.

POWER AND INFLUENCE

For the rest the times were quiet, undisturbed by internal dissension or foreign war. A law was passed stopping the wandering of free peasants from village to village, thus fastening serfdom on a greater number of poor people. Much was done to help agriculture, especially on the poor estates. The frontier defences were better organised and plans were approved for converting Smolensk into a stone fortress. In 1595 there was another serious fire in Moscow and the whole of the Kitai-gorod—the market adjoining the Kremlin—was burned to the ground, but Boris had this famous place rebuilt in stone. Incendiaries were arrested and executed. Probably the crime of designing to set Moscow on fire was fastened upon innocent persons whom for other reasons it was desired to remove. Prince Vasilly Shchepin was one of those who paid the supreme penalty.

The Tsar, when he was not on pilgrimage, and Boris Godunof, kept up a considerable court in Moscow. There was little private dining. Everyone of any importance went to dinner in the Kremlin palaces where they sat down to meat in hundreds. There were few absentees from religious and court ceremonials. The gentry had to move about in masses and no opportunity was given to groups to meet secretly to conspire against the state. In the intrigue which has always ravished Russian court circles lay the greatest menace to the power of Godunof, but he was successful in suppressing it.

XI.

PERSIA ASKS FOR FRIENDSHIP

THE whole of the Volga, even to the estuary at Astrakhan, had become Russian during the preceding reign of Ivan the Terrible. The Russians had fought their way through to the Caspian and made contact with Persia. On the other hand, the Black Sea remained immutably Turkish and the Sea of Azof was Tartar. There was no Odessa, Nikolaef, Sebastopol, Taganrog, Rostof on the Don. The Turks who occupied the Balkan territories were in possession of Bessarabia, Rumania and Eastern Transylvania and were arrayed in battle against Hungary and Austria. Turkey was at war also with France and Spain and was considered to be a menace to the whole of Western Christendom. The Sultan Amurath, though hostile to Russia, was more concerned to destroy the great Catholic powers of the West than to make good the failure of the Khan of Tartary. He bitterly reproached the Khan for his cowardice in fleeing from Moscow when the Russian capital was in the hollow of his hand, but he did not invade Russia to revenge the insult on Mahomet.

Russia as we know it to-day, like England, France, Italy, Germany, Spain and almost every other land, is a north-south country. One thinks of the north as the head, the south as the feet, and east and west as the two sides. But in those days it was a lop-sided west-east country. It had no north: Archangel was just being built. It had no south: Moscow could almost be called a southern city. The vast black earth region of present southern Russia was a debatable land liable to be overrun every summer by the Tartar. Kursk and Voronezh were abuilding but could not yet be considered places of military importance. Russia had developed via her rivers, the Oka and the Volga. Her forests were a defence but also a hindrance. And with her small standing army she could not organise lines of defence across the vast, open treeless regions south of the forest lands. The best she could do was to colonise with fighting men such as the Cossacks and leave it to them to ward off attacks or invade new territory. Such fighting communities, especially the Cossacks, were a law unto themselves and their doings were seldom reported to Moscow either for approval or censure. In their growth and activity they were a menace to the Moslem. When the Sultan demanded that certain new forts on the Don should be dismantled the Russians replied in all innocence that no such forts existed. Very probably, to the knowledge of Moscow, no such forts did exist.

It suited Russia to nibble at the territories of the Khan and to take them piecemeal, using the Volga bases and her military colonists. But it did not suit her to be over-run by great armies plunging northward over the undefended plains. Therefore she steadily sought peace both with the Sultan and the Khan. She did not greatly care what happened to Western Christendom, and though both Godunof and Fedor were flattered by the presence of a Papal legate in Moscow, they would rather have peace than holy war.

We have a series of intrigues, lying offers, bluffs, chicanes, false truces. The Khan resented the imputation of cowardice made by the Sultan and pretended to offer Moscow an assured peace. He said the Sultan intended to dethrone him. Therefore he would abandon the cause of the Sultan. He would evacuate the Don Steppes and the Crimea and establish his headquarters on the Dnieper where he would protect Russia from invasion by the Turks. All he asked was money to defray the expense of building fortresses on the Dnieper when he would become the Tsar's vassal. As a guarantee of good faith he would at once move north and lay waste part of Lithuania. The Russians replied that although they were at peace with Lithuania they would not be at all averse to seeing it laid waste. But the peace proposal of the Khan was humbug. Even while discussing it with a Russian envoy his sons were raiding Russia in the good old style and filling their baskets with children for slavery. The raiders reached Riazan and returned to the Crimea without conflict, bearing with them large spoils. The Khan reproved his sons and followers publicly, but privately was entirely pleased. His cynical comments on his perfidy did not please Boris Godunof, who at once switched his peace negotiations to the court of the Sultan himself. The Tsar sent a personal message to the Sultan; Boris to the Grand Vizier. The bearer of the messages was Nashchokin who invited the Sultan to send an ambassador to Moscow. The Sultan replied that he was neither in the habit of receiving ambassadors nor of sending them.

The tenor of the Russian messages was that the Sultan might see in Russia a friendly neutral who had not listened to the overtures of the Pope, of the Emperor of the Holy Roman Empire, the King of Poland and

Grand Duke of Lithuania or of any of his other enemies. In consideration of this neutrality the Sultan was asked to stop the inroads of the Tartars. The Grand Vizier replied: "The Sultan will believe in your sincerity when you agree to hand over to him Kazan and Astrakhan. As for your neutrality, we fear neither Europe nor Asia. Our forces are so innumerable the earth can scarcely bear the weight of them. We shall proceed overland against the Shah of Persia, against Lithuania and the Emperor. Spain and France we shall attack by sea. We admire your prudence in attaching yourselves to our cause and we will willingly call off the Khan if you surrender Kazan and Astrakhan and destroy the new fortresses which have appeared on the Don, the object of these fortresses being apparently to bar our way to Derbent and the Caspian. Do these things or worse shall befall you in the future."

This was not a very promising beginning for peace negotiations. Instead of any advantage arising from the overtures, it appeared that Nashchokin had attracted the Sultan's rage toward Russia. The Russians feared both Turk and Tartar but they were firmly established in Kazan and Astrakhan and could not easily have been dislodged by force of arms. But Nashchokin did not show himself dismayed. If he could not get a treaty of peace he could at least start a long parley such as Russians loved. He seems to have argued that the Russians considered Turkish goodwill the greatest guarantee for security and peace and that the Tsar might even part with Astrakhan and Kazan to obtain it. He was not abashed by the proud boast that the Sultan did not send ambassadors. "It might be worth your while. Why abandon a potential ally for the sake of an old custom?" The Turks were bluffed and sent their envoy extraordinary to the Tsar.

The Sultan did not wish peace with Russia and was too much preoccupied in the West to make war. But he had long viewed with misgiving the Russian development toward the southeast. When Ivan the Terrible had taken Astrakhan it had not been thought probable that he would keep it long. But now the Russian occupation had an air of permanency. The Khans had repeatedly terrorised the Russian centre where plunder was great and opposition slight, but they had left the Russian strongholds on the Volga alone. Russia had opened a trade route across the Caspian into Turkestan, even to distant Bokhara. Russian influence was slowly permeating the Terek Steppes and was felt in the foothills of the Caucasus. The King of Georgia had asked and obtained the protection of the Tsar. It seemed to the Sultans that communication by land to the Mahometans of Central Asia would soon be entirely interrupted by the Russians. For that reason Sultan Amurath was willing to do much if he could get Astrakhan into his hands, the more so as he was at odds with the ambitious Shah of Persia who contested his hegemony of the Mahometan world.

But nothing came of the parley. The Sultan sent his envoy. Godunof replied by sending another. Amurath died and was succeeded by Mahomet III. No peace was made but no war was proclaimed. The Khan obtained the Sultan's permission to conclude a false armistice and there was a peaceful meeting in barbaric splendour of Tartar and Russian princes. The Russians were lavish of gifts and although it was the Khan's intention to cheat he proved in the long run too venal to resist the Tsar's gold. He was in effect bought off and undertook no further enterprise of great moment against Muscovy. The greater part of his following went to fight under the banner of the Sultan against Hungary.

The Russian southeastern development remained unchecked. Abbas, Shah of Persia, hostile to the Sultans, conceived great respect for the Russians and with oriental readiness of phrase proposed eternal brotherhood. Azi Khozrov, the Persian envoy, came to talk with Boris Godunof in August, 1593, and flattered him, calling him the guide and support of the Russian Tsar, letting him know that Persia regarded him as greater than his sovereign. "You with but one hand support the great Russian land, deign to lend the other hand in loving support of my sovereign the Shah!"

Boris, with masked expression, replied discreetly that both his hands belonged to his master the Tsar. He might be the hands of Russia but the Tsar was the head. But Azi Khozrov had not come to Russia without something in the nature of an invitation from Godunof. The initiative was not entirely Persian. The Russian territory in the southeast must be guaranteed against the pretensions of the Sultan. If a large Turkish army crossed the north Caucasian plateau and destroyed the power of the Shah, it would inevitably proceed afterward against Astrakhan. An understanding with Persia had become Russian policy.

The Shah was ambitious, bloodthirsty and capable. Like Boris, he had been holding the Turks in parley in order to gain time. Before entering the field he wished to dispatch what enemies he had in his own country. He had agreed to an armistice with the Sultan, but intended to break it directly he was ready for war. He had given one of his nephews, a six-year-old boy, as hostage. . . . "Directly we unsheathe the sword, cut his throat" . . . but the envoy explained that the Shah had enough nephews and to spare, and they caused him trouble, anyway.

In May, 1594, Prince Andrew Zvenigorodsky was deputed to go to the Shah and treat for a military alliance. Khozrov returned to Persia with him. The journey seems to have taken a long time, for it was not until November that they were received by the Shah. The light of history lies on the west in the fifteenth and seventeenth centuries, and little is known of what was happening in Southern Asia. At the Persian court were Bokharese and Khivans, Afghans and Indians. "Do you see that man?" asked the Shah, pointing to one in his court. "He is the ambassador of India. His sovereign, Jelladin Iber, is in possession of unmeasured lands, perhaps of two-thirds of the inhabited world, yet I esteem your Tsar more than I do him."

The curtain lifts on Persia of those times. The Shah, swollen in bulk of quilted silks and damasks, sat on a throne in Kashan, with jewelled scimitar on his hip, bow and arrow on his knee. One bare foot was exposed for the Russian to kiss, but when Zvenigorodsky objected to that oriental obeisance the Shah good-humouredly offered him a fat brown hand, all ringed and jewelled, and the prince kissed that instead. There were present many representatives of the nations of the East, but those considered to be hostile to Russia had been eliminated. There were no tale-bearers to the Sultan.

The Shah showed him the gold-studded saddle of Tamerlane and possibly the chariot in which Tamerlane had driven with twenty kings harnessed to it. Shah Abbass recalled the greatness of Persia and expressed his will that she should become under his rule as great as she had been under Timour. He would drive the Ottomans out of Western Persia. He would conquer Khiva and take back Khorassan from the Emir of Bokhara. "I have 40,000 horse, 30,000 foot, 6,000 musketeers, and when the time comes and I have settled with my enemies at home, I will unite my army with the Tsar's and we will share the glory of conquering Turkey."

All went well. Prince Andrew knew that Godunof had no intention of starting a war with Turkey, but Russia would stop the Turks if they attempted to reach the Caspian. There was a common cause. There were feasts and games in honour of the Russian ambassador. The Persians were not strict Mahometans and they drank freely with the Russian prince. Even the Shah himself lifted a glass of wine and drank the health of Tsar Fedor and Boris Godunof. The Persians were careful not to omit to do as much honour to Boris as to the Tsar.

The festivities were transferred to the open and there was carnival at night. The Shah took the tambourine and danced in the light of naphtha flares. The drummers beat a terrific hullabaloo and there was trumpeting from enormous horns. There were reed lights along all the walls, volumes of blue flame and suffocating smoke from burning sulphur which nobody seemed to mind, drinking from rams' horns, the carving up of enormous melons from the Oxus shores, the pouring forth of thick honey upon musk melon, singing, sword dancing, explosions, fireworks, in all of which, of course, men only took part, the women being shut in their houses and under guard.

By day the Shah took the Russian to the great bazaar and turned over with him innumerable bales of silks, showed him the most magnificent carpets and jewelled daggers and swords, and saddles, and girl slaves offered as merchandise. Then he went to Prince Andrew's lodging and danced for him again in private. He had the reputation of being a remarkable dancer in the Persian style. The dangerous potentate, merciless in war, had evidently great heartiness of disposition and having made a friend became a brother and stood no longer on ceremony of any kind.

There was some dividing of spoils in anticipation of victory over the Turk, and Russia was to have Derbent and Baku. It was arranged that the nomadic tribes of Central Asia acknowledge the Tsar as their sovereign. The Khan of the Kirghiz became Fedor's vassal. Zvenigorodsky returned to Moscow with promises and gifts. Godunof heard his recital and was well pleased. Another prince was sent to the Shah, Vasilly Tiufiakin, to confirm the alliance. Unfortunately, Tiufiakin and his party were attacked and murdered on the way. The Shah waited some time for the Russian reply, and then losing patience decided to make war on Bokhara instead of Turkey. The military alliance lapsed for the time being, but it did not matter very much because the Sultan's army was mutinous, not having been paid wages for a long time. The greater part of it was engaged in the European campaign and there was not sufficient force at the Sultan's disposal to embark on the hazardous enterprise of enforcing his will upon Persia and Russia.

XII.

THE DEATH OF FEDOR

TOWARD the end of the year 1597 the Tsar Fedor became seriously ill. Possibly the symptoms were those of poisoning. Physicians gave no name to his disease, but there was a suspicion of poison. If it was poison, it was slow in its working, as it was twelve days before the Tsar died. He fell ill on the 27th of December; he died on the 8th of January.

From the first moment of his sickness there was sorrow and anxiety in Moscow. Fedor was idealised by the common people. His piety approached sainthood. His alms always had been liberal. He had not scourged the city as his father had done. His simplicity and sweetness of disposition showed itself as God's mercy to Russia after the terror of Ivan. The prayers for his recovery were more sincere than the prayers on such occasions usually are. It was soon learned that not only was Fedor ill but dangerously so. Almost at once the Patriarch and the court seem to have grasped that the Tsar was about to die.

Sorrow was linked to fear and apprehension. With Fedor the dynasty of Rurik was coming to an end, a matter of indifference to historians, but something like the end of the world to young Muscovy. Moscow had risen from nothing under this line. Its triumphs, humiliations, bondage, freedom, victory, were bound up with the rule of the Grand Dukes and the Tsars. It had grown with them from being a church in a wood and a castle on a hill to a great metropolis. It regarded the dynasty as sacred. The Tsar was nearer to godhead than patriarch or metropolitan. James I was about to expound the divine right of kings to a sceptical England, but Ivan, when he assumed that the people were given to him by God and he had the right to do whatever he liked with them, met with no objection. His victims died in torment praying for his long life. Thus it will be understood that with Fedor dying, God's dispensation to the Russian people seemed to have been withdrawn. It is easy to see that the child Dimitry, had he lived, would have been advanced to the throne, whether considered legitimate or illegitimate, that the ancient line might be continued.

This devotion to the dynasty was one which had been shared equally by the monarchs themselves. But for Ivan it could not be said that they had been in any sense suicidal. And Ivan had put the question of succession before all others in his mind. In cold blood he would never have murdered his eldest son, Ivan. But he was a supreme egotist and such supreme egotism as his sometimes has the same result as supreme abnegation. He had destroyed the heir presumptive, Vladimir Andreyevitch and his sons, that the succession might be safeguarded to the direct succession of his own sons. Then in mad rage he had struck down the heir apparent. His mother before him, the Regent Helena, had also done much to extinguish the dynasty by destroying the brothers of Vasilly III. Actually, with Fedor, the dynasty was extinct.

And Ivan had gone further: he had prepared the way for Boris Godunof. His personal policy had been one of centralisation of power. He had exalted his title by making himself Tsar. He had then proceeded to alienate all power from the feudal aristocracy. He had destroyed whole families. He had sequestered large estates. He had degraded and humiliated. He had taken all executive power and control into his own hands and Russia had become more of an autocracy than ever before. He died. The simple Fedor was incapable of manipulating the one-man machine. But all was arranged for one man ruling Russia. The new machine passed to the man capable of using it, Boris Godunof.

The old year, 1597, passed; the new year, 1598, came on, packed with problems and surmise. Fedor lay on his death-bed and each day it was hoped or feared that he would make a pronouncement regarding the succession. The redoubtable Godunof was waiting, cat-like, for any mouse to jump. There was no mean danger in any mention of a name by Fedor. Vasilly Shuisky boasted descent from Rurik and had a claim to the throne. But he had no following. The great Shuisky clan had been dispersed and partially destroyed. He was himself a pardoned man who had obtained high office merely by indulgence. He was secretly hostile to the usurper of power, but feared him. It would have been very dangerous for him had Fedor named him as the next Tsar.

At the bedside court were many of the kindred of Ivan the Terrible's first wife, Anastasia, the Romanofs. That they imagined at that time that they would provide the next long line of tsars is not probable. There is a story that the dying Fedor offered his sceptre

THE DEATH OF FEDOR

to Prince Fedor Romanof. It seems that the sceptre lay on the bed beside the powerless arm of the dying man, and his crown reposed on a pillow above his head. Thus we have the picture. A high bed with gorgeous draperies; ikon of the Virgin, with lighted lamp, over the Tsar's head; ikon at his feet; a cross in his hand; ikons with lighted lamps on the walls; a room surcharged with incense; lamp reflections in the dim mica windows; the black-robed clergy and chief among them the Patriarch Job, all praying; men-at-arms; courtiers. The story goes that Fedor indicated Fedor Romanoff, who at once said he had rather his brother Alexander took the sceptre. But Alexander offered it to his brother Ivan, and his brother Ivan offered it to his brother Michael, who also refused it. This is dismissed by Russian historians as an old wives' tale. But it has some substance in it. None of those Romanofs nor any other noble present dare touch the sceptre if it were offered, and none dare aspire to the throne for fear of Godunof.

It is generally assumed that Fedor had no interest in this world whatsoever, and left all tacitly in the hands of Boris and Irene. On the evening of the 7th of January he asked to be left alone for a while with the Tsaritsa, and the priests and the courtiers removed themselves. It was Fedor's last night. At eleven the Patriarch returned and anointed the monarch's temples with holy oil and gave him the Bread and the Wine. Peace settled on the pale face of the Tsar and did not leave it; a vague shadow lifted from it at one in the morning and he was dead.

The lugubrious tolling of the Kremlin bells in the middle of the night told the prayerful populace that the end had come. The people rushed out of doors over the deep snow to the Kremlin bridges and gates. The gentry, sitting up, waiting the event, surged to the palace. All men-at-arms were on duty in the Kremlin and had their orders from Boris Godunof. Irene had swooned at the death of her husband, and had been carried to her apartments. But there must be no hiatus in Tsardom. Boris at once assumed the direction of affairs. He did not lose his head at that moment. He knew the procedure which he intended and he had in advance communicated it to the Patriarch, who agreed. To the boyars assembled in the presence of the dead Tsar, he said that all must now swear allegiance to the Tsaritsa. To that there was no demur. The Patriarch then received each noble in turn. One by one the Shuiskies, the Romanofs and the rest came and kissed the cross in the hand of the Patriarch and recited an oath of allegiance to Irene, who became Tsaritsa in her own right.

Irene, when she recovered, declared that she would enter a cloister and henceforth renounce the world. But her brother persuaded her or seemed to persuade her to take the throne. But she was mad in her grief, shrieked and tore herself with her fingers, and blood and saliva were running from her lips.

And the grave of Ivan the Terrible was opened and the body of his son was laid with him.

XIII.

INTERREGNUM

THE Tsaritsa Irene was not in that state of mind in which she might have been capable of ruling Russia. Boris did not need to use his persuasive power to make his sister abandon the throne. Her psychological state led her inevitably to a refuge from the world. She had long sought compensation for childlessness in communion with the saints. The religiosity of her husband had led to an exaggeration of her own piety. Too much pilgrimage and prayer and pre-occupation with death and the unseen had weakened her resistance to grief. Instead of emerging purified and calm in mind after the emotional crisis of Fedor's death she gave way to sobbing and hysteria. Only the church and the veil could give her peace. She fled from the funeral feasts; she put her fingers before her face to hide from funeral pomps. She was at once at Novodevitchy Convent grovelling prostrate before the ikons. The Church had pity on her and took her to itself and she became Sister Alexandra.

The people of Moscow at that time are pictured as possessed of a purely animal grief. Men sobbed because the dynasty was dead. A whole people asked: "What will happen to us now that the family of the grand dukes and the tsars has perished?" God, it seemed, had withdrawn that particular blessing which is associated with the birth of royal children. The Muscovites looked pathetically upon themselves as a nation of orphans.

Godunof steered the course of affairs but men looked more to God than Godunof and there is even a story that at Fedor's funeral there appeared a heavenly stranger whom no one recognised as belonging to the court. God had withdrawn the offspring of Kalita but had vouchsafed an angel to govern Russia. It was characteristic of the Russians even then that they believed that God took a special interest. That came of centuries of struggle and battle against the Moslem, an enduring holy war which caused Russians to identify their cause with that of the Almighty.

As was natural under the circumstances the position of the Patriarch Job became greatly magnified. There is something in name and rank even within the Church. A holy man as Metropolitan is still more holy when he is called Patriarch. To be patriarch means to be father of a people under God. It is a fine exalted word commanding respect, obedience, devotion. This was the first great moment of the influence of the patriarchs in Russian history. As tsars could only be vouchsafed by God they would most probably come by way of the man who stood nearest to god, the Patriarch. The men of Moscow raised their bowed heads and all eyes rested upon the Patriarch Job as the one who must guide the nation in its bewilderment.

The Patriarch prayed to God that having taken the sovereign He would not at the same time withdraw His mercy from Russia. The funeral of the last of a line must lack something of the pomp of a funeral

THE PATRIARCH JOB

which has an heir as chief mourner. It is a more tragic event when it is not possible to rush from the dead to the living shouting: "The Tsar is dead, long live the Tsar!" The chief feature of the funeral of Tsar Fedor was the great alms given by the Patriarch's orders to the poor. There was such bounty that many men made themselves beggars to partake of it. At the same time on the day of the funeral all prisoners throughout the land were made free by proclamation. The dynasty was dead: all prison gates must open.

Boris Godunof followed his sister to Novodevitchy Monastery, leaving the throne vacant and all authority either in the hands of the Patriarch or the Council of Boyars. It must have seemed to some that he also was about to abjure all worldly vanities and obtain the sanctuary of the Church from his own ambition and from his enemies. But as Vasilly Shuisky could rightly remark: "Why did he have the Tsarevitch Dimitry removed if he did not intend to become Tsar?" The boyars were well aware of the craft and guile of Boris Godunof but were helpless in their collective stupidity. There were several of them who felt that they had at least as much right to become Tsar as Boris had. Shuisky felt it; Mstislavsky felt it; more than even these Fedor Romanof felt it. The story was already abroad that the dying Fedor had offered his sceptre to Fedor Romanof and the Romanof was popular. It is probable that he could have obtained the suffrage of the boyars had the council been empowered at once to choose a new tsar. But the choice was not in their hands. Moreover they had been quickly sworn to allegiance to Irene and although the Tsaritsa had fled to a convent she had not made an official renunciation of the throne.

The rivalry of the would-be tsars was increased by the re-emergence of Bogdan Bielsky who at Nijni Novgorod had been keeping quiet ever since his disgrace and banishment at the outset of the reign of Fedor. He had heard that the tsardom was a-begging, that both Irene and Boris Godunof had renounced the throne. Ivan the Terrible had entrusted the security of the realm to a Council of Five and with Boris turned ascetic it seemed to him that he had a sound claim to be made the unique ruler of Russia. He brought with him from Nijni a large number of followers. No one placed him under arrest though he had not permission to return to Moscow. Boris in retirement probably surmised that the presence of another jealous competitor could only weaken the position of Fedor Romanof and strengthen his own.

To what extent Boris was secure of tsardom is difficult to gauge. We have the beginning of what are called the "Confused Times" in Russian history and the period is well named. A spectre was already stalking in the consciousness of Russia, the Tsarevitch Dimitry supposed not dead. We take three stories, none worthy of literal credence, yet part and parcel of the conjecture of the times. Boris was said to have in reserve, in safekeeping, either the young Tsarevitch Dimitry who was not dead or a lad who resembled him sufficiently to be used as a pretender. In the case of Fedor Romanof being proclaimed Tsar, Boris would bring this double forward and declare that Dimitry had not died and that he must be Tsar. Similarly it was said that Fedor Romanof had the double of Dimitry in reserve and intended to spring him as a surprise upon Boris. Also it was said that at the Chudof Monastery near Moscow there was a mysterious novice who at the death of Tsar Fedor said that he was the Tsarevitch Dimitry and the rightful heir to the throne. The name of this lad was Gregory or popularly, Grishka Otrepief. It was considered by the abbot that his statement that he was Dimitry showed that he was possessed by the devil, or that he was in league with the devil. He fled toward the Lithuanian frontier, but with a price on his head and if arrested he was to be executed forthwith.

Boris Godunof was staged at prayer at Novodevitchy Monastery. Thousands of petitioners arrived but he must not be disturbed. The whole government of Russia had depended on him for thirteen years and did so still. It is not surprising that he had callers. In reality he conducted affairs of state from within the monastery walls and could have had but scant time for his devotions. He had information from his spies; he received his agents; he gave his orders. What interested him especially was the basis of support which he would have as Tsar. It was easy to take the Tsardom; it might not prove as easy to keep it. Then the status of a proclaimed Tsar might not be the same as that of a Tsar by divine right. He was soon informed that certain of the boyars envisaged a limited monarchy such as that of Poland where the sovereign was bound to the will of Parliament. It was far from his ambitious mind to accept that form of royalty. And yet as he did not inherit the throne, he must somehow obtain suffrage. The problem was to obtain suffrage without conditions.

The *dyak*, Vasilly Shchelkalof, became the spokesman of the senatorial movement and tried to obtain from clergy and laity alike an oath of loyalty and obedience to the Council of Boyars. But as Boris must have foreseen, he failed. The Council of Boyars had lost under the ruthless government of Ivan the moral and physical authority of a previous generation. The princes were impoverished by repeated sequestrations, their retinues were decreased. And there was not among them any single personage of outstanding talent capable of leadership. The Patriarch was for Boris and the rest of the clergy, taking their guidance from him, would give no countenance to the pretensions of the Council of Boyars. In the administrative services there was a multitude of men who owed their position to Godunof and they naturally cried for him to rule the land. In the general hubbub there were always more voices for Boris Godunof than for anyone else. Sister Alexandra added her voice to the rest and prayed her brother to take the throne which the Patriarch offered him.

But Boris with mock humility refused the offer, refused it again and again, making the sign of the Cross and asking the suppliants why they troubled him when all he wished was to be left alone with his God. It was a difficult situation because to the simpler mind of the Patriarch it must have seemed possible that some change had taken place in the soul of his friend. He must have clung to the belief that Boris would ultimately consent because, as will be seen, he was ready to stake his patriarchate upon it. If Boris would not be Tsar, Job would not be Patriarch.

Foreign observers of incidents give quaint details of Boris' hesitancy, but it is always possible that they misunderstood what was going on, merely setting down the interpretation they put upon it. Thus the Ikon of Our Lady of Vladimir was brought to Boris to persuade him. Boris prostrated himself in tears before the holy picture asking the Mother of God why she pursued him thus. But it is not probable that he asked such a vulgar question. He was in an agony of prayer, for among other things he must convince Russia that he was a holy man. January and February passed and all the while he played the world-forsaker. He mumbled in supreme mockery the words of Christ. "Lord, if it be Thy will, let this cup pass from me!"

On the 20th of February, 1598, there was great prayer to the Virgin for intercession and a church parade in which Boris appeared in public view, still in mourning for Tsar Fedor, with bowed head and half closed eyes. On that day he wavered. The National Assembly had taken place on the 17th. It was composed of "serving-people," priests and monks, merchants and magistrates, to the number of about five hundred. It cannot be thought that such an assembly had in those times much authority. But it was all-Russian in character and may have appealed to the popular imagination. At its sessions it did not vote. The Patriarch said that he named Boris to be Tsar and the members of the assembly gave their assent by acclamation. The presence of this queer Duma in Moscow was in itself an affront to the boyars. But the latter saw the cause of Boris advancing all the while and they were helpless. Armed men increased in number within the city which swarmed with Cossacks, archers and musketeers, all adherents of Boris Godunof. Any rising in favour of one of the princes must have been put down instantly.

Boris remained for the rest of the great fast of Lent at the monastery and he kept Easter there. It was only on the 30th April that he came out of retreat and made a solemn entry to Moscow, though even then he was not determined to be crowned at once. He bade all and sundry to a great feast. "Let no one think he is not invited." He was not going to sit down to meat with the boyars alone and perhaps be assassinated at table. He was not going to be the Tsar of the boyars but of the Russian people. It is said there were 70,000 guests at this feast. There followed the presentation of an oath of allegiance more formidable in its wording than any which had previously been required by Russian monarchs of their subjects. The weakness of Boris' position as a merely elective monarch demanded a much stronger oath and the penalty for perjury was eternal damnation. Nevertheless there were extraordinary scenes of enthusiasm at the taking of the oath in the Cathedral of the Assumption and other places. The people swarmed in, striving as to who should be first. There was even some unseemliness in the way the recital was shouted, with gusto, with triumph, by the haters of the old *régime*.

The boyars were not backward in giving their oaths of allegiance to Boris. No one at the time dared make any objection to its terms, but actually there was a new

INTERREGNUM

development in their councils. Seeing that all went the way of Boris Godunof and that the cause of the individual princely candidates was hopeless, the boyars had secretly made common ground by deciding to invite the blind Tartar Simeon to become Tsar. There would not seem to have been much danger to Boris in this plan, but he was alarmed. It was popularly believed that he had caused Simeon to lose his sight and the presence of the blind Tartar in Moscow would be a reminder that Boris was not such a holy and humane man as he was pretending. He postponed his coronation. He had resolved on yet another measure for the guaranteeing of his position. Suddenly he startled Moscow by the intelligence that the Crimean Tartars were once more on the war-path and that the Khan was advancing upon the capital with an army greater than he ever put into the field before. This was bogus news but it gave him a reason for organising a vast army of defence, an army for the defence of Moscow, yes and for the defence of Godunof.

He left Moscow to join his army at Serpukhof. There was no fighting because there was no invasion. But the Khan had been invited to send emissaries to discuss an armistice with Godunof. What took place actually was a great military parade. The "children of the boyars" pranced about on fine horses. Boris reviewed and flattered regiments every day. There was much feasting and every day there assembled to dinner some ten thousand who were served on silver plates. Boris was extremely hospitable and liberal and did everything possible to make himself popular with his army. There were six weeks of merrymaking on the banks of the Oka, one of the most pleasant campaigns any army withstood. Russia was saved by caviar and wine. Finally on the festival of St. Peter and St. Paul there was a monster banquet when it is said that half a million guests were mustered, though one can hardly credit the figure. Presents were made to all commanders and Boris made an eloquent speech thanking his forces for what they had done and assuring the assembly that he was the soldiers' Tsar. And he was rapturously applauded. He had the army behind him.

The Patriarch meanwhile had been getting more and more impatient, especially as he soon learned that there was no actual danger of a Tartar invasion. He worked like a pack-horse to help Boris and could never understand the crafty dilatoriness of his friend. Boris was Tsar but the Patriarch feared that Boris might still shuffle out of the responsibility and go back to a monastic cell. He was anxious that his voice should be ratified and confirmed by solemn coronation. At length he was to be comforted. In August Boris considered that the time was come when he could safely have the diadem set upon his brow.

XIV.

BORIS IS CROWNED TSAR

IN the *Travels of Sir Jerome Horsey* the rise of Godunof is thus described:

"Boris and his family, growing mighty and very powerful, suppressing and oppressing by degrees, and making away most of the chief and ancient nobility, whom he had wonderfully dispensed, long tormented with all impunity, to make himself redoubtable and fearful, removes also now the Emperor Fedor Ivanovitch [it was rumoured that Boris had poisoned Fedor], and his sister the Empress into a monastery, though himself was Emperor in effect before; causeth the Patriarch, metropolits, bishops and friars, and other new upspring nobility, his officers, merchants, and all other his own creatures, to petition unto him to take the crown upon him. Their fear and time appointed, he was solemnly inaugurated and crowned, and styled, from a gentleman, with open acclamation, Boris Fedorovitch, Emperor and great duke of Vladimir, Moscow and all Russia, king of Kazan, king of Astrakhan, king of Siberia, and the rest described.

"He is of comely person, well favoured, affable, easy and apt to evil council, but dangerous to tend to the giver; of good capacity, about forty-five years of age, affected much to necromancy, not learned, but of sudden apprehension, and a natural good orator to deliver his mind with an audible voice; subtle, very precipitate, revengeful, not given much to luxury, temperate of diet, heroical in outward show; gave great entertainment to foreign ambassadors, sent rich presents to foreign princes. . . ."

Actually Boris Godunof was forty-seven or forty-eight years of age when he took the crown of Russia, middle aged but well preserved, not subject to recurrent illnesses. He was tall, athletic looking, with scant black hair, a coppery-coloured dark visage, close-shaved, somewhat of a round head.

The title of Boris to the throne was pronounced to be that of natural reward for the services performed by him for Ivan the Terrible and his son Fedor. Besides that the Patriarch found warrant for the choice by citing Holy Writ, the example of the choosing of David and so forth. The Patriarch also explained that when after the victory over the Khan Tsar Fedor had put his fur cloak upon the shoulders of Boris Godunof it was an inspired symbolic act and the late Tsar had at that moment been inspired by the Holy Ghost. How the great nobles, Vasilly Shuisky, Vorotinsky, Sitsky, the Romanofs and others regarded the validity of the title of Boris may be guessed but is not recorded.

The coronation took place on the 1st of September, 1598. It was accompanied by great magnificence of parade. Russia and Boris believed that they were starting a new dynasty. Boris had with him his young son Fedor who gained a new significance in men's eyes as the heir to the throne. The solemnity of the occasion was enhanced by the fact that Boris Godunof was the first Tsar to be crowned by a patriarch. And the authority of the Church had steadily increased throughout the reign of Fedor. It had made good all it had lost during the iconoclastic second part of Ivan's reign. The aristocracy had not so recovered its position in the realm. Humiliated by Ivan, it had been constantly harassed and degraded by Boris Godunof. Now in Russia the Church came first, the people second, and the nobility third. Marshals had been withdrawn and the question of precedence in rank had been waived. Nobles might quarrel among themselves as to precedence but they could not bring such a dispute to the arbitrage of Boris who, having become Tsar, was pleased to think that all men were equal in the sight of God. Boris, without reading Sir Thomas More—he was still illiterate—and probably without converse on the subject, had arrived at the idea of Utopia, the democratic conception of the Golden Age, even interrupting the liturgy of the coronation to proclaim the equality of man. It was a striking interruption of the ceremony. The Cathedral of the Assumption was packed with a mixed assembly such as never could have found place at the coronation of a tsar of the blood royal. There were many nobles there, but cheek by jowl with them merchants, shopkeepers, even beggars. Boris suddenly took the arm of the holy Patriarch in his and declaimed in a loud voice: "Oh, holy father Patriarch Job, I call God to witness that during my reign there shall be neither poor man nor beggar in my realm, but I will share all with my fellows, even to the last rag that I wear." And in sign he ran his fingers over the jewelled vestments that he wore.

There was an unprecedented scene in the cathedral, almost a revolutionary tableau when the common people massed within the precincts broke the disciplined majesty of the scene to applaud the speaker.

Encouraged by this popular success Boris then promised to abolish capital punishment. The worst punishment he would inflict on any man was to banish him to Siberia. Several Russian Tsars after Boris bound themselves to a similar undertaking and such even was the law under the last tragic Romanof, Nicholas II. But Boris did not keep the promise, nor was there any Tsar after him who could be pronounced "innocent of his country's blood."

But the new Tsar enjoyed a great popular success. He had completely overborne the bad opinion which had grown during the years of his regency. The death of Dimitry was forgotten and indeed no one seemed to remember anything against Boris Godunof. He had made himself a reputation as an uncommonly clever man, a genius; he had made himself a reputation as a soldier and organiser, a capable defender of the fatherland; he had made himself a reputation as a holy man, one who in reality preferred a monastic cell to a throne; and he had made himself a reputation as a lover of mankind.

With the crown of Monomakh on his head and the purple on his shoulders and the sceptre of the Tsars in his right hand he paced in solemn procession out of the cathedral, while his subjects shouted their delirious joy and Prince Mstislavsky threw handfuls of gold coins over him, tinkling against his crown. Then he hastened to take up his position in the royal palace and proclaimed open house for all, signalling his accession by making rich gifts to the boyars and the representatives of foreign powers and distributing an unheard-of largess to the poor.

It was a brilliant first day. It seems clear he desired to be a great tsar of a new type. He had realised the impossible honour of tsardom and in return would give back much. Yet he must have known that he promised himself and Russia more than he could fulfil. The way was not clear; the times were confused. Splendour broke upon the outset of his path but darkest shade would succeed. And still he could not disguise it from his conscience that he was an upstart. The throne of Ivan the Terrible was not his and ghosts were arrayed against him. He had long had the freedom of the palace and there was no closet where Ivan held his secrets that had not long been open to him, under leave from Ivan's son. But now the "guardian angel" was dead. On his own responsibility he passed through the hangings of tapestry behind which the dread Ivan had withdrawn, trod the deep carpet that those feet had trod. That night the ghost of Ivan the Terrible might have appeared to him, saying with dangerous smile: "Thou puttest thyself above us?"

XV.

THE NEW ERA

A SECOND oath of allegiance was exacted after the coronation. In this oath the subject was bound to renounce any plan, wish, or thought of making the Tsar Simeon, or any one of his sons, Tsar. It is surprising that Boris Godunof took such precautions against a rising in favour of Simeon, but it shows that there had been a considerable movement in favour of the blind Tartar and that Boris felt danger would approach him from some quarter, probably from that of the boyars who had promulgated the candidacy of Simeon for the throne.

The date of the second oath is the 15th September, 1598, and it may be presumed that the swearing in continued for the greater part of the month. Not only must the people of Moscow take the oath but many in distant places and at the outposts of empire. On the other hand it is possible that the new oath was tabulated during the preceding summer while Boris was feasting his armies and that the swearing in began months before his coronation. The first oath had been taken as early as February of that year.

The month of September was one of peaceful consolidation. To ingratiate himself further with the merchant class the Tsar decreed that trading licences should be free of tax for the two ensuing years. He rewarded the serving-people who had stood by him by doubling their wages. By "serving-people" is to be understood not only civilians, civil servants, but soldiers. The army was put on double pay. Boris to make good his promise sent out to inquire into destitution and lavished much money on the poor. Certain provisions were also made for widows and orphans. At the same time the Tsar tried to win over to his side many of his opponents in the Council of Boyars, honouring some, adding to the estates of others. He took over the amassed gold of Ivan the Terrible and was most lavish with it. Had he continued to dispense benefits throughout his reign at the same rate as he began the treasury must soon have been emptied. This is the more remarkable because there is much evidence that Boris loved wealth and he had never missed an opportunity of adding to his immense personal revenue. He seems to have had a profound intuition that he had no inherent right to the throne and that his position must be bought. From the moment he became Tsar money took a second place. He put his throne and his family and the prospect of continuing a dynasty of Godunofs first and was ready to sacrifice all else to these.

The reign seemed to begin brilliantly and a less suspicious and watchful man than Godunof might have been content with the outward show of national enthusiasm. But he was aware of the brooding discontent of the boyars. They had hoped for a limited monarchy. Fedor Romanof had implied that if he were chosen Tsar he would restore the ancient privileges of the boyars. Many of them would from the first have been willing to accept Boris as Tsar if he had been ready to subscribe to constitutionalism. But one of the reasons which had prompted Boris to refuse the throne so often was his desire to hold out for unimpaired autocracy with all its powers and privileges unshorn. He had had his way: he had been elected without conditions. He had sworn to obey no one but himself. Despite his democratic impulses expressed at his coronation he had shown no inclination to share his power with others. It seems Godunof made a mistake. Certainly his sagacity failed him in this matter of conciliating the boyars. That he could remain ruler over Russia was clear; the question was what was the maximum power he could arrogate with safety. His *idée fixe* overbore his judgment. We believe that even during the reign of Ivan the Terrible he had imagined that he might one day be Tsar of Russia. He had lived twenty years with that goal in view. He had attuned his great sagacity to that and to that alone. It is perhaps not surprising that the thing itself obsessed him and became finally master of his judgment. Had he compromised with the boyars he might have had a united nation behind him and have become one of the greatest and most popular of Russian monarchs. But instead, he must perforce inherit with the autocracy the fear and suspicion that went with it. His spies must be increased in number. Every chance word let drop by potential enemies must be reported to him.

He took over the Tsar's apartments in the palace. His wife, Marya Grigorievna Skuratof, was not as popular a Tsaritsa as Irene had been, but she was quiet and virtuous. The daughter of the vicious Skuratof inherited none of her father's evil characteristics. She was a good mother, simple and religious, and it is thought she did not share her husband's counsel, being entirely passive to his ambitions. But she brought up her children well and in that was encouraged by Boris, who, illiterate himself, nevertheless wished that his son and daughter should be well educated. The best teachers were sought for Fedor and Xenia and they were given what may be called a European education. The Godunof family, which was very numerous, had the run of the palace. Several cousins had been made boyars during the reign of Fedor. Others were honoured or promoted at the accession of Boris. Dimitry Ivanovitch, Boris' uncle, became the most important man in Russia after the Tsar, being made *Konyushy* (master of the horse), a very high title and position vacated by Boris on becoming Tsar. Semyon Godunof was one of the most capable of Boris' watchdogs, but the whole clan were on guard for Boris, since if ill befell him ruin must ensue to them.

The Godunofs stuck together. There is no instance of disloyalty among them. They had a strong tribal sense. And what was tribal in their instincts became dynastic in those of Boris. Hardly had he become Tsar than he was consumed with anxiety as to whether at his death the succession would remain in the family. Fedor was eleven or twelve years old and it seems a healthy sturdy boy. That this child would be Tsar after him, Boris firmly believed, but he intended to take precautions to preserve the new dynasty and not allow it to go the way of Ivan's family. Fedor might die, or in marriage might have no heir. To guarantee the Godunofs against that eventuality Boris decided to seek for little Xenia a husband from some royal house of Europe. Such a bridegroom having been found, he would be invited to make his home in Russia, become a Russian appanaged prince, with the succession to the throne, failing offspring from Fedor, bound in his issue. Boris would also raise his own name and prestige by being thus united through marriage to a reigning house in Europe. With this in view he approached first Gustavus, the exiled son of the King of Sweden, and then when that failed, John, the brother of the King of Denmark.

Directly after his coronation Boris ordered that the frontiers of Russia be open again for foreign intercourse. They had been shut and no foreigner had been allowed to enter Russia during the suspense period when the throne was vacant. It had been feared that if Sigizmund of Poland or the King of Sweden grasped the state of affairs they might either of them invade Russia forthwith and seize the tsardom. Now Russia took her shutters down and disclosed a new shopfront with Boris Godunof in royal attire. Foreign powers were notified of his accession and accepted it without demur. Godunof had the reputation in Europe of a man of genius. Foreign powers had for long dealt with him rather than with the reigning Tsar and no one was surprised. It was certainly not regarded as a revolution nor was Boris called a usurper then as became the fashion to call him after his death. It must have been thought that Russia had done wisely in choosing him and that she would flourish exceedingly under his governance. That certainly was the opinion of Queen Elizabeth who watched Russian affairs with keen interest.

The peace in the west which had endured throughout

the greater part of Fedor's reign still continued. The internecine quarrels of Poles and Swedes, Lithuanians, Livonians and Germans kept the enemies of Russia engaged within their own territories. No army leader of note had arisen since the death of King Stephen of Poland. Russian armies had ceased to be aggressive and there was consequently peace. But Russian trade had suffered a reverse through the loss of Baltic ports. Boris sought by craft rather than by war to regain the lost hold on Livonia. He had no success and he increased the hostility of Poland. The Romanofs and other disaffected families were soon looking to Poland for aid to rid them of Boris Godunof.

XVI.

THE BETROTHAL OF XENIA

I

KING ERIC XIV of Sweden was deposed by his two brothers, Duke Charles and Duke John, in the year 1568, and his children were disinherited. The elder brother became King John III. King John had a Polish wife who bore him Sigizmund, who in 1587 was elected King of Poland. Both father and son were hostile to Russia. King John died in November, 1592, and Sigizmund came to Stockholm to be crowned. Thus began a short period in history when Sweden and Poland were united under one king. The union was not however characterised by peace, but by civil turbulence and religious disputes. The Swedes were mostly Lutherans but Sigizmund was a devoted Catholic anxious to serve the Pope and cleanse the country of heretics. Duke Charles headed the movement for religious freedom and it seemed likely that Sigizmund would soon be deposed. It must have appeared to Boris Godunof to be not outside the bounds of possibility that Gustavus, the unfortunate son of Eric XIV, might at some time be restored to his due position at the Swedish court and even that he might become king. Boris decided to offer the young duke a permanent refuge in Russia. If he consented he was to receive a large estate and the revenue appertaining thereto and he would be received at the Russian court with the honours due to a prince of the blood royal.

In the year 1599, Gustavus, who was living with a mistress at Danzig, decided to accept the Russian offer. It was a great change in affairs for him. The emissaries of Boris met him at the frontier with magnificent gifts and a suit of gold brocade to wear. He cast aside his threadbare garments and his old hat. Barbers attended him. He washed off the soils of banishment and stepped forth a Russian prince. A fine carriage was in waiting and accompanied by certain Russian dignitaries he set out on the long journey from the confines of Novgorod to the capital of Russia. He could speak some Russian and probably expressed his sense of exhilaration in the change of circumstances, though he may have wondered why the Muscovites were so generous. The Swedes were a hospitable people but this oriental magnificence of treatment was not in the tradition of the north and could hardly have been accorded by the court of Sweden to an outsider such as he considered himself.

His reception at Moscow was in keeping with the richness of his escort. Boris received him in a full court. Hundreds of boyars, princes, *dyaks*, all in cloth of gold, sat down to dinner in the palace in a state of grandeur not seen since the days of Ivan the Terrible. For now that the Tsar Fedor was dead there was one court in the Kremlin instead of two and Boris expressed both his personal wealth and the wealth of the Tsardom in his feasts. It is said that never before had the dinners and receptions of the Kremlin been attended with such pomp and ceremony as in Boris' reign.

Gustavus and Boris Godunof dined at a table apart. His gilded chair had a pillow headrest sewn in cloth of gold. He kissed the hand of the young heir, the Tsarevitch Fedor. He drank the health of the Tsar and his family. The whole court drank his health. He made them all a speech of thanks in broken Russian.

He was made prince of Kaluga and given the revenue of three towns and of the surrounding rural areas. He was received into a large house in Moscow with many servants. It was furnished with gold and silver plate and had many rich carpets and other ornaments. Boris cultivated him and saw him every day, conversing with him concerning his travels, Swedish history and the troubles of that country, probably picking his brains. Since Boris could read no books he was at special pains to glean reliable information in conversation. And this Gustavus was no fool. He was shrewd and witty and pleasant and somehow he had picked up a good education despite the ruin of his mother and himself after the fall of Eric XIV. He knew Italian, French and German, evidently having a facility for languages. But besides that he was especially versed in chemistry which at that time of course was allied to alchemy. There was a common ground which had no political significance. Boris had dabbled in alchemy with Ivan the Terrible. Necromancy was his hobby and he was deeply interested in the qualities of substances, in poisons and elixirs, in the water of life. The vagabond prince passed as erudite and evidently had a mind stored with curious lore. Add to that he was gallant and honourable and we see a personality which is remarkable. Having been deprived of a throne and exiled from his country had not made him unscrupulous. He was in fact too sincere to lend himself to Godunof's crafty plan for rehabilitation.

Gustavus was treated as Boris' right hand man and it soon became clear that it was intended to offer him the hand of the Tsarevna Xenia in marriage. And Boris would first have him made King of Livonia. We see here Boris Godunof copying his master Ivan the Terrible who successfully worked a similar trick, giving his niece Marya to Duke Magnus of Denmark on the assumption that he would conquer Livonia for himself and Russia. The loss of Livonia to Sweden and Lithuania in the latter part of Ivan's reign rankled in the Russian mind and it was a serious set-back to commerce and development. The hope of a "little window on Europe" had been frustrated. The great towns of Novgorod and Pskof languished beside a dead frontier and much of the foreign trade of Russia had been diverted to Archangel and the route of the north. It is nevertheless surprising that the pacific Boris hankered after a restoration of the lost Baltic territories. Was it in order to add to his titles of which he had become as vain as Ivan himself? It was partly that and partly due to an intuitive understanding of the hostility of the Catholic thrones of Poland and Sweden. Catholicism, shorn of glory, territory and adherents in the west, looked to the east for compensation. It therefore became part of Boris' policy to protect the rights of Protestants. Although Protestants were every whit as heretical as Catholics from an Orthodox point of view, nevertheless Germans and Livonians were given complete freedom of worship in Russia. Boris even fancied himself as the protector and champion of the oppressed Lutherans in Livonia.

A considerable number of Livonians with their wives and families were at that time in bondage in Moscow. They had been captured during the wars in Livonia and had never been repatriated. Boris rounded up all these people and told them he had decided to liberate them and allow them to return home. They must first promise to be his faithful servants wherever they went and each would be given a bag of silver to be used to start afresh in life. It was something for nothing and the poor exiles very gladly agreed. At the same time a frontier proclamation was made to Livonia that shortly Duke Gustavus would arrive with a Russian army to guarantee religious liberty and take over the rule of the country from King Sigizmund.

Gustavus was not told that one of the conditions of Russian support would be his agreeing to marry Xenia. He thought all was being done merely for love of himself and the cause of liberty. The knightly rôle appointed him pleased him. Actually in 1599, the same year in which he had come to Russia, the rulership of Livonia had again become divided. Duke Charles met Sigizmund in battle and overthrew him. Sigizmund abdicated the throne of Sweden and became simply King of Poland and Grand Duke of Lithuania. Duke Charles became King Charles IX of Sweden. The change neither benefited Gustavus nor made the lot of the Livonians more covetable. Gustavus wrote a challenging letter to his uncle in which he naïvely mentioned the compassion of the noble Boris who had given

THE BETROTHAL OF XENIA 135

him the honour due to him by his fatherland and taken upon himself the protection of the unfortunate Livonians.

The Livonian propagandists with their bags of silver returned to their country and did apparently work for Boris there, apprehending advancement and protection for themselves if the scheme of a Russian protectorate should be realised. But they did not find their fellow countrymen enraptured by the plan. The memory of the cruelty of Ivan the Terrible in Livonia had not been effaced. Russians were hated with a hate which was to last for centuries. Few were found ready to believe in Boris Godunof as an impartial champion of religious rights or in the pretensions of the Swedish nominee he had found to do his work. Livonia did not wish to be assimilated to Russia on any terms. Then the use to which Ivan the Terrible had put Magnus made them suspect that Gustavus was a cat's-paw also.

Still, Gustavus with the aid of a Russian army and a treasure chest might conceivably have made himself master of the Baltic shores. The plot broke down because of the condition which Boris Godunof attached to his support. The Swedish prince must change his faith, embracing Orthodoxy. He must marry Boris' daughter Xenia and become to all intents and purposes a Russian. It was a great honour to be asked to be the son-in-law of the Russian Tsar but Gustavus did not see the matter in that light. First he was bound to a previous love and would not be parted from her. Then he would not exchange his religious sect for that of Orthodoxy, probably considering that there was too much superstition and idolatry connected with it. And finally he would not take over the Baltic littoral merely to betray its inhabitants to Russian rule.

With that the favour of Boris Godunof at once vanished. Semyon prepared a *dossier* of the unfortunate things that Gustavus had said about the Livonian project. He was arrested and kept under guard in his own house in Moscow. Then the city of Kaluga and the rich estates were taken from him and as if in mockery the ruins of Uglitch were granted him. Uglitch after the chastisement which had followed the death of Dimitry was scarcely worth having. The chagrined Swede was however allowed to take up residence there. He ceased to play a political part and buried himself in the study of chemistry. He ended his days in poverty, deserted, it is said, by the woman for whose sake he had renounced a throne. He was a man of a type completely opposite to that of Boris Godunof. It may have been a romantic attachment which stood in his way. One may judge that the attachment was strong because by all accounts the Tsarevna Xenia was uncommonly beautiful and desirable. But we suspect that besides being romantic Gustavus was obstinate and devoid of ambition.

II

The adolescent Xenia, still in her teens, was reputed of great beauty. She was dark and striking. Her long black hair hung in curls like trumpets down her back. There was no trace of the Tartar in her. Her skin was very white and she had a vivid complexion. Her eyebrows met over her eyes. She had long eyelashes which made her irresistible when there were tears in her eyes.

THE BETROTHAL OF XENIA 137

She was of medium height, but full-breasted in the Russian style. And she sang very sweetly. So at least wrote the chronicler in that time. One may surmise that she was attractive. It might seem she was designed for happiness and that would probably have been her lot but for her father's ambitions and the Tsardom. A husband could quickly and easily have been found for her among the princes of Russia and she would have had protection in time of trouble. But this innocent child had been marked out for a cruel destiny. Whatever was planned for her went wrong, even to the end when she was poisoned and then cured, perhaps in order to be debauched.

Disappointed in Gustavus, Boris sought a bridegroom for his daughter at the court of Denmark. In this again he was swayed more by political motives than desire for the happiness of the Tsarevna. As a preliminary he ceded to Denmark the Kola peninsula and the waste northern region of Lapland, including however the ancient Russian monastery of Petschenga. It was claimed that the name Murmansk means Norwegian and after some parley Boris seems to have agreed. His territorial ambitions were nearer home, the coveted southern Baltic shore. Russia must have Narva and Reval and might get Riga. The nations of the north were at odds. Charles IX believed that nothing less than the complete sovereignty of the north would satisfy Christian IV of Denmark. Charles was at war with Sigizmund of Poland and Lithuania and at enmity with Russia. It seemed to Boris Godunof that by aiding and abetting Denmark in her ambitions Russia might obtain a substantial Baltic dividend. And so the hand of Xenia was offered to Duke John, the younger brother of King Christian, and the Danish court approved.

Duke John was to become a Russian appanaged prince and a subject of the Tsar. Once more, as in the case of Gustavus, there was a grand frontier meeting. But Duke John, arriving at the mouth of the Narova river in a ship of the Danish fleet, was no vagabond. He brought something of the majesty of Denmark with him and there was no need for him to be presented with magnificent attire. As he stepped ashore there was a salute of guns. Prince Michael Saltikof welcomed him in the name of the Tsar and the *dyak* Vlasyev read to him a manifesto from the Council of Boyars. He was conducted to a luxurious pavilion and among the gifts sent to him from Boris were eighty of the finest sables in Russia. Next day he was escorted to a gilded carriage drawn by many horses and commenced a long processional drive to Moscow.

There were several carriages and mounted escort. Accompanying the prince were three Danish senators and other dignitaries of Copenhagen. In the towns they stopped for banquets and to receive addresses; in the villages they stopped to listen to the singing of the peasants. In the forests hunting parties were organised. On the rivers there were boating parties and fishing. The Dane wished to familiarise himself with the life of his adopted country. It will be understood it took him a long while to reach Moscow and his betrothed. He arrived at Ivangorod on the 10th of August, 1602; he reached Moscow only on the 20th of September. He was given a fine house adjacent to the Kremlin, on the corner of the Kitai-gorod. Russian formalities were somewhat curious. Duke John was not received at once at court. But his dinner was sent to him, borne by many servants, some hundred heavy golden platters with viands, great numbers of golden goblets and stoops of wine, and bread which the Tsar had tasted. It was evidently desired to impress the foreigner with the wealth and grandeur of Moscow. Duke John, for a week, was shown the sights of the city and received Russian princes in his house. Semyon Godunof and his spies watched him and remembered all his conversations.

The report which Boris received was that he had an entirely loyal and faithful ally, accomplished, handsome, friendly, in every way fitted to be the husband of Xenia, appanaged prince and son-in-law to the Tsar. On the 28th of September he was received at court.

There was a guard of honour from his doors to the palace. Each of the great boyars had his appointed station at the Tsar's house, at the threshold, at the head of the stairs, at the antechamber, Vasilly Shuisky, Mstislavsky, Golitsin, Trubetskoy, Cherkassky. There were no Romanofs, for that family was already in disgrace. But Boris seemed substantial enough on his golden throne. There was no hint of disaffection in his court. It must have seemed to Duke John that he was marrying into a well established royal house with some prospect of his children having the throne of Russia in their succession.

All the wealth of the Tsar was on parade and both he and the Tsarevitch wore immense sapphires and diamonds. There was a great display of emeralds. The Tsar's table was silver. The drinking vessels were of jewelled gold. In these days gold was not hidden away in bank vaults, and if kings had it they made a show of it. If a digression may be pardoned, that may be held to explain the grandeur of the theatrical setting of the court of Denmark in former productions of Hamlet in Moscow. The king sits with all his courtiers arrayed in cloth of gold. It was assumed that in former times kings always sat down to dinner in that magnificent style.

Duke John embraced the Tsar and the young Tsarevitch and they were soon engaged in a lively and happy conversation. Evidently the Dane was one whom one loved at first sight. He was extremely handsome and very charming, a man in whom there was no guile. It is possible he awoke some paternal affection in the breast of Godunof, for Boris, though he was ready to sacrifice Xenia's future to political considerations, was nevertheless extremely fond of his beautiful daughter. Duke John scanned the faces in the palace and looked for some feminine form. His curiosity regarding his bride, which at first had been slight, had been awakened by the oriental hyperbole with which she had been repeatedly described to him. But Russian convention stage-managed the appearances of the princess. The beauteous virgin must not be exhibited like a slave in the bazaar. Xenia was not on view at the great reception. And she herself was not allowed to see the chosen groom except by stealth, through some little window or crevice in the walls.

The luckless Danish prince was further from felicity than anyone could have dreamed at that great court reception.

> "There is a road to happiness
> But the way is afar."

THE BETROTHAL OF XENIA 141

The betrothal and marriage were postponed for a little while, probably on the recommendation of the Patriarch that the bridegroom might first be received into the Russian Church. It was important to Boris that Duke John's status as a Russian should be complete. Xenia's future household must be indubitably Russian and Orthodox. It would also be helpful if the young husband could obtain at the outset a reputation for piety. Only thus may be explained the immediate programme set out for the Dane after his reception.

Boris, as we have seen, was prodigal in feasting and banqueting. He had consummated his accession to the throne by marvellous hospitality. But that was not because he was in any way a glutton or a wine-bibber. On the contrary, he was one of the least intemperate of Tsars. It was a matter of policy. Similarly, when Boris cut the feasting and merry-making and prescribed devotional exercises for Duke John, it was policy. It did not come out of any great piety on the part of Boris Godunof.

Confessors waited upon the young man and put liturgical books in his hands. Interpreters came to read with him and expound the canon of the Orthodox Church. He took lessons daily in Russian and Church Slavonic, that he might fit himself to become an Orthodox prince, and it is assumed by the chroniclers that he was anxious to change his faith. At the same time, he may have become spiritually intoxicated by Russia, and as he lay each night in his voluptuous bed, between sheets embroidered in silver and gold, he may have earnestly wished to become one with the mysterious people into whose royal house he was to marry.

Within a week of the reception at Court, a great parade pilgrimage to the shrine of St. Sergey was organised. To this, curiously enough, Duke John was not invited, perhaps because he had not yet been received into the Church. But the object of the pilgrimage was to pray to St. Sergey that he would bless the coming union and ensure its fruitfulness. It was a repetition on a much more magnificent scale of the yearly pilgrimages which the ex-Tsaritsa Irene had made to the same shrine praying St. Sergey for a child. It seems almost that for some reason best known to himself Boris anticipated that if his son Fedor married he would be childless and the succession would pass to the offspring of Xenia and Duke John. In the care taken about this proposed marriage there is something exaggerated which is not explained in history.

The pilgrimage to St. Sergey was a grand turn-out. There were two carriages, drawn each by six beautiful horses. In one sat Boris Godunof. The other, which belonged to the young Fedor, was empty. Fedor was on horseback and two civil functionaries led the horse by the bridle. The procession therefore went at a foot pace. But there were six hundred horsemen resplendently attired. One of the court secretaries was in charge of a large red box, and it was his task to gather the petitions of the populace. Boris, since his accession, had become steadily more suspicious and recluse, and had hid himself from the people who had elected him with approbation. But now, to make a good impression on the foreigner, he renewed Ivan's good custom of receiving petitions. Duke John must have been a witness of the setting forth of this religious cavalcade.

But again Xenia, the bride-to-be, was not on view. It had been announced that she and the Tsaritsa Marya were also going on the pilgrimage. But they were not included in the first party. It was some thirty minutes after they had left the Kremlin that mother and daughter set forth. The mother's carriage was drawn by ten white horses; the daughter's by eight. But Xenia's carriage was completely closed and neither Duke John nor anyone else caught the slightest glimpse of her.

They had an escort of ancient men on horseback, their long beards reaching to their horses' manes. But the carriages were surrounded by three hundred magistrates on foot, bearing wands in their hands.

The great company wound its way over the plain and through the woods to the white walls and golden cupolas of Sergey-Troitsky Monastery, and it stayed there nine days, fasting and praying. But there was a dreadful answer to prayer. The superstitious might well say that God and St. Sergey were not on the side of Boris Godunof. While the Court was thus interceding for the happiness of the coming marriage, the princely suitor in Moscow was suddenly stricken with some mortal malady.

The court had arrived at Troitsky about the 5th October. On the return journey, on the 16th October, Boris learned the tragic news. What exactly was the matter with the young man is not set down, though there is a suggestion that in the first place he was suffering from surfeit. There was little to occupy him in the Court's absence. Boris had given orders for luxurious and superabundant meals to be carried to his house every day. That may have been his undoing. The first message to Boris did not suggest that the prince was in danger of death, and the Tsar was afterward angry that he had not been told the truth. Of course, all medical aid, both German and Russian, was mobilised for the patient, and the Church and the people were set to prayer. But Duke John did not mend. Fairy-tale rewards were offered to anyone who could come forward and heal him. But there were no miracles either of medicine or of religion. He became so weak he was bereft of voice, and then death set its seal upon his brow. At six in the evening of the 28th October, exactly one month after his brilliant reception at Court, Duke John of Denmark was dead. And he was only twenty years of age.

It seems probable that he had never seen the beautiful Tsarevna, to marry whom he had come from distant Denmark and for whose sake he was prepared to renounce family, fatherland and faith. One can believe that Boris wept and that Xenia fainted at the news of his death. It was a tragical drama calculated to move most men's hearts. And it was much more than a domestic calamity. Boris may not have been superstitiously religious but he believed in the stars. The stars were against him, and the death of Duke John dealt a shattering blow to his mentality.

XVII.

THE FAMINE OF 1601–1602

THE reign of Boris Godunof was already in deep shadow before the death of Duke John of Denmark. For more than a year there had been dire famine in the land. Famines were regarded as visitations of God's displeasure, and one must add to the physical calamity a spiritual prostration.

There had been in the summer of 1601 a climatic disturbance in Russia, observed but unexplained. It started with a dense mist in the month of May. Then it rained without ceasing until the second week in July. There was no harvest either of hay or grain. There was no fruit. Livestock perished in the floods. The whole peasantry was rendered idle. And in July the weather did not mend. It was unseasonably cold, and on August 15th there was a very severe frost. The ruined fields had been feverishly re-sown from the reserves, some say with rotten and empty grain, though the fact that it came to nothing might as easily be explained by the blighting cold as the inferiority of the corn. But in any case the common people sowed the corn which might have fed them in the autumn and winter. The large estates were in a state of decay. Much encouragement had been given to small farming, but it may be observed that small estates are less able to weather agricultural calamity than large ones. Farming communities living from hand to mouth are ruined by one bad year. Ruin swept Russia in the winter of 1601–1602. The winter crops were not sown and a great famine became certain.

The rich ate; the poor people starved to death. In Moscow the price of bread rose to a point where only the rich could buy it. Livestock was slaughtered because there was no fodder. There was a glut of horse-flesh and then there was a glut of beef. Then milk disappeared and children died like flies. The people ate their dogs and cats and the rats and the mice and the sparrows and the crows, even the sacred pigeons. They gnawed the bark of birch trees and pines. They dug through the snow and ate the frozen grass. Dead people lay in the streets of Moscow with their mouths full of chaff or grass. Many of these probably died of panic, which in time of famine may cause more deaths than actual starvation.

The people were reduced below the level of the beasts of the field. They hauled the dead from the streets into their yards and fed on them. New-born babes were eaten and human flesh was on sale in the market-places. Peer Persson, the Swede, recounts having seen a mother eating her still-living child in the street. The Frenchman Margeret tells a story of a woman of Moscow ordering wood from a peasant. When the peasant arrived with the wood she sprang on him and strangled him. Then she put his body on ice. It appears the peasant had a horse which in the course of the winter she ate also. It is possible, however, that the many gruesome stories of the kind may be justly reduced to the vague sentence: there were some instances of cannibalism. If, on the one hand, there was some eating of the dead, on the other, by order of the

Tsar, there was the enforced burial of great numbers of corpses. The death-men went from house to house each week routing out the dead. The graveyards of the four hundred churches of Moscow were stacked with dead waiting to be buried. And according to the chronicler Palitsin there were counted 127,000 burials.

No such calamity had visited Russia since the destruction of Moscow by the Tartars. We have the paradox that more people died in Moscow than the total population and there were probably more people in the city after the famine than before. That was due to the swarming in of famished provincials and peasants. It became a city of beggars, bandits and cut-throats. Many thousands of whining, emaciated people besieged the doors of churches and monasteries or dragged themselves along the streets. It was the strangest comment on Boris' coronation vow that he would not rest while there were any poor and that he would share his last penny with the poor. Actually, that declaration of Boris' was not characteristically Russian. The Russians have generally understood that you cannot get rid of the poor, "the poor always ye have with you." Humanitarianism, the familiar spurious coin in the hands of modern politicians, must have been a novelty in the sixteenth century. It was a fine pose. There may even have been a genuine and sincere impulse, but it showed the groping political blindness of Boris Godunof. Despite his apprenticeship to Ivan the Terrible, he had not learned the way to hold himself as Tsar. It is much better to give, not having promised, than to promise and then not give. His promise must have been remembered with bitterness by the poverty-stricken people in

1602. At this time, despite his immense efforts to relieve suffering and to combat the famine, he lost the whole of his cheap popularity.

In the first year of his reign he had given great alms. He had also entertained all and sundry most prodigally. That is not to say that he gave the poor man his coat. His court, in its show of gold and finery, was soon more magnificent than that of any previous monarch. He manifested a taste for grandeur which was expressed in gems. He remained liberal, not to say orientally profuse in generosity. He was not niggardly in his gifts. We see that in his first treatment of Gustavus in 1599, and again in his treatment of Duke John in 1602. In the famine year he sent eighty of the finest sables to Duke John. Certainly you cannot eat sables, but they can be sold for corn, and the German grain merchants were selling rye at not too extortionate a rate.

The measures which Boris took were inadequate. Probably any measures would have been inadequate, but he did not seize his god-given opportunity to make himself one with the suffering masses and share the famine. He ordered the monasteries to disgorge their grain reserves. He put the army supplies of hay and corn on the market. He punished thieves, incendiaries, engrossers, profiteers, probably punished some of the cannibals. Leaders of revolt and banditry were tortured, boiled in oil, burned at the stake. But Boris did not lead the boyars to a simple life. There was no famine within the Kremlin walls.

We do not say that Boris ought to have acted up to his professions. But he had chosen the common people

THE FAMINE OF 1601-1602

as the buttress of his throne. The nobility was disaffected at the time of his accession and had grown more so throughout these first three years. He was endeavouring by marriage to raise his family high above them. He took his position as Tsar more and more seriously and comported himself as the sainted autocrat. He became a stickler for court convention. It is true that he gave positions of responsibility to men of humble rank, but he could not dispense with the background of the aristocracy. He would have felt his throne less splendid if it had only a background of clerks and officials. Therefore, he kept the race-proud boyars doing homage to him without in any way convincing them that he was their ultimate master.

There must have been a large number of petitions presented by the populace when Boris and the Court set forth on the great pilgrimage to the shrine of St. Sergey to pray for the happiness of Xenia and Duke John. There may also have been murmurs against the display of wealth. The people would not have dared to murmur against Ivan the Terrible, or if they had, he would have stopped the procession to have the malcontents publicly mutilated. But Boris had started the poor thinking he intended to give them all his wealth, and if you start giving money in that way, you may be torn to bits if you do not continue. Boris was not torn to bits, not assailed, probably not even insulted. But all his subjects had grievances and he was fast becoming a monarch without a friend.

God also had withdrawn His favour. One ought to renounce the evangelical misconception concerning Russian religious feeling. It is not made up of good works, nor is it chained to the Teutonic sense of sin. It is preoccupied with the miraculous and the immanence of God. The foul greed and selfishness and brutality of the Muscovites during the famine did not prevent the people from feeling that the Almighty had a daily and constant interest in their affairs. Boris Godunof, as Tsar, was an experiment, at first thought acceptable to God, but after not.

Now men remembered the stories which they had tried to forget. Some said that Boris Godunof had had the rightful heir to the throne, the Tsarevitch Dimitry, put to death, and God was punishing him and Russia for the crime. But a greater number contradicted this story and said that Boris had wished to kill Dimitry but had failed. The living Dimitry was in hiding but was about to appear and claim his heritage. Others said that to hasten his accession, Boris had put poison in the cups of the late holy Tsar Fedor. God's vengeance on the usurper must be explained.

It is not to be thought that the popular interest in Duke John amounted to more than curiosity. It had been much more politic to have found a Russian prince as husband for the Tsarevna Xenia. Indeed, at that moment that was what was required to rekindle national feeling. The common people did not add their prayers to those of the Tsar and Tsaritsa and the Court at the shrine of St. Sergey. But God's answer to the prayer by striking the bridegroom dead struck conviction to the heart. What further proof was needed of Boris' unpopularity in heaven!

Boris then tore the rich raiment from his shoulders and put on weeds of mourning and hid himself in his despair. The winter of 1602–1603 was one of great gloom in Moscow. The Tsar in this state of mind became stupid. That he was obstinate is clear: a man set on an idea and determined to realise it in the face of Fate. He would make reparation to himself and to his daughter. He sent to Christian IV of Denmark for another prince to make Xenia happy, to take the place first planned for Gustavus of Sweden and then for Duke John.

XVIII.

BIELSKY LOSES HIS BEARD

THE Tsar was uneasy. Someone kept always saying that the Tsarevitch Dimitry was alive. The alarming whisper coming from outside Moscow would not die away. "I charge you, Shuisky, on your soul to tell me the truth. You saw him dead. It was Dimitry dead and none but he?"* Boris could not be absolutely convinced that the Tsarevitch was dead. Vasilly Shuisky, who had been sent to make the inquest at Uglitch in 1591, was smooth spoken, slippery and treacherous. He was cunning and had been at pains not to break with Godunof. They plied one another with honeyed words, but knew all the while that they were enemies. Shuisky had the power to blackmail Boris by threatening a *volte-face*. He was the highest authority on what actually happened at Uglitch. He had exonerated Godunof, but if he fell into disfavour he had it in his power to proclaim that the child had been murdered. Or if he fled from Court he might even say that Dimitry had not been killed but had been spirited away and would shortly rise to claim the throne. Undoubtedly, there was lurking somewhere a man who called himself the Tsarevitch Dimitry. There was such unceasing rumour and whispering going on in Russia that weak-minded individuals began to ask themselves pa-

* See Pushkin, the drama *Boris Godunof*, conversation between Boris Godunof and Vasilly Shuisky. These are not historical words but I use them here to indicate the Tsar's state of mind.

thetically were they not perhaps that Dimitry. The whole Russian people began calling the ghost of Dimitry; it is not surprising that that ghost ultimately appeared.

Up to the time of Boris Godunof there had been no ghosts. Ivan the Terrible had killed thousands of innocents, but their ghosts did not rise to trouble him. But one night in the year 1601 the *strieltsi* on guard in the Kremlin reported: "We were standing sentry at midnight when we saw come through the air a carriage drawn by six horses. The driver, dressed like a Pole, carried a long whip in his hands and, striking the Kremlin walls as he passed over them, yelled horribly."* But why? There is no particular interpretation except that a cold wind from the spirit world was blowing into the kingdom of Godunof.

The illiterate monarch was uneasy. He had no relief from reading. He could not retire to a quiet cabinet and read again all the reports which had been made to him. He was reliant upon the spoken word. Script has a legal advantage over speech in that it is generally toneless. The mind mechanically registers the meaning of the spoken word, but the subliminal consciousness is affected by the tone and accent with which it is spoken. The written words "Beware the Ides of March" are dead, but spoken aright by actors or soothsayers, trouble the soul. The words were informed by Doom. And such words kept coming to the ears and consciousness of Boris Godunof.

It had evidently been his intention, at the beginning

* Kostomarof: *Smutnoye Vremya.*

of his reign, to propitiate everyone. He had some gratitude to the country which had elected him, but more than that, he believed he could more successfully govern the country and strengthen himself and his family in an atmosphere of general goodwill. In some Western state such as England such a man, with such a policy, might conceivably have succeeded and been blessed contemporaneously and posthumously. But it is doubtful whether, even without the complication of Dimitry's ghost, he could have held turbulent Russia by humanity and love. It is notoriously a country where ruthless monarchs have succeeded and idealists have been murdered. Tyrants rule by virtue of a faith which is not Christian when they believe sufficiently in themselves to execute great numbers of their subjects. Boris had not that type of faith. He had, in fact, no blood lust, and there are some instances when he actually stopped a public torture and tried to comfort the victim. He was merely unscrupulous and unimaginative. If originally he ordered the killing of Dimitry, or like Henry II with Becket, hinted the expediency of such a murder, he did so to remove a danger of sedition, without realisation of the possible consequences. He could never have committed such a murder with his own hands. He was logical without being imaginative, and the logic of certain situations forced him to acts of violence which were opposed to his peaceful instinct. And his violence lacked the dramatic force to strike terror into men's hearts.

At the moment of his accession the Dimitry legend seemed negligible. Boris attacked the wrong phantom and bound everyone by an oath not to talk about the blind Tartar, Simeon. It is plain that there had been more talk of the Tartar being made Tsar than of any double of the Tsarevitch Dimitry. Dimitry was seven years old when he was supposed to have died. In the year 1598, if still alive, he would have been fourteen, still too young to be embarked on the dangerous adventure of pretension to the throne. But the boyars knew the story and sniggered at Boris' self-glorification. "Dimitry is growing up. The time will soon come when the blood of Ivan the Terrible will triumph over this parvenu."

The Romanof family seem to have held the Dimitry secret. Whatever it was, they shared it with Vasilly Shuisky, who was clever enough to appear a friend of theirs and a friend also of the Tsar. When Bogdan Bielsky arrived in Moscow from exile, thinking the boyars might make him Tsar, he must have been aware of the Dimitry legend and may have had his own special version. He had been in "honourable" banishment ever since the troubles of the year 1584. He had been opposed to the banishment of the Tsaritsa Marya and her child Dimitry. He even declared that Ivan the Terrible had confided to him the protection of Dimitry. He had not been able to avert the banishment of mother and son, and later, banished from the centre, he could not save the child from being murdered nor Marya from being forcibly shorn and shut off from the world. Nor had he any power to intercede for the Nagy family when Boris took vengeance on them. Bielsky was a born organiser and leader who might have gone far but for his love of sumptuous living. He did not waste his time as voivode at Nijni Novgorod, but gathered wealth and adherents there, made himself a man of power. Although not a noble, he was able to return to Moscow with the following and trappings of a great Russian prince. He had once been on intimate terms with Godunof, but it cannot be thought that any feeling of friendship remained in 1598. He had had the story that Boris had ordered the murder of the Tsarevitch. He knew that Boris had punished the unfortunate Marya and struck her family down. He knew that Boris was a hypocrite and wanted the throne, though he pretended he did not. It is likely therefore that he asked many questions regarding the fate of Dimitry, and gained some information which historians do not possess.

Boris had his way and was crowned, but did not at once treat his rivals as his enemies. They were his enemies, but for the moment they were powerless. Boris began to rule without their co-operation in government. Bielsky, with his brilliant suite was impotent and idle. He was not sent back forthwith to Nijni Novgorod, but nothing responsible was found for him to do in Moscow. He was allowed to eat, drink and make merry with the Romanofs and others, while the spies organised by Semyon Godunof watched and listened. The harvest of eavesdropping was the Dimitry legend, which self-sown multiplied itself prodigiously. There was also an ill will which could not be dissolved by favour. Left to themselves and unused in state service, the rivals of Boris were bound sooner or later to contrive something against him.

Boris became aware of the danger lurking in the story that the Tsarevitch Dimitry was alive. Although there is no historical warrant for the supposition, he must soon have ordered his agents to find the lad who was supposed to be Dimitry. If so, he had no success; the child must be far away. There was a danger near at hand and that must be dispersed. That danger was inherent in the councils of his rivals.

There had been three who were mooted for the throne, Bielsky, Fedor Romanof and Fedor Mstislavsky. Of these, only Mstislavsky had been sincerely unwilling to be elected. Either of the others would have taken the throne had it been offered to him. The spies gave Mstislavsky a clear record, but there were many denunciations of the Romanofs, and probably some of Bielsky. Bielsky was more easily dealt with. Still Boris flattered him and assumed terms of friendship. Bielsky had shown his capacity as a soldier and organiser, would he undertake valuable work for the state in the south? In the far south? He was asked to go and build a town and fortress in Boris' name on the Donets Steppes. The place was to be called after Boris, perhaps at Bielsky's suggestion, though at the time the new Tsar was causing many buildings and places to be named after himself or his patron, St. Boris.

Apparently the date of this mandate to Bielsky was July, 1600, though the original order contains an ambiguity, being dated both 1600 and 1599. The date 1600 is generally assumed to be correct, but it may have been 1599. If it was 1600, then Bielsky had been at court for a year and ten months following Boris' accession and had done nothing in that time worthy of record. Yet he maintained at least as great an establishment then as during the days of his candidature for the throne. He was evidently more powerful than he had been at the death of Ivan the Terrible, when his association with the leadership of the *Opritchina* caused him to be hated by the people. Either the people had forgotten or his bodyguard was more numerous. When he obeyed the command of the Tsar to go build Tsar Boris Gorod, he moved out of Moscow with an immense retinue and with great show of wealth and arms.

One can see that the authority of the Tsardom had greatly weakened since the time of Ivan the Terrible, when Russians even in the remotest places waited his personal orders before obeying or serving strangers. Bielsky behaved like a little Tsar himself, raising an army and making financial levy as he went along. He arrived on the banks of the Donets more like a conqueror or a great feudal lord than a servant of Boris Godunof. He proceeded at his own charge and with his own men to build the new town and was reported to have said: "Boris may be Tsar in Moscow, but I am Tsar in Boris Gorod," in itself a fairly harmless remark, though his disgrace was pinned on to it.

Actually, he had been sent to a disaffected area. The prestige of Boris Godunof had not been built up throughout Russia, and it did not exist on the borders of the Ukraine. The Cossacks required a more barbaric and terrible lord. They did not understand the course of history and the chance by which the parvenu who was not a soldier had obtained the throne. Bielsky carried the gossip of Moscow to the wild southwest. And he showed by his bearing that he considered Boris Godunof of little account and himself as probably much better.

He cold-shouldered Boris' men on the Donets and on

the Oskol tributary, where he laid the foundations of the town. They were allowed no part in the planning and building. But he overlooked the activities of the spies. Soon there were runners hastening from his camp back to Moscow to report on his doings and sayings. They brought back incautious words let fall by Bielsky concerning the Tsarevitch Dimitry. It is possible that Bielsky had assured the Cossacks that "the Tsarevitch Dimitry still lives." It did not need much clear-sightedness on the part of Boris to realise that if someone did appear, sponsored as the lost Dimitry, it would not be difficult for him to raise an army and start civil war. With the nobility still disaffected and the power of the legend growing, this danger was manifest.

Boris was very angry with Bogdan Bielsky. He showed him that the power he mocked was a reality by having him bound and sent a prisoner to Moscow. When he had him there he rated him. It is said he was put to the torture and flogged with wire whips. If so, it was not simply as punishment, but to gain information from him. Did he know something about the Dimitry which Boris did not? The chronicler relates that he was chastised for calling himself Tsar of the new town. But that is not in keeping with Boris' character. He knew well how to laugh at nonsense of that kind. He was infuriated by something that Bielsky had done, what it is is not recorded. The bearded voivode, with arms and legs tied, was in his presence and at his mercy. There was a strong Scotsman in the palace, a certain Dr. Gabriel. Boris sent for him and bade him pull out Bielsky's long beard by the roots, hair by hair. There must have been some terrific upheaval in the peaceful soul of

Boris Godunof for him to have committed this barbarity. It is for a moment as if the terrible Ivan had risen to do this deed. The Tsar was possessed of a great new fear, and this fear had made him cruel. But he did not put Bielsky to death, as Ivan would have done. He sent him in irons to a prison far from Moscow. Numbers of his adherents at Tsaref-Borisof were also seized, including his chief henchman, Afanasy Zinovief, and they were banished to distant parts. It is curious. Directly after the supposed murder of the Tsarevitch Dimitry, hundreds of people had their tongues cut out so that they might not tell whatever story they had to tell. But at this later and more dangerous time Boris distributed enemies in banishment to all sorts of places, and they carried their stories with them.

XIX.

THE DISPERSAL OF THE ROMANOFS

THE Romanof family, which included the Koshkins and the Zakharins, derived from a certain Andrew Kobila, who was supposed to have come out of Prussia about the middle of the fourteenth century. Their connection with the throne and claim to the succession was due to the first marriage of Ivan the Terrible. The young Tsar chose Anastasia Zakharin, a paragon of beauty and virtue. The Zakharins and the Koshkins and the Romanofs came to court and obtained great influence. As they did not join the *Opritchina* they obtained a certain secret popularity. Ivan in his rages for the most part spared them. Everyone connected with his beloved and sacred first wife had exceptional treatment. Apparently the name of Zakharin was waived by Anastasia's brother Nikita in favour of Romanof. This Nikita married a Shuisky, who bore him six sons, the eldest of whom, Fedor Nikititch, became the head of the house. Fedor, Vasilly, Alexander, Ivan, Michael were cousins of Tsar Fedor.

Fedor Nikititch Romanof was the most gifted of the brothers. He was very handsome. He was the best horseman among the boyars. He was well educated and could even speak Latin, which was remarkable in Russia of those days. First and last he had a remarkable career, governor of Nijni Novgorod, voivode in the Swedish war, Governor of Pskof, forced to lead a monastic life by Boris Godunof, made archimandrite, archbishop of Rostof, patriarch of Russia. He was the great grandfather of Peter the Great.

Immediately after the interrogation and punishment of Bielsky, the Romanofs were placed under arrest. Concerning the reason for the arrests there is no reliable written record. According to one account, they were charged with sorcery, but that, even if true, explains nothing. It was a common practice to invent a charge of sorcery when punishment for other reasons was required. Semyon Godunof persuaded a retainer of Alexander Romanof to denounce his master. Alexander was supposed to have obtained from wizards a sack of magic roots. With the help of these he was going to make Tsar Boris Godunof suddenly disappear. Alexander was sent to a lonely place on the shore of the White Sea and there strangled. But one can be quite sure this was not done because he was a sorcerer. The other brothers were punished at the same time. There is no suggestion that they were sorcerers, and if Fedor Nikititch had been pronounced a sorcerer he could not very well have been made a monk.

Fedor Romanof was about twenty-six years of age at the death of Ivan the Terrible. Throughout the succeeding reign of Fedor, Boris used the Romanof brothers and showed them friendship. He needed their support. Boris' friendships were not of the heart, but there seemed to be almost an affectionate relationship between him and Fedor Nikititch. On the other hand, Fedor Romanof was not allowed to augment his power and influence in Russia by a distinguished marriage. He married a poor girl of humble family, the ward of his sister, Princess Cherkassky. These Romanofs were not related by blood to Fedor, but they must be watched. If on his deathbed Tsar Fedor did offer his sceptre to Fedor Romanof in the presence of Boris Godunof, one can understand the pretensions of Romanof to the throne after the Tsar died. It is probable that Fedor Romanof failed to penetrate at once the hypocrisy of Boris when the latter retired to the monastery and refused to have the throne. He may have assumed that Boris had not the courage to take the throne which was his for the asking. Or he may have thought that Boris was so appalled by the meanness of his birth that he dared not aspire to wear the crown of Monomakh. Fedor had an unwarranted sense of his own superiority. He was a clever and accomplished boyar, but Boris was deeper than he. During the strange moulting season of Boris Godunof, when he was putting off his former estate, and men had difficulty in saying what he was going to be, a monk or Tsar, Fedor drew his dagger on him in the course of a dispute, and would have struck him but that others present intervened.

What was the subject of the conversation which led to violence is open to surmise. It was probably the question of the guilt or innocence of Boris Godunof with regard to the supposed death of the Tsarevitch Dimitry. Boris was supposed to hold in reserve another illegitimate son of Ivan the Terrible, and to intend to bring him forward at the psychological moment to thwart the ambitions of the Romanofs. But Fedor Romanof was supposed to have in his household the double of the Tsarevitch Dimitry, or perhaps the Tsarevitch himself who after all had never been killed.

Whatever the dispute, peace was made. Boris was

crowned and Romanof gave oath of allegiance. Godunof took no immediate revenge: he bestowed great honours on the Romanof family and Alexander was raised to be a boyar. The Tsar seemed to bear no grudge. The years 1599 and 1600 passed in amity. But the year 1600 saw a great increase in credence of the legend that the Tsarevitch Dimitry was alive, that he had august protectors and would shortly make himself known. Boris had Bielsky arrested and put to the question. His next step was to arrest the Romanof brothers. There was a pretender in hiding and Boris told the Council of Boyars that it must take measures to suppress any conspiracy on his behalf. The Romanofs were such an important and influential family that he thought it better to let the boyars try them and sentence them. The details of the hearing of the case are lost. But it appears that Boris was successful in fomenting partisan feeling against the Romanofs. He had his claque in the senate and at times during the trial it was impossible for witnesses to be heard above the shouting in the chamber. Many retainers and poor relatives were suborned to speak against their masters. At least Fedor Romanof said so bitterly afterwards.*

There was much torturing to obtain evidence and some of the family serfs died in torment rather than say anything against their masters. But others doubtless gave away the fact that a boy with the likeness of the dead Dimitry had been sheltered for a while in the household of the Romanofs. Where was that young fellow now? That no one could say. Possibly none of

* *Akti Süskago Monastirya.*

THE DISPERSAL OF THE ROMANOFS

those put to the question knew. It is certain that no pretender was arrested following upon the trial.

Sentence was promulgated by the Council of Boyars in June, 1601. The brothers and their families and their near relatives and their families were banished. Their estates were at the same time sequestered and either taken over by the Crown or awarded to others—mostly awarded to others—that they might not go back on the judgment they had given. Alexander as we have seen was strangled on the White Sea. Vasilly was sent to far Yarensk where he was brutally beaten and tortured; afterwards he was removed to Pelym where he soon died of his ill-treatment. Ivan, a sick man with a paralysed arm, was sent to Pelym also. Michael, who was the strong man of the family, was confined in a subterranean prison in the district of Nyrob and had twelve great iron fetters on the upper part of his body and nineteen on his legs, all being fastened together to a lock which weighed nearly a stone. It is said that the ill-treatment of the Romanofs in banishment was contrary to the will of Godunof, but one can hardly believe that.

The fate of hundreds remains unrecorded. A feature of the dispersal was the separation of fathers and mothers and their children. They were sundered far and wide and precautions were taken that they should have no further communication with the world they had left behind. Of course had Boris been Ivan he would have had them murdered, and there is a difference. He even scrupled to remove the head of Fedor Romanof, the man he feared most, the one against whom he had the bitterest grudge. Fedor was sent to a monastery in the forests of Archangel, Siisk on the Northern Dwina, in the region of Kholmogory. In the words of the chronicler of Siisk: "In the reign of the sovereign Tsar and Grand Duke Boris Fedorovitch Godunof the boyar Fedor Nikititch Romanof was sent to Siisky Monastery, with orders to make him a monk. For that reason he was made a monk and given the name of Philaret."*

His wife, Xenia Ivanovna (Shestof) was sent to Zaonezhie; his children, Tatiana and Michael (who afterwards became Tsar) to the Monastery of St. Cyril at Bielo-Ozero. Two guards, Durof and Voikof, were sent with Fedor Romanof to the monastery to make sure that he did not escape and to prevent communication with anyone beyond the monastery walls. They were enjoined to see that the monastic prisoner was treated with respect and that he had clean clothes. The main object of Boris Godunof was to keep the head of the house of Romanof *incomunicado*.

Where the purposes of Boris Godunof stopped, the zeal of Semyon Godunof went on. Retribution came upon such an unlikely person as the mother of Xenia Ivanovna. The old mother-in-law was seized and taken to a nunnery and shorn. As she had no family connections other than that of the Romanofs into which her daughter had married and no political significance one is led to surmise that she had in some way been responsible for bringing up the legendary Dimitry who was becoming such a menace to Godunof's peace of mind.

* *Akti Siiskago Monastirya*. Fedor was banished under an order dated June, 1601, but according to the Monastery Chronicle he arrived in 1599, an example of the confusion in the records of the era.

THE DISPERSAL OF THE ROMANOFS 167

Great numbers of friends and adherents followed into banishment. Prince Ivan Sitsky was brought in chains from Astrakhan and sent to Kozheozersky Monastery, and his wife was sent to the Sumsky wilderness. Princes Repnin, Shestunof, Cherkassky were banished. The whole nobility of the time was combed out by Boris and his agents. These operations took place during the famine year of 1601. In the following year some leniency was shown to a few of the prisoners. Prince Cherkassky seems to have been reprieved for we find him in a post of honour at the reception of Duke John of Denmark. The paralysed Ivan Romanof was moved to easier quarters at Nijni Novgorod. But Fedor Romanof, as Father Philaret, remained immured at Siisk.

XX.

FIRST INSURRECTION

THE persecution of the nobility continued throughout the first year of the famine. The motive was the protection of the throne and the new dynasty. Both Vasilly Shuisky and Fedor Mstislavsky were forbidden to marry lest they beget sons who might be a danger to the Godunof succession.* One observes a remarkable degeneration in the mind of Boris under the influence of dynastic fear. It was not fear for himself. Boris Godunof may not have been very brave but he was self-sufficient. The man who by craft had ruled Russia for sixteen years could not believe he would be worsted in any conflict with his subjects. He feared for his son and daughter in the time coming after him. The Romanofs threatened them; the phantom Dimitry threatened them; everyone of power seemed to threaten them. But instead of building up a support for his progeny he rendered their position yearly more precarious by the alienation of the great families.

He made a particularly obnoxious practice of encouraging false witnesses by giving them the fortune of the people they denounced. Denunciation became a profitable business. Boris was not unreasonable but he made no effort to curb the malevolence of Semyon Godunof, now head of a great political inquisition so

* Margeret: *Estat de l'empire Russe.*

unjust and cruel as to be called a new Maliuta Skuratof.

The Tsar was extremely secretive. He caused much to be expunged from the records. It was as if by the mere mention of the Tsarevitch Dimitry corporal substance might be given to the phantom. This secretiveness is a very important factor in the character of Boris Godunof and explains much. He believed he could overcome rumour by silence. He believed he could hide self-evident truths by national pretence. The famine brought beggary and misery upon his reign and the injury to his good name as sovereign mortified him much more than the famine itself. He feared lest the catastrophe be noised abroad. So he organised prosperity parades before the foreign ambassadors in Moscow to make them think things were not nearly so bad as they had been told. At the beginning of 1603 it was forbidden for anyone to appear in rags in the streets. Conversation with foreigners was forbidden lest someone should tell them of the ruin that had befallen Russia. The penalty for chattering to a foreigner about the famine was death.* Directly the famine showed signs of abating the import of foreign grain was stopped so that Europe might think that Russian agriculture had made a sudden and complete recovery. In effect recovery was greatly retarded by this act of false pride.

The same psychological characteristics mark the struggle with the Dimitry legend. Every story must be stopped. It was sedition to talk about the Dimitry. Boris sought the source of each of the stories. Hence

* Kostomarof: *Smutnoye Vremya*.

the secret inquisition. He sought also the person, real or imaginary, who called himself the Tsarevitch Dimitry. It is also possible that he sought a young man who had once been his prisoner but had escaped. There was a round up of wizards and sorcerers and the charge of having dealings with magicians was preferred against many people. Godunof believed in the dread power of sorcery yet it is not to be imagined that he was afraid of sorcery in the abstract. It seems possible that he believed that sorcery had been employed to raise Dimitry from the dead or to provide a double. Miracles were being wrought at the grave of the Tsarevitch Dimitry but that does not seem to have convinced the popular mind that the child had died. If Boris Godunof was in doubt about that it is quite likely that instead of asking Shuisky to swear on his soul about it, he had the grave secretly opened and the body examined. If so, he found that another child's body had been substituted in the tomb, one holding a cluster of nuts in his hand. The records of the prosecution of the Romanofs have much mention of sorcery and nothing about the Tsarevitch Dimitry, but when at last a pretender claiming to be Dimitry announced himself, Godunof declared the "impostor" to be a young man brought up in the household of Fedor Romanof. It seems most probable that the charge against the Romanofs had much to do with the whereabouts, identity and purpose of that young man.

All those most concerned with the secret were dealt with by Semyon Godunof. The *dyak*, Vasilly Shchelkalof, shared the fate of his brother Andrew and was removed from his high office. He had been much in the

FIRST INSURRECTION

confidence of the Romanofs. The Pushkin family was banished and their estates confiscated. No particular reason is given, but the poet Pushkin in his drama, *Boris Godunof*, makes one of his ancestors have the first news of the appearance of the Dimitry and he communicates it to Vasilly Shuisky. Semyon Godunof has intercepted the intelligence or at least suspects it and warns Boris. It began to be clear that the phantom or dreadful reality was beyond the Russian borders in the west and Boris ordered that the frontier guards all along the west be reinforced and that a special watch be kept on persons coming into Russia. Every traveller was stopped at the frontier and kept there while a description was dispatched to Boris Godunof for his consideration. Similar precautions were taken in the large cities of Russia. All people departing were questioned as to their destination and visitors were examined as to whence they had arrived. It was said that search was being made for an important criminal but further information was not vouchsafed.* The streets of Moscow became infested with professional eavesdroppers picking up tittle-tattle to sell to Semyon Godunof. Many were brought to the torture for hints let fall about the Dimitry. There was a great season of blackmail and hush-money was demanded by many villains. Tale-telling infected the monasteries and spread disaffection in the Church. There was great disaffection and confusion throughout the land, says the chronicle of Nikon. "Wives denounced their husbands, children denounced their parents, fathers denounced their children."

* Margeret: *Estat de l'empire Russe*.

Banditry broke out partly as a result of the famine and the looting of granaries and the plundering of merchants and partly because of the general confusion. The forests were infested with armed bands and no roads were safe. Boris Godunof was so preoccupied with political persecution that he had little time to give to the capture of robbers and cut-throats. Robber gangs came into conflict with the soldiery and often got the better of the conflict. Russia was out of hand and the time was ripe for a rising on a large scale. The robber chieftain Khlopko was suddenly found in control of a great body of armed men marching upon Moscow to loot it. Boris was forced to mobilise an army to fight Khlopko. A bloody battle was fought in the environs of the capital. The commander of Boris' army was killed but Khlopko after a severe struggle was beaten. The robber chief was himself taken prisoner. He died of his wound or was done to death in prison. Boris Godunof sought information from many prisoners who were put to the torture. It is not clear that the Tsar by torture elucidated any better reason for the rebellion than starvation and a determination to sack the capital. The prisoners were hanged and provided the spectacle of the first public executions since Boris had at his coronation abrogated the death penalty.

The main part of the robber's army had not however been taken prisoner but had found refuge in flight. They fled to the main centres of discontent and took with them the story of their dangerous assault on Moscow. What Khlopko had attempted on a small scale might be attempted on a large scale with more probability of success. With the phantom Dimitry as a leader, insubordinate Russia might advance like an elemental force and sweep the Godunofs away.

The rebellion of Khlopko took place in the autumn of the year 1603. It is thought that there were in the robber army many of the runaway serfs and retainers of the Romanofs and other families ruined by the political inquisition. Because of the famine in the villages Boris Godunof had been obliged to repeal his earlier law which bound each peasant to the district where he lived. It would have been broken, anyway, by swarms of famished people going from region to region seeking food. In 1603, although the famine had abated, the breadseekers had not returned to their villages and the land they tilled. The insurrectionary bands were therefore recruited from economic as well as political victims.

It is not recorded that Boris Godunof took special precautions for his personal safety or that of his family. Possibly he was confident that Basmanof with his disciplined troops would deal effectively with the insurrectionaries. But it may be also that Boris was losing his grasp. Just before the appearance of Khlopko he suffered a great personal loss. His sister, the ex-Tsaritsa Irene, then the nun Alexandra, died at Novodevitchy Convent. It is said that her end was hastened by anxiety and grief and that she repented having relinquished her throne to her brother. But the surmise may merely be born of the Tsar's unpopularity. She had shared power with her brother for many years before she renounced the world and more than any other knew his sagacity and strength of will. It is more likely that she blamed his enemies than that she blamed

Boris. But her death was sincerely mourned. Irene was remembered as a good woman. Her virtues were exalted to the detriment of Boris. Great crowds followed the bier. There was little pomp or show. Boris did not go on foot but followed, muffled, in a sledge. Possibly he was suffering from gout which in these latter years was affecting him seriously. He was silent and gloomy and the other mourners imagined him possessed of melancholy self-condemnatory emotions. The mourners whispered that God had taken Alexandra from this vale of tears to spare her the anguish of witnessing in the flesh the fall of the house of Godunof.

XXI.

DIMITRY RISES FROM THE DEAD

IN the late summer of 1603 a man arrived at the house of Adam Wisniowiecki at Brahin in the Polish Ukraine, and announced himself as Dimitry Ivanovitch. He said that the hirelings of Boris Godunof had come to kill him at Uglitch in 1591, had visited his bedroom in the dead of night, but had been cheated by the substitution of another child. The body exposed in the cathedral for Vasilly Shuisky to report on had not been his. He had passed the fourteen years in various households and had finally crossed Russia as a pilgrim to the catacombs of Kief. He did not incriminate the Romanofs by his explanation of his past, but the time of the arrest of the chief members of that family would seem to correspond to the period when, disguised as a monk, he made his way across Russia to the wild and confused territory of the southwest. It is possible he was a whole year in the environs of Kief before he went to Brahin, and seems to have been employed on the estates of Prince Constantine of Ostrog, a militant champion of Orthodoxy against Roman Catholicism, but it seems unlikely that he announced his alleged birth or origin either to this prince or to his quartermaster, Gabriel Hoscki, where he obtained a job in the kitchens.

The household of Gabriel Hoscki was given over to disputes upon religious dogma. It is possible that the Dimitry worked there still clad in monkish attire.

Hoscki was an Arian heretic and though Arianism was far enough from Orthodoxy, anyone who was opposed to the Catholic Church was *persona grata* to the Prince of Ostrog. The Hosckis were champions of freedom of conscience, and even Protestants were welcomed at their houses. The Dimitry was employed in a household where questions of religion were naturally considered the most important in the world. He arrived at the house of Adam Wisniowiecki in a state of theological preoccupation. It is possible that even at the outset he professed to be in a state of doubt as to which was the true Church of Christ, Greek Orthodoxy or Roman Catholicism.

He crossed the frontier from Russia to Poland. The vigilance of Boris Godunof's wardens of the Marches had been in vain. Possibly they were led to expect the arrival of the Pretender from Poland rather than his exit from Russia. But they were supposed to stop all and sundry going either way. Their task was too difficult: the dangerous man got through.

Adam Wisniowiecki was an important landowner with large frontier estates. The family was one of ambitious and intriguing soldiers of fortune, established on both sides of the Dnieper river. The uncle, Dimitry Wisniowiecki, had been an aspirant for the throne of Moldavia. They were leaders of faction, with influence both in Poland and the Russian southwest. The estate was the centre of a wild, unpacified region.

The pilgrim must have brought letters with him establishing his claim, or Adam Wisniowiecki must have been informed in advance that he would come to him. The latter seems more likely, because it would

THE DIMITRY, BY SOME SUPPOSED
TO BE THE FORSWORN MONK
GRISHKA OTREPIEF

have been more dangerous for the Dimitry to carry letters on his person when at any moment he was liable to be arrested and searched. But the names of his actual sponsors have never been revealed.

According to one version, the pilgrim did not reveal himself at once, but obtained the post of page to Adam Wisniowiecki, but this may be dismissed, for it was quite unnecessary. In some way or other, the Pretender gained access to the Polish seigneur and announced his claim to be the Tsarevitch. He showed a jewelled cross given him at baptism by Ivan Mstislavsky. He pointed to the mole on his left cheek and the red birthmark on his right hand, and he showed that he had one arm longer than the other, well established identification marks of the Tsarevitch Dimitry. Leon Sapieha, who may have carried the message announcing the coming of the Dimitry (he had always been particularly interested in the Dimitry legends), produced a certain Petrushka, who had been a servant at Uglitch, attached to the young Tsarevitch. He was brought to Brahin and introduced to the Pretender under another name, but the latter instantly recognised him. That was dramatic and seemed a convincing proof of the identity of the stranger, but it is possible that the scene was staged with the connivance of the man who was to be identified. The news was then bruited across the frontier that the true heir to the Russian throne had arrived at Brahin. Russians of various rank flocked over the border to see him. Adam Wisniowiecki kept open house for Russian visitors.

From the first the Wisniowieckis acted as protectors of the Pretender. He was given raiment more becoming to a prince and given the respect due to high rank. The Poles are gifted flatterers. It was easy for them to treat this stranger as if he were the rightful Tsar of Russia. If the Dimitry lacked assurance, it was provided for him by his host. When it was necessary to announce him, he certainly looked the part. It is said that he was ugly, but he was evidently striking in appearance. He had a presence and was convincing. It is clear also that he was no fool. He had somehow learned how to comport himself with persons of high or low degree.

The Russian visitors from over the border were not necessarily predisposed to hail the man as the son of Ivan the Terrible and their true Tsar. They risked severe punishment, probably death, for such disloyalty to Boris Godunof. Had the pretender exposed to their gaze been an obvious simpleton or rascal, it is unlikely that they would have agreed that the Pretender's claims were just. But the behaviour of the Wisniowieckis and the way the mysterious stranger comported himself, convinced them. None of them had ever seen the Tsarevitch Dimitry before the drama of Uglitch, but they said they recognised the Prince; he was indeed the long-lost son of Ivan. Some of them did homage to him as to their true Tsar. Some attached themselves to him and decided to remain with him. One can imagine that the Wisniowieckis were not particularly anxious to entertain together with the Tsarevitch a large Russian retinue such as immediately began to form about the young man. But they were partial to the pretensions that he made and what could be more convincing to other Polish gentry than to see numerous Russians converted by a nod into abject slaves?

The Pretender, encouraged by the court thus forming around him, announced his firm intention of recovering the throne which was by rights his. "I am not prompted to this by ambition, but by the desire that right may triumph. Many of the Russian boyars wish it and they know that I am alive. They are awaiting me; they hate the tyrant and are ready to welcome me as their true sovereign."

On the 7th of October, 1603, Wisniowiecki was sufficiently convinced of the presentability of Dimitry to affirm the authenticity of his claim to be the Tsarevitch, and he wrote to John Zamoyski, Grand Chancellor of Poland, to that effect. He demanded for the Pretender the protection of King Sigizmund. It is clear that Poland was not originally responsible for the conspiracy to put the Pretender on the throne of Russia. The initiative was Russian. Neither Zamoyski nor the King of Poland was in the secret. The coming of a claimant to the Tsardom was a surprise to them. Wisniowiecki's letter awakened no enthusiasm on the part of the Chancellor, who replied coldly that it would be necessary for the man to come to Cracow to have his claims investigated by a committee of inquiry.

Had this been done, it is not outside the bounds of possibility that in consideration for a certain sum of money or certain political favours the Pretender might have been surrendered forthwith to Boris Godunof. The hubbub at Brahin and on both sides of the frontier had been great, and Boris had been informed by his agents that someone calling himself the Tsarevitch Dimitry had made himself known. He at once demanded of the Wisniowieckis that they deliver the

Pretender a prisoner to the Russian frontier police. In the event of his refusing to do this, Boris threatened instant reprisals.

Adam Wisniowiecki was not prepared to take orders from the Tsar of Russia, and he probably did not believe that Brahin would be raided by Russian soldiers. Nevertheless, he took precautions for the immediate safety of his protégé and got him invited into the interior of Poland. First, he introduced him to his cousin Constantine Wisniowiecki, an ardent Catholic who was married to Ursula Mniszech, who belonged to another important and influential family. Apart from the narration of the Pretender's adventures incognito, the religious talk went on, and it is possible that the Dimitry gave Ursula Mniszech a vague hope that some day he might renounce Orthodoxy and be received into the Catholic Church. Constantine Wisniowiecki and his wife were as much impressed by the Pretender as Adam had been, and entered into the conspiracy with the fullest zest. There was certainly no idea of sending the young man to the cold John Zamoyski at Cracow. Access would be obtained to King Sigizmund by a roundabout way. The Mniszech family were well placed at Court. It was decided to take the Dimitry to the headquarters of the family at Sambor in Galicia. It was a long journey, some hundreds of miles, more than half of the way to Cracow. The arm of Boris Godunof could not extend to Sambor. There was no further likelihood of a troop of Cossacks being sent to capture him and hale him to Moscow.

The frustrated Boris laid waste the estates of Adam

DIMITRY RISES FROM THE DEAD

Wisniowiecki, which were on the left bank of the Dnieper, but he had little satisfaction in that. He must have known that the Pretender had been moved into the interior of Poland, but he does not appear to have addressed a remonstrance to the King. Russia had concluded a twenty years' pact of peace with Poland and he did not expect that pact to be broken. Nevertheless, he seems strangely remiss in not demanding the surrender of the Pretender from the supreme authority. At the end of 1603 Poland had not realised the possibilities of using the claimant to the Russian throne, and it is possible that prompt action would have stopped the development of the conspiracy.

The state of Russia is well exemplified by what happened to Semyon Godunof in the spring of 1604. The rumour of the discovery of the Tsarevitch Dimitry had spread with rapidity throughout the whole of the south of Russia. Semyon Godunof had been sent to quell a rising in Astrakhan. By the time he arrived at Saratof on the Volga he learned that the Cossacks were in a ferment of revolt. He was warned against proceeding further downstream. He continued on his way, but was soon set upon by the marauding Cossacks. The force with him was captured or dispersed. Semyon Godunof fled for his life. But the Cossacks sent a party of the prisoners they had taken and gave them an audacious message to the Tsar. "Tell him we follow soon to Moscow in the army of the Tsar Dimitry Ivanovitch."

Poland had mobilised no army in support of the Pretender, but the latter had got in touch with the

Cossacks of the southwest and these wild horsemen had already carried the flaming torch of insurrection from camp to camp throughout the south. Independently of Poland, Russia was rising against the Godunofs.

XXII.

CONVERSION TO ROME

THE adventure of the young man who called himself the heir to the throne of Russia developed romantically like the plot of a novel where to hazardous enterprise must be added love interest and inner conflict. From his first days in Poland the Pretender seems to have progressed in the grand style. There was no shabbiness or indifference in the way he was taken up by the families which sponsored him. Life in southeastern Poland was spacious. The gentry was rich, social, hospitable and idle. The coming of the Pretender awakened a grand excitement and curiosity, associated with goodwill. When Constantine Wisniowiecki set off with his protégé for Sambor to visit the Palatine George Mniszech, he did so accompanied by pretty well all his retainers and a large number of friends. Some went in carriages and some on horseback, all finely arrayed. There was no haste. The party journeyed from landowner to landowner, often going considerably out of its way to visit connections and acquaintances. And wherever they stopped it was a festival and there were dances and banquets. Constantine Wisniowiecki had someone to show, the rightful Tsar of Russia, no less. He never exhibited the slightest doubt of the validity of the claims of his guest. Most of the gentry he visited took the Dimitry equally on trust and were glad to give him the respect due to a Tsarevitch. They must have sensed the mortal danger to Boris Godunof implicit in the man's pretensions. An enemy of Boris Godunof must be *persona grata* to a subject of King Sigizmund.

Sambor, apart from the gentry, was almost entirely a Jewish town, a trading centre. It is finely situated over the river Dniester. Mniszech lived in an immense wooden palace with many towers, one of which was gilded. Over the main entrance was his coat-of-arms, not unlike the Prince of Wales' feathers. It was a colourful establishment with gilded ceilings, stained-glass windows, portraits of ancestors in gilt frames, rich tapestries and hangings. George Mniszech held the palace in fief for his sovereign. There were two royal suites of apartments, one for the King and the other for the Queen of Poland, but as these were never requisitioned by the sovereign they were occupied by the Mniszech family. The magnificence suggested wealth, though in fact George Mniszech had run through a fortune by living lavishly and had become extremely impecunious. He had failed to extract much largess from his master, Sigizmund III. The King of Poland was parsimonious to a degree. But Mniszech must live in style, and he had had the wit to capitalise his charming daughters. That was how it came about that he was ready to gamble on his daughter Marina becoming Tsaritsa of Russia. He had got the elder Ursula married to a rich and influential aristocrat. He soon conceived the plan of marrying the younger to the Pretender, Dimitry.

In Poland, young ladies were not held so strictly in reserve as in Russia. The young Marina, aged about eighteen at that time, must have been witness of the exaggerated homage and respect paid by her father to the adventurer when receiving him under their gates. The father was an expert courtier who knew how to deal with kings and all people whose importance must be enhanced in others' eyes. The man he welcomed and accepted was striking in appearance and royal in his demeanour. There is no gainsaying the fact that whether he was or was not an impostor, he looked the part he chose to play. The *cortège* of Constantine Wisniowiecki which accompanied him set off his pretensions. He came, as it were, with an imperial retinue. He was dazzling and romantic; it is no wonder the eyes of the young girl filmed when his gaze rested upon her.

"We have brought him to you and you are going to make him a Catholic. That battle is half won. And you are going to get him to His Majesty. . . ." Constantine Wisniowiecki was proud of the thing he had started.

Ursula, we can believe, sang the praises of the Dimitry. She had begun the good work of converting him to Rome. The force of love, if that could be enkindled, would do the rest. One can imagine that Dimitry himself was rather cynical in religious matters and that when he took the welfare of his soul seriously he was hypocritical. Henri Quatre had said a dozen years before that Paris was well worth a mass. Dimitry could have made much the same utterance. Actually, to obtain the goodwill and support of Poland it was necessary for him to be received into the Catholic Church. That must have occurred to him in the first stages of the adventure. That was why he had allowed himself to appear troubled in conscience with religious doubts. And he was clever enough to realise that a ready promise to abjure Orthodoxy in favour of Catholicism would not serve his purpose so well as a studied inner struggle. Promises lightly given were apt to be lightly broken and he did not wish his Polish hosts to think that directly he had won the Russian throne he would go back on his conversion and become a Greek Orthodox once more. At the same time he was aware of the fact that it would be difficult for a Catholic to be Tsar of Russia in opposition to the patriarchate, the Church and the traditional religious ceremonies of Russia. He was in no haste to be converted. Conversion might gain him the support of a Polish army but would almost certainly lose him Russian adherents.

But he fell in love with Marina Mniszech and she with him. As far as we can judge by the subsequent behaviour of the pair this was true love. Nature aided the conspirators. The romantic young man was thrown into the company of the romantic young virgin and like Othello he told her the wondrous story of his life. With such a tale, real or imaginary, he was well equipped to win a lady's heart. She thanked the Almighty for his preservation in all manner of dangers, from the first attempt on his life by the agents of Boris Godunof to his safe passage across the frontier to Poland. She was pure and pious. He told her of his adventures and ambitions; she talked to him of her religion. She was a tiny creature, almost doll-like, with almond eyes and dark arched eyebrows and very little mouth, a whisperer. He was bold and manly and forthright in action and utterance. It was not for him to

MARINA MNISZECH

deceive her about his religious scruples but if she wished him to be converted that was yet another reason for his abjuring the Church of his fathers and making obedience to the Pope.

But in strictness marriage with Marina Mniszech was not part of his plan, nor could a union with this lady be helpful to him in the long run. It was not an alliance with a great Polish family. Mniszech was Czech by origin. It was not an alliance with a wealthy family. Marina must prove somewhat of an encumbrance at Moscow. It had been better for him to wait and marry into one of the great families of Russia and thus obtain some sort of constant support among the boyars. But he was caught in the snare of his own emotions and very soon after meeting Marina wished her for his bride. George Mniszech was pleased. So far, so good; things were going the way he wished. He had been confident that the young man would be ready to buy his support at court by making an alliance with his daughter merely as a political transaction for their mutual benefit. But since romance had entered into it so much the better! Marina must use her power in love to bring the Dimitry quickly to the One True Altar of the Catholic Church. The father did not give his consent to the union out of hand. He felt sure of the potential bridegroom. He could afford to wait till it was certain that there would be official backing for him. The King and the Diet must approve the enterprise and give him an army. He was not willing to risk losing his profitable daughter to an adventurer who with the aid of a few bands of Cossacks proposed to attack the serried armies of Boris Godunof. George Mniszech required a guarantee of success and some prospect of a dividend when the wealth of the Kremlin was at the disposal of his daughter.

Nevertheless an engagement was allowed to be understood. Many jolly monks reinforced the religious persuasiveness of Marina and he must soon have given her assurance that he did not intend to allow his soul to remain in a state of damnation. If she would give him her body he would give her his soul to keep.

The year 1603 passed. January and February, 1604, were spent at Sambor. Like a characteristic Slav the Pretender might easily have forgotten his high designs in the rapturous pre-occupation of love. He had thought he craved Moscow and a throne but all he asked was to remain at Sambor with the Polish maid. His adherents grew restive. The romantic side in which they had no share, displeased them, and many must have denied the advantage of their leader being affianced to a Mniszech. But the initiative was not left with Dimitry. He had started a movement which went on by itself. His name was bruited over Russia and Poland. Whether indeed the lost Dimitry or an impostor, he was a child of Destiny and had henceforth little control of the forces which would raise him to a throne and then betray him to hideous death.

Others uninterested in the delights of love were developing the plot. George Mniszech was active. As steward of the King of Poland he had access to the councils of Sigizmund III and it was easy to get past the unsympathetic John Zamoyski and fill the ears of the sovereign with the curious tale of the risen Dimitry. The King's mind was good soil in which to plant Dimitry's hopes. He was a zealous Catholic who had however failed Rome in losing Sweden. He had also, despite pacts of peace, been constantly threatened or embarrassed in Livonia where Boris Godunof had chosen to be a champion of heresy. It was known also that the Tsar had encouraged the Tartars to attack Lithuania. Also he was painfully aware of the reputation of greatness which Godunof had obtained in Europe and of his own intellectual inferiority. He disliked the upstart and had been irritated by the attempts which Boris had made to have his daughter Xenia married to Gustavus who as the price of union was to invade Polish territory and make himself King of Livonia, still more annoyed by the project of marriage with Duke John of Denmark. He was predisposed to do Boris Godunof an injury when the opportunity offered itself. At the same time it must be remembered he was bound by a treaty of peace and he was a monarch of limited power, tied to the Diet in all matters of active foreign policy.

Sigizmund from the first must have caught the infection of the great conspiracy and determined to help the Pretender if he looked capable of causing trouble in Russia. It is not to be supposed that he troubled himself much about the authenticity of Dimitry's story or the validity of his claim to the throne of Russia. Zamoyski wished a committee of inquiry. A few lawyers would at least have pointed out the discrepancies in the Pretender's story and have called upon him to elucidate much which remains now an insoluble problem for the historian. If indeed the Tsarevitch Dimitry did not die at Uglitch and the stranger was he then much could have been done to place his claim on a more solid basis. But it seems that if the Pretender were willing to become a Catholic all else could be gladly taken for granted.

Zamoyski and Chodkiewicz, both possessed of great influence in Poland, besought the King not to lend himself to the designs of Mniszech and the Pretender, but Sigizmund was not willing to listen to their sage advice. And the court camarilla was all for the adventure. The Jesuits seized upon it as something entirely to their liking. For them of course the main prerequisite was that Dimitry be received into the Roman Church and directly the Pretender was brought to Cracow they set about the task of conversion with methodical earnestness. Father Bartsch, the King's confessor, charged himself specially with this task.

Both the Diet and the Senate were hostile to the pretensions of the Dimitry. The Senate took a vote and there was only one who voted the claim of the Pretender authentic, John Tarnowski, archbishop of Gniezno. It was however Zamoyski who obtained this negative vote and Sigizmund was not deterred by it. Mniszech with his protégé arrived in Cracow and the first thing the father of Marina did was to invite the greater part of the senators to a banquet. It was the clever and audacious move of a diplomatic gambler. He had brought with him a number of distinguished Russians who were slavish believers in the claim of the Dimitry. Mniszech knew how to order a feast; it was superb. The pretendant Tsarevitch bore himself well, every inch a Tsar's son, and after libations of Tokay the whole dinner-party was rapturously won over.

There was no mistaking the feeling that the Russian guests were not accidentals. They were representative of the emotional excitement of their country. Dimitry might be an impostor but the Russian visitors were sincere. It began to be clear to the Poles that Russia was tired of Boris Godunof and desired the leadership of Dimitry to overthrow him. The impression was confirmed by the arrival of further delegations from Muscovy, chiefly from the Don Cossacks who unanimously offered their services.

The banquet took place on the 10th of March, 1604; five days later King Sigizmund received Dimitry. It had taken the Pretender six months since his first arrival and announcement to achieve that end, six months in which it might seem Boris had time and opportunity to have used energetic measures to avoid civil war. But Godunof as if oppressed by a sense of Fate had ceased to be a vigorous sovereign.

King Sigizmund was indulgent and friendly. He did not make any declaration which would offend the Diet or those of the senators who were opposed to Polish participation in the conspiracy, but he let the adventurer understand that he was sympathetic to his cause. The presentation was not made in a full court but in a private cabinet of the King. The papal nuncio Rangoni accompanied. Rangoni had been one of those who before seeing the Dimitry had dismissed him as an impostor, but he had been won over and at the Mniszech banquet had been especially struck with the possibilities of the young man. He had had private talk with him and had convinced him of the necessity of embracing publicly the Catholic faith. He had had him as guest of honour at another banquet and now, in a way, vouched for him before the King.

Dimitry made a very flowery speech which it is thought had been composed for him by some erudite friend of George Mniszech and at the conclusion of this address he was requested to retire to another room while the King conferred with the nuncio. After a few minutes he was asked to return to the presence. Then Sigizmund rose and lifted his hat and made a speech in his turn: "May God assist you, Dimitry, Prince of Muscovy! We have listened to what you have said and have considered the testimony. We see in you without doubt the son of Ivan and as a token of our good will assign you the sum of 40,000 zloti per annum, for the upkeep of your position and to defray expenses. We also grant you full liberty to enter into relationship with our nobility and to profit by their assistance."

This income was to be a charge on the royal demesne of Sambor which Mniszech farmed to his profit. The King must have thought "our George Mniszech stands most to profit by this adventure, should his daughter become Tsaritsa of Russia. We will charge the expenses up to him."

Dimitry was so moved by the King's bounty that he was bereft of speech but he showed his gratitude by his distraction. The nuncio conducted him from the cabinet, assuring him that he had made the best possible impression and that now the most imperative thing was that he be received into the Catholic Church with all celerity.

The Society of Jesus founded by Ignatius Loyola in

SIGIZMUND III, KING OF POLAND

1534 had grown to be one of the most powerful instruments of the Catholic Church and it was a militant ecclesiastical force in many countries. What had been lost in the Reformation seemed more than compensated in the zeal of the Jesuits whose ambition for Mother Church was unbounded. It did not seem to them beyond the power of faith and action to bring the millions of Russia into the True Fold. In their reasoning the most striking point of departure was that in Russia all depended on the will of one man, the Tsar. If the Tsar woke up one morning and said: "By evening all my subjects shall be Catholics," his will would be done. In 1580, when by the good offices of Pope Gregory XIII a tentative peace was made between Ivan the Terrible and King Stephen of Poland, it was thought that the Russian Tsar might perhaps be persuaded in his decline to become a Catholic. The Jesuit father, Anthony Possevin, was sent to Moscow to endeavour to achieve that end and to facilitate a union of the churches. He failed, but upon his return to Rome reported favourably on the prospect of Russia becoming Roman at some near future date. He lit a lamp for Russia at Rome and the possibility of the conversion of Russia had been kept alive throughout the reign of Fedor and had not died during the unsympathetic rule of Boris Godunof. With the rise of Dimitry the faith seemed justified. To some pious Catholics it must have seemed that God had raised Dimitry from the dead in order that Russia might be saved. Possibly the Jesuits were already too cynical to believe that in all sincerity. But by the mechanism of their conscience they were predisposed toward the Pretender. "The Cause of

Christ always justifies the means." It did not so much matter if the Dimitry were an impostor, or if he merely thought he was the son of Ivan the Terrible. What mattered was that he would bring Russia into the Catholic communion. Once Tsar his word was law. He had but to command his subjects to abjure Orthodoxy to be obeyed.

But the conversion could not be consummated with indecorous haste. The process of conversion must be staged in keeping with the dignity of the act. On each successive day after the reception by the King the Pretender received the holy fathers and conversed with them seriously of "difficulties." The season of Lent does not appear to have been observed with much austerity. Dimitry was the hero of Cracow and every night, if the chronicler is to be believed, there was feasting and dancing. But every morning there were religious conversations and preparation for conversion. Into these conversations the Dimitry entered with much zest. He had evidently disputed religious matters much in previous years, with monks and priests and pilgrims, and like a true Slav, he at times forgot that in any case he had to be converted and defended the Orthodox position with such enthusiasm that the Jesuits did not know what to make of him. They could not compromise on the *filioque* clause or the infallibility of the Pope even for the sake of Russia. And it proved extremely difficult to make the young man agree that the Holy Ghost proceeded from the Father *and the Son*. It appeared moreover that Dimitry was tinged with the Arian heresy. But at length he surrendered to the Faith, as of course he must, and Holy Thursday was the final

CONVERSION TO ROME

day of the conversations. It was agreed that the Tsarevitch should be received into the Catholic Church on Easter Eve.

There were difficulties which foreshadowed much greater difficulties to come. The Russian visitors in Cracow must be kept in the dark. How it escaped their attention that their leader was preparing to become a Catholic it is difficult to say. Possibly they regarded a flirtation with Catholicism as politic. Some may have felt that no Poles were necessary for the conquest of the throne, but these visitors were on friendly terms with the Poles and had enjoyed Polish hospitality. It is not likely that they renounced the idea of military assistance from Poland. Differences of creed were minimised in order that a common ground for co-operation might be found. But the Russians might be shocked by the actual conversion of the man who was to be Tsar. Dimitry insisted that the ceremony of his being received into the Catholic Church be kept secret.

The Pretender put off his princely garments and wore a beggar's rags and hid his face that no one might be perfectly sure they had seen him in the act of apostasy. It seems a little superfluous but there was something of the past in this behaviour of the Pretender. His claim to be the Tsarevitch Dimitry owed much to the fact that perhaps no one had actually seen the face of the young Tsarevitch dead. So now it must have occurred to him that he might at some future date defy anyone to come forward and say that with his own eyes he had seen him forswear his church. Paradoxically enough he became much more of a convinced Catholic after his conversion than he was at the moment of his renunciation, but that was possibly due to the influence of Marina Mniszech.

The conversion took place in the house of the Cracow Jesuits on the 17th of April, 1604. Dimitry chose his father confessor and made his confession and renounced Orthodoxy forever. Besides the Jesuit fathers there were present a few Polish aristocrats also in rags. In this disguise they had previously made a round of the Cracow streets with Dimitry seeking alms for the Church. At the door of the Jesuit College when asked what was their business they had proclaimed in a loud voice that they were strangers and foreigners travelling for the love of God. The scene was mysterious and dramatic. The Pretender put off his rags and in a dark cell, in his underclothes, made his humble confession, his chief sin apparently being that he had previously confessed to Orthodox priests. Besides renouncing the Greek rite he renounced also personal ambition, which seems strange, seeing that his whole position at Cracow expressed personal ambition, and upon his personal ambitions were centred the hopes of the Society of Jesus.

He obtained absolution from his sins and confirmation in his new faith. The fathers were well pleased by the youngest son of the Church.

Dimitry re-assumed his rags and slunk away home to do the first bidding of his advisers and compose a letter to the Pope Clement VIII, asking his Holiness for his protection and benediction. He hid himself from his Russian adherents and neither gave nor received the Easter kiss. All Easter Day he stayed in the privacy of his apartments and was seen of none. He was not communicated. His confessor, Savitsky, held that it

CONVERSION TO ROME

was better to reserve the blessing of the Sacrament to the actual day of his leaving Cracow and setting forth on his perilous and glorious enterprise.

It still remained doubtful what military aid, if any, he would receive from Poland. The King remained studiously non-committal. The Diet was hostile. But the conditions on which aid would be given were communicated. Dimitry, should he be successful in wresting the throne from Boris Godunof, must cede to Poland half the province of Smolensk and part of the Novgorodian lands. There was to be an economic union of Poland and Russia, with free ingress and egress for subjects of either state. Jesuits should be free to establish themselves in Moscow. Permission should be given to build Catholic churches in Russia. Dimitry should engage to assist Sigizmund to recover his lost realm of Sweden. Dimitry promised all these things, but still it was not clear that he was getting much in return except the moral backing of the King and the Catholic Church.

On the 24th of April, 1604, Dimitry despatched his famous letter to the Pope, asking for blessing and probably hoping for financial aid. The Pope had given money to King Stephen for his campaign against Russia; was it not possible that the papal coffers might be opened again for this even brighter hope. "The poor lost lamb" bleated to the shepherd of the one fold; Dimitry put himself at the feet of his Holiness as at the feet of Christ himself. Having found an eternal kingdom, he was even ready, if it pleased God better, to renounce his claim to an earthly kingdom. But he was sworn to devote the rest of his life to bringing the erring Orthodox to the true faith.

On the same day as he sent this letter, he received the Holy Sacrament and departed from Cracow. He was probably anxious to remove himself from the scene of his conquest by the Jesuits and eager to return to Marina. His offer to the Pope to renounce his earthly kingdom may have been mock humility. He was embarked on the great enterprise and could not turn back from it. But he had found something which was perhaps more satisfying than Tsardom, Marina Mniszech. Had it been possible to continue his days as a Polish rentier married to Marina Mniszech, it is possible that he might have let the Tsardom go. But that was not to be. He journeyed to Sambor with George Mniszech and two Jesuits watching over him. And Sambor was the rallying ground for all Russians in Poland and all Poles and Ukrainians willing for the adventure. The standard of the Pretender was raised at Sambor. There was no possibility of retiring from leadership. George Mniszech was, moreover, flushed with the success of his mission to Cracow. He never wavered. He did not grudge the grant from the Sambor estates, though in a way the money was taken from his own estate. He believed that all he expended he would get back a hundredfold. And it is possible that the little Marina herself was ambitious. She would rejoice that her fiancé had become a Catholic. That made it easier for their marriage. Now, all she wished was the diadem of Russia.

XXIII.

THE MOTHER OF DIMITRY

DOUBT, as a mental disease, afflicted Boris Godunof, paralysing his will. He became extremely morose, avoided conversation with the boyars, hid his face from the people. He remained for long periods in the privacy of his palace apartments and allowed subordinates to rule the country in his name. Petitioners assailed his gates in vain. The people brought grievances, but they were beaten off with sticks. Crimes of violence increased. Still nothing was done to check the banditry which had begun to flourish in the famine years. The measures taken against Dimitry were pitiful in their inadequacy. People caught talking about the Pretender had their tongues cut out. Some were sent to prison in Siberia; others suffered death by impalement or at the stake. The frontier service between Russia and the Polish Ukraine was doubled and orders given to prevent emissaries of the Pretender from entering Russia. But it is probable that the frontier guards themselves became quickly disaffected.

In March of 1604 Boris had the nun Martha brought under escort from the Vyksa wilderness to Moscow. Sister Martha was the ex-Tsaritsa Marya Nagy, the mother of the Tsarevitch Dimitry. She was brought secretly to Novodevitchy Convent and her coming to Moscow was in no way advertised. Godunof still pursued his policy of secrecy. He was even loath to utter the name of Dimitry as if by speech he might perchance show that he believed the Tsarevitch was alive. Ever since 1591 he had tried to make his position safer by cutting out tongues. Sister Martha was brought secretly at night from the Novodevitchy Convent to his bedroom in the palace. He wished to ask her definitely: had she seen her son dead on that fatal day at Uglitch, the 15th of May, 1591?

Thirteen years cloistered, shut away from the world, the ex-Tsaritsa Marya must have brooded considerably on her wrongs. She believed that Boris had sent agents to kill her child. She at least did not believe that the Tsarevitch in a fit, fell on a knife he was holding and killed himself. But supposing the wrong child had been killed and that the Tsarevitch had been at once taken into hiding by her kindred, she would naturally have allowed it to be said that the murderous Boris had succeeded and would not have breathed to anyone that her child still lived. The immediate vengeance on the Nagy family and the chastisement of Uglitch must have convinced her that the boy had little chance of living if Boris discovered him. And Boris was still her enemy: he sat on the throne where her son should be sitting.

No one knows whether Boris Godunof brought Sister Martha to Moscow to satisfy his own mind or to use her testimony to kill the claim of the Pretender. Had the mother been willing to make a public statement that she had seen her son dead, it must have been of some value to the Tsar. Vasilly Shuisky and others might have been mistaken as to the identity of the body of the dead child they saw, but it was not to be thought that a mother could be mistaken as to her own child.

The method of Boris Godunof was not that of the characteristic tyrant. No matter what the mother said, it had been possible to make a public proclamation in her name that the Pretender was an impostor and that she had seen her son in death. One must surmise that Boris feared to take this step lest the importance of the conspiracy in Poland should be magnified in the popular estimate.

The actual conversation between the Tsar and the mother of Dimitry is not very well authenticated. Boris made no announcement nor was any record kept. What is written must be derived from what was said by the ex-Tsaritsa when she was taken away from the presence of the Tsar. But it is certain she was actually brought to Boris to be questioned. The story goes that she was brought to the Tsar's bedroom and that the Tsaritsa Marya Skuratof was also present. Boris asked Sister Martha, had she with her own eyes seen the Tsarevitch Dimitry dead. The black veil of the nun was lifted that Boris might see her face as she replied. One sees the faded eyes, shrunken features and puckered brow of an old lady worn by her sorrows and the ascetic life. The nun was silent. "Is he alive or dead?" shouted Boris wrathfully. "I do not know," answered the nun.

"What! You say you do not know; you know well enough," shrieked Boris' wife, and snatching the lighted candles from the table, flung them in the mother's face.

Probably the nun's veil or her hair caught fire, for Boris intervened to save her from being burned.

Then the mother said: "I was told that my son had been secretly removed from Russia. But those who told me that are now dead."

Boris obtained no information that could dispel his doubts, nor any declaration which he could use against the Pretender. It is probable that he offered the mother liberty and an income on which to live, had she been willing to make a useful statement, but that is not recorded. She was sent back to a more rigorous confinement than she had previously undergone.

What Godunof discovered was that the mother thought her son to be alive. She knew he had not died at Uglitch. It must have added very greatly to his mental distress. Whether his wife actually threw the candles in the face of Sister Martha may be doubted, but there was severe tension and heart-searching in the palace. It was not that Boris Godunof might lose his throne. He still did not believe that. But the future of his children was placed in great jeopardy by the existence of an authentic Dimitry. All that he and his wife had worked for was threatened by the Pretender. The forces at their disposal were unreliable. The boyars gave lip-service but were disloyal and might go over to an insurrectionary if the cause of the latter were assured.

So much conflicting evidence regarding the Dimitry had been collected that it was difficult for Boris to make up his mind regarding the Pretender in Poland. The Romanofs had employed great chicanery. They knew something of the true story of what had happened to the Tsarevitch Dimitry. Perhaps they knew the whole story. But they had also sheltered a double, a candidate for imposture, though why they had was difficult to understand. Boris may have come to the conclusion that there were two dangerous men living; one was the authentic Dimitry, the other was an impostor with a striking resemblance to Dimitry. There was no other course open to him, for his own security and peace of mind, than to declare that the man who had shown his face in Poland was an impostor, he was the double.

The name of the double was known. He was Grishka Otrepief, in childhood in the household of the Romanofs, afterward a monk who had secretly dabbled in magic and the black arts, hoping by the aid of Satan to raise himself to the Russian throne. The monk had been at the Chudof Monastery whence, after his dark designs had been discovered, he fled in pilgrim guise to Kief. From Kief it is thought he crossed to the Polish Ukraine, and it was Boris' assumption that he and the Pretender Dimitry were one. Boris declared that the Dimitry at Sambor was Grishka Otrepief, a runaway monk.

A near relative of this Grishka was found, Smirnoi Otrepief, an uncle, who said that he knew his nephew well and would recognise him in an instant. The difficulty was that if Grishka was exceedingly like the Tsarevitch Dimitry the uncle might conceivably make a mistake when confronted by the Pretender. Boris probably doubted whether this uncle would do much good. He had him expedited to Poland, but he lacked the courage to give him an official and expressed mandate to expose the true identity of the Pretender. It was possible that Smirnoi when he got to Sambor might declare: "This is not my nephew. It must be the Tsarevitch Dimitry: long live his Majesty!"

The endorsement of Smirnoi Otrepief's frontier pass was characteristic of the strange secretiveness of Boris Godunof. It was stated in the *gramota* that he was sent to adjust boundary disputes with Polish and Russian landowners whose property abutted on the frontier lines. Nothing was hinted of his ulterior mission. Under the circumstances, it is not surprising that he failed. Free passage into the interior of Poland would naturally at that time be denied to a servant of Boris Godunof unless his purpose was deemed friendly. But whatever the cause of his failure, he returned to Moscow without satisfaction for the Tsar.

In October, 1604, Boris prepared to send another agent into Poland, Postnik-Ogarof, but he changed his mind and did not send him. Khrushchof was sent to the Don Cossacks to inquire into their alleged disloyalty, probably to inquire which Cossack families had fallen upon the party of Semyon Godunof and sent prisoners with impudent messages to Moscow. What was required was a punitive expedition, but Boris sent one man. Three years previously Boris had arrested Bogdan Bielsky and chastised his adherents in Cossack country with the greatest of ease. His authority was intact. But in 1604 at a distance of a week's journey from Moscow the Tsar was mocked. Khrushchof was seized and bound by the Cossacks and they sent him to Dimitry for examination. The Pretender obtained from him much useful information.

The futility of the measures taken by the Tsar is further exemplified by the hiring of an assassin to go to Sambor. It appears an attempt was made on the life of the Dimitry during his second sojourn at the house of George Mniszech.

XXIV.

THE STANDARD OF REVOLT

IN May, 1604, George Mniszech with the Dimitry and their large party, arrived safely home at Sambor. Marina was there and the lovers were reunited. The hero returned with an enhanced glory, for he had seen the King and won him to his side. And he had gained a spiritual victory which meant even more to Marina Mniszech. He had embraced her faith. He had become a Catholic and the saints and relics of her church would work for him. The fairy prince had become crusader and had promised to bring Russia to the feet of Rome.

The meeting of Dimitry and Marina was no doubt rapturous and it might normally have been assumed that an early marriage would have been arranged there and then. But George Mniszech was not impulsive and it depended on him. Had the father said the word, the marriage would have taken place. It must have occurred to the father that Dimitry would prosecute his great enterprise more valorously if Marina was withheld. "Gain your kingdom first," said he. "And then you shall have my daughter." Love is a greater force than ambition. Marina and not Moscow should be the prize. Moscow in short should be a means to Marina, not an end in itself.

It was agreed that Marina should be his wife in the event of his being successful in his enterprise. But if he failed, she should not be his. Marina was George Mniszech's chief asset, and if all this came to nought, she might still be advantageously married to someone else. But a pact was drawn up and on its basis the lovers were betrothed. Dimitry must have manifestly been greatly infatuated to have agreed to everything the father suggested. And Mniszech would not have demanded such a high price for his daughter had he not observed that the young man was passionately attached.

The following were the terms of the marriage pact:

"I do give my faithful and true princely promise that I will take in marriage the Lady Marina. If on the contrary I do not, then I wish that I might give this as a curse upon my self.

"Also, as soon as I shall make entrance into our kingdom and heritage of Moscow, then will I give the Palatine, the Lord, her father, a reward of ten thousand pieces of Polish gold.

"And to the Lady Marina our wife, in consideration of her great and long journey, as also for the providing and furnishing of herself, I will give out of my Treasure Velvets wrought with silver and gold.

"And the messengers that shall be sent to me from the Lord her father or from the lady herself I shall not hold or keep, but shall let them pass, and will reward them with gifts, which shall be a token of our princely favour.

"As soon as we shall come to the imperial throne of our father, then presently will we send our ambassador to the resplendent King of Poland to certify unto him, as also to entreat him to take knowledge of this business now passed betwixt us, and withal that he would be pleased to suffer us to conclude and effect this our said business, without loss or hindrance.

"Also unto the forenamed Lady Marina our wife, we give two lordships, viz., Novgorod the Great and Vobsko, with all the provinces belonging to the same, with counsellors, gentlemen, yeomen, and priests, fitting for a congregation, to rule and govern freely with full authority in the same form and manner as if we ruled. And myself to have no more right or title nor authority in the said two cities of Novgorod and Vobsko. . . .

"But if by chance our wife hath not by us any children, then in those two Lordships before specified, she shall place men of authority of her own . . . as though it were in their own true and lawful dominion, and to build monasteries and to set up the Romish religion and to have Latin and Romish priests and schools. But she herself to abide and remain with us.

"We will likewise with earnest care, seek by all means to bring all the Kingdom of Moscow to the knowledge of the Romish religion and to set up the Church of Rome.

"If God should not grant us good success . . . within a year, then it shall be at the pleasure of our father to separate me and his daughter Marina. But if it please him to forbear till another year, then do I pass this my bill with my own handwriting, and thereunto I have sworn my self and have given a vow according to the holy order, and in all this bill to hold and keep carefully: as also that I shall bring all the Russian people to the Latin religion.

"*Written at Sambor, the five and twentieth May, in anno* 1604. *Dimitry of Uglitch.*"*

* From a translation sent by John Merrick for the perusal of King James I.

This did not comprise the whole of the deal. Palatine Mniszech considered that he ought to be himself rewarded and reimbursed. King Sigizmund had earmarked half the province of Smolensk as his own perquisite. This somewhat annoyed George Mniszech who had hoped that he would have had most of that for himself. He sought compensatory estates and revenues and pored over the map of Russia for weeks trying to decide on what territory he could most advantageously put his little fat hands. Dimitry was not quite so obliging in dealing with the father on his own account. He had been ready to sign away anything and everything for Marina, but he showed a bargaining spirit in raising objections to the father's demands. However, about the 15th of June, this matter was settled also. All was clear; it remained to put the adventure to the test of action.

The recruiting and organising of an army of invasion now commenced in earnest. Eastern Galicia and the Ukraine were up in arms. Poland proper stood aloof; most of the ferment took place on Lithuanian territory, under King Sigizmund of course but not responsible to the Polish Diet. Zamoyski and other Polish leaders still thought that Poland would be mad to embroil herself with Russia by the military support of the Pretender. It is interesting to note that informed opinion in Warsaw and Cracow was to the effect that the Dimitry had not a chance. Mniszech was looked upon as a crazy and ambitious busybody ready to risk the peace of Poland for his personal aggrandisement. But King Sigizmund lay low and let Mniszech prepare for war. Poland wished the mobilisation stopped but the

King delayed action till Dimitry with his forces had crossed to the frontier regions of the Dnieper banks.

Apart from the Cossack detachments it was a nondescript army which Dimitry led to the invasion of his country. It is always thus in the first stage with the armies of pretenders. The first force is made up of adventurers and camp followers, as Richard III said of Richmond's army, "a sort of vagabonds, rascals and runaways." Success depends on who comes over from the other side. Dimitry published a number of manifestos and sent copies over the Ukraine and into Russia. Boris' agents had been instructed to stop these sheets coming across the frontier. But Russia, not yet fully recovered from the famine, was importing grain, and the manifesto was commonly smuggled across in sacks of flour. Mniszech and Constantine Wisniowiecki sent messages to their estates and wherever they had influence. Adam Wisniowiecki was at first disgruntled by the fact that although he was the original patron and protector of the Dimitry he was apparently to get no share in the ultimate spoil. But he also was brought into line and helped raise part of the army. Constantine Wisniowiecki had by far the greatest territorial interest and found the largest contingents of recruits. The manifesto was posted on the walls of the churches. The cause was in many places recommended by the priests. Secretly or openly sponsored by the Jesuits, Dimitry's cause was carried far beyond the local sphere of influence. A godly business in which there was scope for plunder appealed to many valiant Catholics who came riding in from the Carpathians. Southeastern Poland and Lithuania abounded in men ready for an adventure. The free lances did not expect much in wages; all they asked was a share in the spoil. To these must be added numbers of Russian peasants who despite precautions streamed across to Wisniowiecki's estates to line up and await the true Tsar. The Russians were even more convinced of the rightness of the cause than the Poles. There seems to have been something in the personality of the Pretender that won allegiance at once. Khrushchof when he was brought before him took a good look at his face and exclaimed: "I see at once that you are the true Tsarevitch, your father Ivan's lineaments are written in your features," and it would not be fair to assume that this noble was just a coward saving his head in the readiest way that occurred.

It became necessary for the Pretender to hurry toward the frontier with his forces. It was manifest that the Polish Diet would pronounce the mobilisation illegal and take steps to disperse the army of invasion. And despite the zeal of the Jesuits the Catholic Church as a whole had not made the Pretender's cause its own. Pope Clement VIII was cautious. When he received Dimitry's letter of the 24th April there was rejoicing in Rome and his Holiness gave thanks to God. But Clement in his reply did not give his blessing to the enterprise nor promise financial assistance and he avoided recognising specifically the validity of his claim. This lukewarmness of the Holy See was bound to encourage those Poles who saw in the adventure a danger to their country. The patriotism and good faith of the latter is not in question: they did not wish to give Russia a pretext for making war on Poland.

About the 30th of July, 1604, with the aid of his

confessor Savitsky, Dimitry wrote a new letter to the Pope in Latin. Some say he had been busy learning Latin in his spare time and this epistle in that language was his own unaided effort. If so it is a sign that he was becoming a more hearty Catholic than he had been at the time of his conversion. This letter contained a promise to consecrate his youth and health to the cause of Christendom and the apostolic throne. He thanked the Pope for his kind words and appealed for financial backing. Russia might in the long run be worth a few gold pieces to his Holiness.

Zamoyski sent a haughty letter of reproof to Mniszech. Even Sapieha who had in the first instance helped considerably to establish the claim of the Pretender, gave an adverse opinion on the adventure. "The palatine of Sandomierz (Mniszech) is about to embroil us with the Tsar of Russia," wrote he. "If he succeeds the result will be equally unfortunate for the fatherland and for us all." The obstinate Sigizmund was being badgered by his senators to do his duty and stop Dimitry while there was time. But he was hard to move, having set his heart on the conversion of Muscovy. The Emperor Ferdinand said of him that he thought so much of the Kingdom of Heaven that he lost the kingdoms of the earth, referring to the fact that he had lost Sweden and that if he had been politic he might have had the dominion of Russia but he lost that also.

In August, Dimitry departed for Russia with all the forces which had been mobilised. On the 7th of September, a royal order was issued demanding on pain of the direst penalties the dissolution of the Pretender's

THE STANDARD OF REVOLT 213

armies. It was issued too late, for the army had departed and was already on the banks of the Dnieper, and it was issued without the signature of the King. Sigizmund was evidently determined that in the event of the Pretender's success he was not going to compromise his claim to a share in the plunder nor renounce the glory of having assisted in the conversion of Russia.

Sapieha estimated the number of men at the disposal of Dimitry at 20,000. The number depends on where the army was counted. Possibly at Sokolniki on the Dnieper there were several thousand if all the camp followers be included. But the Polish contingent was merely three squadrons of hussars and 200 foot. George Mniszech commanded 2,600 men. It was neither a numerous nor effective army which in the first place attacked the power of Boris Godunof.

Dimitry reached the Dnieper north of Kief and had much to fear from Prince Ostrozhsky who was violently opposed to Roman Catholicism. Ostrozhsky had an urgent message from the Patriarch Job to seize and bind the runaway monk, Grishka Otrepief, and send him to Moscow for the punishment he deserved. Ostrozhsky had control of most of the armed forces in and around Kief and could certainly have dealt with the small invading army. It is said that he feared to embroil himself with the powerful Polish families but that seems insufficient excuse for his dilatory behaviour. He was far from believing in the claims of the Pretender and as a champion of Orthodoxy against militant Catholicism it would have needed no encouragement for him to deal with the invader on his own responsibility. He must have been aware of the astounding disaffection in the neighbouring Russian territory beyond Lithuanian jurisdiction. At that time Kief, though largely Orthodox, was not in Russia, but still part of the Grand Duchy of Lithuania. The only thing he did to frustrate the expedition was to withdraw from service all the ferry boats of the river. It had been better to allow the invaders to embark on these and attack them while they were astream. The withdrawal of the ferry boats did not deter Dimitry. Rafts were quickly improvised and the whole force crossed the river without a shot having been fired, without the passage of an arrow through the air. It advanced in a gay picnic spirit through the woods and across the rich corn-lands of the Dnieper valley. Nothing was wanted for its entertainment on the way. The Lithuanian borderland was strongly in favour of the Tsarevitch and no one prevented his progress. On the 16th of October he entered Russian territory and sent the following letter to the Tsar:

"We, Dimitry Ivanovitch, by God's grace Tsarevitch of all Russia, appanaged prince of Uglitch, Dimitrovsk and Gorodetsk, by ancestral right inheritor of the great tsardom of Muscovy, to the usurper of our power Boris Godunof, love and remembrance. We wish the ineffable bounty of high God and propose our clemency. We wrote thee recently a letter, O Boris, reminding thee in a Christian spirit of thy wrong doings and deceits which let them once be made known will appear more serious than you will care to admit. We, thy Tsar, are naturally sorry for thee our subject, that thou wilt shed Christian blood. . . . Bethink thee, were it not better for thee to retire to some place such

THE STANDARD OF REVOLT 215

as we shall appoint, make repentance and save thy soul?"

The text of this letter exists only in a Polish transcript. If it is genuine it can be regarded chiefly as an *aide-mémoire* to Boris, for it tabulates most of the wrongs, real or alleged, committed by Boris during the years of his power in Russia. It repeats the stories that Boris set fire to Moscow and that he invited the Tartars to attack the capital to divert attention from the tyranny of his rule. It accuses Boris of having designed to murder him, the Tsarevitch Dimitry, and tells how he was saved by his teacher and physician, Doctor Simeon. As for Grishka Otrepief: "Thou wilt soon see who is Grishka Otrepief and who am I." Then in quite a friendly spirit he tells the sagacious Godunof what a stupid fellow he has proved himself to be. Perhaps he was right: in his latter years Boris showed extraordinary stupidity and most especially in dealing with the Pretender.

The letter concludes warning Boris lest the indulgence which he feels toward him be changed to wrath. But Dimitry is greatly concerned with the welfare of Boris' soul in eternity. Better to endure some small humiliation than to burn forever in the torments of hell.*

At the same time Dimitry sent a message to all military commanders and officials bidding them renounce their allegiance to Boris Godunof and come over to him, remembering the oaths given to his father, Ivan Vasillievitch. He promised therein to uphold the

* *Historya Dmitra Falszywego.*

Orthodox Church, the first assurance of the kind that he had given, and very important as a means of winning over Russians who had been rendered doubtful by the rumours of the Pretender's conversion to Rome. This assurance did not run counter to the advice of his Jesuit confessor. He had obtained Jesuit consent to his being crowned under the ceremonial auspices of the Orthodox Church. It was expedient that he be firmly established on the throne before he attempted to convert Russia to Catholicism.

XXV.

THE PATRIARCH PRONOUNCES ANATHEMA

IN October, 1604, the adventurous Sir Thomas Smith, ambassador of James I of England, VI of Scotland, arrived in Moscow and was received by Boris Godunof in full court. We have a valuable impression of Boris at this later date which may well be compared with the earlier description by Horsey in 1590.*

Sir Thomas thus describes him:

"For the Emperor's person, he was tall and well bodied, teaching out of his authority obedience, of an excellent presence, black and thin haired, well faced, round and close shaved, strong limned. A prince framed between Thought and Resolution, as being ever in labour, but never till death delivered: never acting, though ever plotting, but in his closet or council chamber. One rather obeyed than loved, being feared where he was not served, doubtless upholding a true majesty and government in every part but in his own mind. . . . A father and a prince whose words, counsels, observations, policies, resolutions, and experiments, were but the life of his dear son, never advising, entertaining, no not praying without him. In all Ambassies and Negotiations, remembering his son's name with his own, loving him (being lovely) for that himself would be loved, unwilling to spare his presence, desirous to have him on all occasions before his eyes."

* *Vide ante*, pp. 119–120.

Sir Thomas brought gifts and greetings from King James and possibly the first news of the death of Queen Elizabeth. Boris was startled by the death of the Queen, as if he had a reminder that to him also death must soon come. The Tsar struck himself on the breast and cried: "Oh, my dear sister Queen Elizabeth whom I loved as my own heart!" and according to the ambassador fell almost into "a weeping passion."

It is probable that the ambassador told the Tsar of the merciful deliverance of the English parliament from the great Papist plot and the discovery of Guy Fawkes about to touch off the powder in the vaults. But Boris was silent about the Catholic plot which threatened him. Of the Tsarevitch "thought murthered at Uglitch and now revived" Smith learned from others.

In the magnificent reception given to Smith there was nothing to suggest the instability of the throne. "Being entered into the Presence, we might behold the excellent Majesty of a mighty Emperor, seated in a chair of gold richly embroidered with Persian Stuffe: in his right hand he held a golden sceptre, a crown of pure gold upon his head. (There was) a collar of rich stones and pearls about his neck. His outward garments of crimson velvet embroidered very fair with pearls, precious stones and gold. On his right side, on equal height to his throne, standing a very fair globe of beaten gold on a pyramid, with a fair Cross upon it, unto which before he spoke, he turned a little and crossed himself.

"Close by him in another throne, sat the Prince, in an outward garment like his father's but not so rich, a high black fox cap on his head, a golden staff with the

SIR THOMAS SMITH, AMBASSADOR
OF JAMES I TO THE COURT
OF BORIS GODUNOF

likeness of a Cross at the top (in his hand)." On the right hand of the Tsar stood two boyars clad in cloth of silver, with long gold chains to their feet, high black fox caps on their heads, and each held a golden battle axe on his right shoulder. On the left of the Tsarevitch stood two other nobles similarly clad but with silver battle axes on their shoulders. "Round about the benches sat the Council and the Nobility in golden and Persian coats and with high black fox caps on their heads, to the number of two hundred, the ground being covered with cloth of arrasse or tapestry."

But this magnificence was a false parade. It was ever Boris' policy to keep up appearances before foreigners. This tableau of wealth could not represent the distraught and impoverished Russia of 1604. The man who wore the golden crown had a head charged with doubt and despair. The hand which held the sceptre was spiritually paralysed. And though Boris, by repute, loved his son more than himself, yet he was losing the power to protect him. Boris, in his low-spirited direction of affairs of state, began to show the mentality of suicide. He passively willed his own destruction and the destruction of his family. Now he pitifully assumed that Fate was in arms against him. The strong self-confidence of his early years had mysteriously left him. The decline in self-assurance seems to have begun with his assumption of Tsardom and it was rapid. In 1604 he was suffering physically. One foot was swathed in bandages; he had gout. But spiritually he suffered more, being unable to face the great danger and call it by its name. When he came at last to the decision to raise an army of defence he must explain that it was to meet the menace of the Tartar. The Pretender was hoodoo to him: he must not breathe the name of Dimitry. Yet nothing was to be gained by lying. It is a curious page of psychology. When he should have composed a national manifesto in his own name he left it to the Patriarch Job. He could not fulminate across his empire as Ivan the Terrible would have done. He had no lightning in reserve.

The conversion of Dimitry and his pact with King Sigizmund and the Jesuits gave to the invasion a complexion of holy war. Doubtless Boris seized on this. The menace was not so much to his throne as to the Orthodox Church. Dimitry had placed in his hands a weapon which Boris had not the energy to use. Orthodoxy might have been mobilised against Roman Catholicism, but that required the vigorous co-operation of Church and State, Patriarch and Tsar. It was an error in judgment to persist in identifying the Pretender with Grishka Otrepief, a runaway monk and thief. The Prince who was leading an army against the throne was manifestly not this Grishka. The anathema which was hurled against Grishka Otrepief left the Dimitry unscathed because most Russians exclaimed: "But he is not Grishka, he is the son of the Terrible."

"The appearance of a Pretender is your business," said Boris to the boyars. "The plan of the Catholic Church to convert Russia to Rome is your business," said he to the Patriarch. Nothing was his business. For a popular appeal to arouse the masses to defend Boris and the Church, the Patriarch's proclamation was a sorry piece of work. Job was too old for his job. He called Sigizmund *King* of Lithuania as if to deny his title of King of Poland, senile and petty. Doubtless, he intended to call him Grand Duke of Lithuania because Sigizmund for a long space of time insisted on calling Boris merely Grand Duke of Muscovy. According to the Patriarch, Sigizmund was a greater enemy than the Pretender, and had contrived the plot against Russia and the holy Orthodox Church, "to set up catholic churches, Lutheran chapels and synagogues."

"Sigizmund has proclaimed the wandering thief Grishka Otrepief, an unfrocked monk and fugitive from the State of Russia, to be Prince Dimitry of Uglitch. But I, the Patriarch, and the whole community of the Church, and the world itself, know that Dimitry the Tsar's son died in 1591, some fourteen years ago. This man who now calls himself the Tsarevitch Dimitry is none other than the monk Grishka. His real name is Yushka Bogdanof. He was brought up in childhood with the Romanofs, began to steal, became a monk, wandered from monastery to monastery, at last appearing at Chudof, where he was novice. He learned to read and write at the patriarchal hostelry. Then he fled from Moscow in company with the monk Varlaam and the chorister Michael Povadin. He stayed some time at Kief in the Petchersky and Nikolsky Monasteries, still as novice. Then he renounced the Christian faith, cast off his black garb, turning to the Latin heresy, black magic and sorcery. At the suggestion of King Sigizmund and certain Lithuanian gentry he began to call himself Dimitry of Uglitch."

Many new details of Grishka's life were communicated in this manifesto. It appears that at the Petcherska *lavra* he ate meat during Lent and was denounced to the Abbot. He would have been arrested but being versed in black magic he knew when the pursuivants were on his track and so escaped. He sold ikons. He was for a time a Lutheran. He continued his thieving when he crossed into Lithuania, but he obtained the protection of Adam Wisniowiecki and by the King's command commenced to call himself Prince Dimitry.

This rigmarole was designed to show most clearly that the Pretender was Grishka Otrepief. It concluded with the statement that the unfrocked monk had been placed under the anathema of the Church. Grishka and all his associates had been publicly cursed by the Patriarch. The holy father therefore gave order that in every church in Russia the excommunication should be read. It extended to Otrepief and to all who called him Prince Dimitry.

It is likely that this denunciation was made at a hint from Boris but without his guidance. It makes the Pretender merely the tool of King Sigizmund. But Boris was aware of the danger of a risen Dimitry long before King Sigizmund took part in the adventure. And it did not much matter in 1604 whether the Pretender was Grishka Otrepief or another. If Russians were willing to believe that the adventurer was Dimitry, the Patriarch's muddled letter would do little to convince them to the contrary. The reason for bell, book and candle should have been that the man who called himself Dimitry was bringing Catholicism in arms against Orthodoxy and Russia. He had been anathematised for calling himself the Tsarevitch Dimitry. Well, perhaps he was indeed Dimitry, and the old Patriarch's reasoning was faulty. Ivan the Terrible had set himself above the Church and had for many years lived without its blessing. He had married the mother of Dimitry without the sanction of the Church's rites. He set himself as nearest to God of all Russians and was beyond anathema. If he was beyond anathema so was also his son. Boris leaned upon the patriarchate because he was not Tsar by divine right. The Patriarch had the unique authority of God only because the stem of Ivan appeared to have been cut off. For that among other reasons, the curse did not affect the fortune of the Dimitry in Russia.

At the same time that the excommunication was launched, Boris requested the Council of Boyars to make representations to Poland. Postnik-Ogarof was sent to Warsaw and Cracow with a missive from the boyars. This was also largely concerned with the identity of the Pretender and the misdoings of Grishka Otrepief. From this it appears in addition that the ex-monk was addicted to drunkenness and that even in his early years he had evoked unclean spirits. The Patriarch had determined to send him to seclusion at Bielo-Ozero for the period of his life, but the monk had fled. The letter complained that no precautions had been taken by the Polish and Lithuanian government to prevent the exit from its frontier of armed forces making inroad upon Russia. It was demanded that the "thief" be arrested and handed over to the Russian authorities, otherwise the armistice between the two countries would be considered terminated.

The boyars went somewhat further than the Patriarch, declaring that the Tsarevitch Dimitry who died at

Uglitch was in any case illegitimate, being the child of a seventh wife, and therefore had no true claim to the throne. Apparently, therefore, it was thought possible that the Dimitry might have convinced some people that he was actually the Tsarevitch. The Poles concluded that Boris Godunof was not himself certain that the rebel was not the prince thought to be dead. But the invasion of Russia had gone a long way before Postnik-Ogarof got to Warsaw to present his ultimatum.

XXVI.

CIVIL WAR

THE army of invasion, having crossed the Dnieper, proceeded along the left bank of the tributary Desna toward the substantial city of Chernigof. On the 18th of October the small town of Moravsk went over to Dimitry. Boris' commander and certain loyal officials were seized and bound by the townspeople and sent under escort to the camp of the Pretender. If instead of civil strife one can imagine the whole affair as a general election, this was the first result showing the way the electoral tide was flowing. "We will serve our lord and master, Dimitry Ivanovitch and none other," said the people of Moravsk. This was an agreeable surprise. A hand came out of Russia to welcome the Dimitry. It is said that the Poles were astonished by the surrender of Moravsk, and yet what could a small band of adventurers expect to achieve in Russia if there was not a popular rising on their behalf?

Some hundred and fifty horsemen were sent ahead to take over the town. Dimitry followed and was received at the gates with bread and salt, the emblems of hospitable service. Dimitry was at least Tsar of Moravsk and he set the captive commander and officials free and won them over to his side. Doubtless they sensed that Dimitry was going to succeed. Suddenly it was not treason to support Dimitry, but it was treason to support the false Godunof.

"Treason doth never prosper: what's the reason?
Why, if it prosper, none dare call it treason."

With Moravsk as a headquarters, scouts were sent over all the country far and near to inquire how the people stood with regard to the cause of the Tsarevitch. It was discovered there was overwhelming and rapturous support. So the army continued its way northward, up the Desna river to Chernigof. Its numbers were augmented by a constant flow of volunteers. The standard of Dimitry began to be raised by independent robber bands.

Chernigof was a fortified place prepared to withstand invasion from Lithuania. It was far removed in status from the almost negligible little town of Moravsk. It had walls and garrison, and its commander, Tatef, must normally have been expected to resist and delay an invading army with all the power at his disposal. Boris, in earlier years, had been at particular pains to strengthen the defences on the Lithuanian front. Chernigof did not capitulate with the spontaneity of Moravsk. A squadron of Dimitry's cavalry was sent to reconnoitre. They rode up to the walls and demanded surrender to the authentic Tsar, but were met by a shower of bullets from Tatef's arquebusiers. It was at very close range and there were many casualties. Mounted men are not equipped to take a city by storm, and it might have gone ill with them had not civil strife broken out within the citadel at the moment the garrison had been commanded to open fire. The horsemen had wheeled about and were attacking the suburbs of the city when the white flag was suddenly hoisted and messengers of peace came forth from the gates. The victory of the partisans of Dimitry within the city had been swift, and one surmises that some of those who had fired on the Cossacks had instantly changed their minds and refused to fire a second time, preferring to join the mob which was howling allegiance to the Pretender.

The Cossacks, enraged by the casualties they had suffered, refused at first to believe that the city had surrendered and did not wish to be baulked of the loot. It proved somewhat difficult to prevent them from massacring their own supporters. Dimitry had to send the Polish colonel, Stanislas Borzha, to restore order and make them give back the goods they had already stolen. The commandant, Tatef, was bound with strong cords and brought out of the fortress. The important city of Chernigof recognised Dimitry as Tsar. The Pretender found when he arrived that Borzha had not been very successful. The Cossacks still held much loot and the townspeople were enraged. The robber horsemen proved obstinate and Dimitry had to threaten that if they did not return the stolen property he would regard them as traitors and set upon them with the rest of his army. It was several days before his authority was completely established. Probably the fact that ten thousand pieces of gold were found in the town treasury helped to convince the marauders. This money was shared out among the troops, who were, we imagine, agreeably surprised at receiving so early some payment for their services. Tatef made oath of allegiance to Dimitry and was released.

Leaving a small force in control of Chernigof, the main army continued northeastward up the Desna to Novgorod-Seversk. It was not war: it was a taking over of the country. Church bells rang the glad tidings of the coming of the true Tsar; the emblems of the rule of Boris were destroyed; delegations from all the villages and estates came to protest their loyalty; recruiting all the while was vigorous. Dimitry was making for the broad highway to Moscow. Of course, there was no such thing as a highway in the modern sense, but the way to Moscow via Kromy and Oryol has been called the *route des ambassadeurs*. The thrust was at the heart. A less impetuous adventurer might have frittered away his chances in guerrilla warfare in outlandish regions. The "wandering thief" or "runaway monk" showed unusual capacity as a military commander.

On the 11th of November, a week after leaving Chernigof, the army of invasion reached Novgorod-Seversk. But that fortress was in command of an experienced soldier, Peter Basmanof, brother of the Basmanof who had perished in the fight with Khlopko before the gates of Moscow. He was son of that infamous favourite of Ivan the Terrible, Fedor Basmanof, but was unlike his father in every way, being a man of integrity and courage. He was able to suppress the movement in favour of Dimitry in Novgorod-Seversk and convince the inhabitants that it was to their advantage to remain obedient to him. He called within the citadel all the burghers living outside the walls and then fired the suburbs so that at least the Cossacks should get no loot. The walls of the city were of oak and mud, but very thick. Dimitry came up with his artillery, which consisted of seven diminutive German cannon. But these popgun pieces could not pierce the wooden walls. The Polish hussars galloped up to the walls, but were met by repeated musketry discharge and soon galloped back again, out of range. The defenders of the walls shouted: "Thief, thief!" Dimitry reproached the Poles for their lack of courage, but could not spur them on to a more daring assault. Then repeated attempts were made to fire the walls. Combustible material was loaded on carts and moved forward to be placed under the battlements. But three times the convoys were beaten off. At this, the first real difficulty, there was much murmuring in Dimitry's nondescript army, and one can see how ill it would have fared with the Pretender had he not had the support of the greater part of Russia. Basmanof was a very exceptional supporter of the power of Boris Godunof.

On the 19th of November, standing below Novgorod-Seversk and not knowing what to do next, the army was cheered by the arrival of emissaries from Putivl, some thirty miles southeast. Putivl recognised Dimitry Ivanovitch and did not wait to be besieged. The commander of the town, Michael Saltikof, was brought into camp bound. The *dyak*, Bogdan Sutupof, arrived and showed himself to be a hearty partisan of the Dimitry. Sutupof was probably responsible for the surrender of Putivl and recommended himself greatly to Dimitry, who marked him out for advancement when he should come into his kingdom. Borzha was sent to take over Putivl.

On the 24th of November emissaries arrived from two more towns which had declared for Dimitry,

Sievsk, ten miles due east of Novgorod-Seversk and Rylsk, twelve miles northeast of Putivl. On the 1st of December the great fortress of Kursk, still farther east, was learned to have abjured the authority of Boris Godunof and come over to the cause. On the 2nd of December it was learned that Kromy, far to the northeast, had recognised Dimitry. The same happened in Bielgorod, far to the southeast. All Russia was being caught up in the movement.

Novgorod-Seversk still held out, though some of its people crawled out by stealth and joined Dimitry's camp. The news of the surrender of other towns was sent by arrow over the walls, but it is possible that Basmanof was slow to be convinced that Russia as a whole was rising for the invader. Still he called him the "thief" and warned those who approached the fortress that their leader and all who served him would be impaled on stakes in due course.

Boris Godunof was by now greatly alarmed and awoke tardily from his apathy. He resolved to trust his fortune in the field to Fedor Mstislavsky. Fedor, although he had good cause to hate Godunof, had remained more faithful to him than other boyars. Boris had banished and caused the death of his famous father, Ivan Mstislavsky. He had had his aunt confined in a distant convent because of the plot to wed her to Tsar Fedor. He had prevented Fedor Mstislavsky's marrying lest his offspring should at some time contest the throne bequeathed to the Godunofs. Boris considered the family dangerous because of its genealogical pretensions. But Fedor, being unambitious, had remained loyal. He seemed to be Boris' best hope. The

Tsar would now make amends to him for the wrong he had done his family. Let him but disperse the forces of the Pretender and his reward should be great. He was to have the unfortunate Xenia to wife, with the dukedoms of Kazan and Siberia as his appanaged right. He was sent into the field with an army of fifty thousand men.

It is said that there was difficulty in mobilising this force. Few wished to go. Recalcitrants were flayed till they had no skin on their bodies. Nevertheless, a well-equipped army did set forth to pacify the insurgent and troubled west, to destroy the impudent Poles and bring the "thief" bound to Moscow.

When Basmanof got the news that an army of relief was approaching Novgorod-Seversk, he became much more daring, opened his gates as if to surrender, let in a goodly detachment of enemy forces and then shut the gates on them. He made frequent sallies to divert the attention of Dimitry's army. December was a month of alarums and excursions. On the 20th Dimitry's scouts reported the proximity of Mstislavsky. It became clear that a battle must be fought. Dimitry sent a message to Mstislavsky to the effect that he was loath to shed the blood of his fellow Russians. He cited what had happened at Kursk and Kromy and asked would it not be better if he bowed to the inevitable and made a submission which sooner or later they would have to make. But Mstislavsky had sufficient mercenaries in his army to control the whole. The secret partisans of Dimitry dare not reveal their sympathies. The advances of the Pretender were rejected with contumely. Nevertheless, it must have become evident to this army in its progress westward across Russia that a vast number of people had fallen away from their allegiance to Boris Godunof. There could have been but little confidence of victory. Dimitry sent a tiny force, some two hundred cavalrymen, against the fifty thousand of Mstislavsky just to see whether the Godunof army would show fight. The gallant two hundred were repulsed. Owing to the activities of Basmanof, Dimitry was obliged to keep a large force on the defensive before the city gates. The infantry remained investing the fortress. The Cossacks and the hussars were sent into action against Mstislavsky.

The army of Mstislavsky was camped at a distance some seven miles from Novgorod-Seversk. It was inactive. An immediate advance was not planned. To make assurance doubly sure, Mstislavsky was waiting for reinforcements. The first skirmish had seemed to show that there was little danger. But in order to capture the Dimitry and not let him escape back to Poland after the rout, it seemed necessary to have a much larger force. Mstislavsky, compared with Dimitry, was dull. The hussars and Cossacks walked their horses to within arrow range of the enemy, and then advancing in a tearing gallop, made a furious charge upon the enemy. And they had complete success, stampeding the army and unseating Mstislavsky himself, who was carried unconscious from the field. The army fled, leaving some thousands of dead and wounded behind them. The losses of their assailants were but slight.

But this victory could not be followed up successfully. Apparently, Dimitry feared to advance leaving Novgorod-Seversk unsubdued in his rear, and he had not enough men to leave the fortress safely invested. The Polish troops demanded wages, and the Cossacks needed plunder. It was far from the will of Dimitry to allow his men to pillage the houses of those who had pronounced in his favour. But where to pick up some money to pacify his followers? There was something like mutiny. "Eh, we'll see you yet with a stake in your rectum," said some of his disgruntled soldiers. If only he had captured the treasury of Mstislavsky, he would have been able to pay a dividend, but his horsemen had allowed that to be borne out of the field. One regiment said: "Pay us and let the others go without! We will stand by you and when the others see that we are staunch they will not dare desert." Dimitry fell for this, but it did not have the desired effect. Dimitry went from man to man among the Cossacks, begging them not to abandon him to destruction, but it was to no avail. His army melted away. Nearly all the Poles returned home. George Mniszech concluded that the game was up and, pleading ill-health, departed for Sambor. He said also that the Polish Diet had now interfered and King Sigizmund had ordered him to return to Poland. It was lucky that Fedor Mstislavsky had been frightened out of action; otherwise, in the forbidding early days of January, 1605, the "thief" might easily have been captured and hailed to execution. There remained with him a mere 1,500 men. How, with such a handful, could he hope to conquer Russia?

The Tsarevitch remained thus inadequately supported for several days, and Basmanof in the fortress was unaware of the defections in the army opposing him. But then Dimitry received new and unexpected aid. Zaporozhian Cossacks to the number of 12,000 came up from the south, bringing with them plentiful artillery. They were ready to support Dimitry without pay. The Pretender rejoiced greatly, raised the fruitless siege of Novgorod-Seversk and departed with his new army southeast to Sievsk, which had already recognised him.

Boris, hearing that Dimitry had been abandoned by the greater part of his army, took heart and sent Vasilly Shuisky with important reinforcements for Mstislavsky. He also sent confirmation of the great rewards which would follow victory. But the whereabouts of the Pretender were not exactly known, nor was the accession of strength realised. Mstislavsky's quartermasters, out scouring the country for provisions and forage, came unexpectedly into contact with the enemy. The Zaporozhians charged upon them, killing several and driving the rest to camp in an infectious state of panic.

There was hope that a great number of the soldiers of Mstislavsky and Shuisky might desert to the Pretender, and some of Dimitry's advisors, especially what remained of his Polish adherents, were in favour of playing a waiting game. But the newcomers were more fiery and were intent on putting the cause to the test of immediate action. Probably the more cautious spirits were right. Mstislavsky had an army of 70,000 men, which must be considered a very redoubtable force whatever the weakness of morale. In the battle which took place on the 21st of January, 1605, Dimitry was routed. The conflict was at first rather a comedy. The army of Mstislavsky was so nervous that it took fright at the number of pennants of Dimitry's cavalry and the blare of trumpets which heralded the onset. Mstislavsky had only three banners, very large ones, it is true, set with emeralds, but Dimitry had sixty or seventy flags. And Godunof's army had no trumpets at all. Dimitry charged upon the bewildered Tartar vanguard and almost carried off a complete victory at one stroke. It is said that it was the Germans in the ranks of Mstislavsky who remarked that after all there were not a great number of the enemy. Some subordinate was responsible for a rapid re-organisation of the panicky army, and a strong counter-attack. Twelve thousand musketeers opened fire simultaneously upon the prancing Poles and Cossacks. Comedy again; it seems they hit no one or very few, but they made such a smoke that one wing of Dimitry's army could not see the other and thought it had fled. There was instant retreat. When the smoke cleared, it was found that it had fled, without casualties. Dimitry, on a beautiful war horse, rode about rallying his men and taking all sorts of risks. He was a brave fellow. His horse was shot under him during the retirement and he would have been captured had not one of his followers immediately given up his own horse and taken that of his groom. The second horse was shot; the Tsarevitch fled on foot.

According to Captain Margeret, who took part, Dimitry lost 6,000 men in this battle. His forces for the time being were shattered. Sievsk was abandoned. Dimitry and what remained of his army retired to the west of Rylsk. But instead of following up the victory by a rapid advance, Mstislavsky and Shuisky wasted much time harrying the supporters of Dimitry in the villages. They began a mild imitation of Ivan the Terrible's chastisement of Novgorod. They had many prisoners as a result of the battle, and these were increased by the numbers taken in the villages. There was an orgy of public torture, impalement on stakes, frying of babies on frying pans, flaying of men and women with wire whips, rape.

The Dimitry, whether he was monk or Tsar's son, had shown himself a humane leader. He had restrained his followers from plunder, he had tortured no one, he had released unscathed all prisoners who professed themselves willing to serve him. He had shown himself brave in the field and intrepid as a commander. The brutality of Godunof's army threw these good qualities into relief. His reputation grew, even in defeat. Mstislavsky sought military information, but many of those he tortured preferred death to betrayal. Poor peasants were found everywhere ready to die for the Tsarevitch. And the cruelty of the expeditionary force increased the resistance of the rebel towns. Mstislavsky moved to the siege of Rylsk and promised much to the inhabitants if they would surrender, but these, guessing what was in store for them, if they made submission, defended their walls with tremendous energy.

Dimitry had retired to Putivl, but instead of pressing on to that fortress, Mstislavsky wasted time besieging Rylsk. In this he showed strange incapacity, and it is not surprising that Boris in Moscow began to suspect this half-hearted soldiering and call it by another name. When Boris heard that Mstislavsky had not taken the legitimate fruits of victory, he imagined treason. It is clear that he was wrong. The ruthless behaviour of

Mstislavsky toward the adherents of the Dimitry proves that at that time at any rate he had no idea of going over to the enemy.

Dimitry was in a sad plight. After the defeat near Sievsk he had been deserted by several thousand men. The Zaporozhians had not proved as staunch as their brave words had suggested. The few remaining Poles wished to return to Poland. It was with great difficulty that the Pretender persuaded Stanislas Borzha to stay with him. But Russia was for him. Two armies had abandoned him. A third army came to support him. The new fortress which Godunof had commanded Bielsky to build for him in the south recognised the Pretender. It was actually called Boris-Tsaref, but it raised the standard of Dimitry. The great city of Voronezh declared for Dimitry, as did Oryol, Yelets, Oskol, and they sent contingents to fight for him and they sent him new artillery.

These surrenders must have given Mstislavsky food for thought. He was stupid, but he had Vasilly and Dimitry Shuisky to advise him. It must have dawned upon him that it was better to play for time and see what was going to happen. He was not so devoted to Boris Godunof as to risk everything for his cause. Dimitry sent 2,000 men to relieve Rylsk, and Mstislavsky allowed them to get inside the fortress and so increase the numbers of the defenders. That in itself might almost deserve a court martial. But what was worse, after a month's masterly inactivity, the siege of Rylsk was raised. The army of Godunof retired northward to Kromy without any enemy attacking them. The petty garrison came out after them, biting their heels like dogs, and they abandoned thirteen cannon in their hurry to get away.

Kromy had long since declared for Dimitry, and on the 14th of March, 1605, Mstislavsky laid siege to it. This was merely a punitive measure and had no military significance. The retirement or advance, whichever it be considered, was conducted in a dilatory fashion. The army plundered as it went. It brought arson and assault and rape into the villages. It became a hunting party, with unfortunate men, women and children as game. And an extraordinary military exploit was achieved by Dimitry. He sent 4,000 men to make a detour of the army of Godunof and they got to Kromy before it did. Mstislavsky received messages from the enraged Boris Godunof, but does not seem to have been spurred to greater activity. He increased his army by uniting with the forces of Fedor Sheremetief, and had some eighty thousand men at his command. It is doubtful whether the number of defenders of Kromy all told numbered more than six thousand, but he could not take it. He had siege guns and siege towers, but he did not use them to any effect. The defenders were allowed to raise earthworks around their walls. Small detachments from Dimitry's camp were allowed to enter the gates of the fortress with cartloads of bread. Boris' spies reported most of this to Moscow, darkening the last days of the despairing Tsar.

XXVII.

TWELFTH HOUR OF THE NIGHT

As yet struggles the twelfth hour of the Night, nocturnal birds of prey are on the wing, spectres uproar, the dead walk, the living dream.

JEAN PAUL RICHTER

THE power of the Tsar failed and the light of his authority faded out in city after city all over Russia. The lights were going out in Moscow, too. Peter Basmanof, the heroic defender of Novgorod-Seversk, had come to the capital; Boris called him to the palace and decorated him and was most gracious to him, seeing in him the one man who in all Russia was indubitably loyal. As a forlorn hope, he offered Basmanof his daughter's hand and half the kingdom if he would take over the command from Mstislavsky and rid him of the Pretender. Such an invitation was equivalent to a command and it is not likely that Basmanof refused, but he was shrewd enough to see that the time was passed when the Dimitry could easily have been destroyed. And although at Novgorod-Seversk, Basmanof had thought that he was dealing with Grishka Otrepief, the "thief," the runaway monk, he had now fallen into doubt. The personality of the enemy was greater than he had imagined. The runagate was clearly a fiction.

Semyon Godunof had returned to Moscow from his fruitless raid on the mutineers of Astrakhan, and was in ill-humour. His baleful activity in the capital had increased. His method of saving his skin and that of the Godunof family lay in ceaseless violence against imaginary enemies. Boris was lethargic; he would certainly not have tortured so many people as Semyon did. The Dimitry got on the nerves of Semyon Godunof. His admiration for Boris failed him. He felt that the Tsar was a bit of a fool. Especially, he resented the offering of the hand of Xenia to Mstislavsky and then to Basmanof. He began to doubt the Tsar's capacity to deal with the Pretender. "I've had a terrible dream," said he to Basmanof. "I dreamed that this fellow was really Dimitry, the son of Ivan." If anyone else had dared to have such a dream, Semyon would probably have had him arrested and put to the torture. Probably he had no such dream, but invented the dream in malice, to see how the new commander would take it. Basmanof shrugged his shoulders: he had had a waking dream to the same effect.

Boris was afraid that he was opposed by a powerful magician. One of his most persistent accusations against Grishka Otrepief was that he dabbled in black magic. That Boris himself did the same was not weighed in the balance. Among the bad news that came to him from the front was the significant item that a famous sorcerer living at Yelets had offered his services to the Pretender. Boris took counsel from his own sorcerers and wrought spells which were curiously ineffective. As fast as one army of the enemy had been dispersed another army appeared out of nothingness. It was like one of those conflicts in an Arabian Nights' tale where opposing genii swarm to the attack. The greater sorcery would prevail, but it seemed as if that might be on the side of the Dimitry. The soothsayers gave warning to that effect.

There was at that time living in an underground cell in Moscow a religious maniac called Alina, a strange woman, probably bearded and ugly and loaded with rusty chains eating into an emaciated body. Alina had second sight and what she prophesied infallibly came about. Her reputation was greater than other soothsayers', for she was reputedly very near to God, who must be supposed to know more than the devil. Boris set off from his throne and went to the hole in the ground to find her, but she drove him off. Then he went a second time. Alina received him. "What is coming?" he asked. But the crone was not friendly. There were other weird sisters at the mouth of the cave and she made them sing part of the funeral service over a little piece of wood which she had found. "You ask what is coming? That is what is coming."

Boris returned to his palace in anguish of soul. He had turned his face away from God and God had turned away His face from him. He could not flee to a monastery and take sanctuary, as he had done when Fedor died. He could not move the great wonder-working ikons into his bedroom. He could not find the solace of personal religion but must send his children to church to pray for him.

But there was no conspiracy against Godunof in Moscow itself. The behaviour of the Council of Boyars, of the other gentry and the officials did not reflect the change in the fortunes of the Tsar. Except for the manifest hypochondria of Boris himself there was no change within the Kremlin walls. The success of the

Pretender was not so clearly recognised by others as it was by the Tsar. Many took malicious pleasure in his troubles: that was all. The situation might have been made more dramatic had Boris declared war on Poland and Lithuania. But he awaited the long-delayed return of Postnik-Ogarof. The latter did not present his message to the Diet and the King of Poland till the 10th and 12th of February, 1605. He did not find Poland hostile to Boris Godunof. On the contrary the Diet was violently opposed to those Poles who had assisted the Dimitry and it criticised the King for countenancing them. Still most of them had abandoned the adventure and had returned to Poland. George Mniszech could be said to have repented his foolhardiness. Poland refused to be embroiled with Russia on account of the Pretender. Sapieha gave Postnik-Ogarof answer: "The man you want is now in Muscovy; he is not with us and we think it would be easier for the Tsar to have him seized and executed than for us to go after him."

That was logical but it was depressing. Unless he went himself to the seat of war, Boris could not make use of the mighty army in the field and deal finally with the Pretender. He had once shown himself a capable soldier, organising the defence of Moscow against the Tartar. He would certainly have done better than Mstislavsky and having the traitor once within his power, would not have let him slip away. But Boris feared to move from Moscow lest in his absence the boyars should seize the city and declare for Dimitry. Probably also he feared being murdered by his own army.

In March he sent three monks to Putivl to murder the Dimitry. These monks were said to have known

Grishka Otrepief by sight. Their mission was to stir up the people of Putivl against the Pretender and if that failed, to poison him. At least they confessed to that under torture and the youngest was found to have poison hidden in one of his jack boots. To discredit them a certain Pole was dressed up as the Tsarevitch and put on a throne. It was expected that when the monks were brought before this person they would say: "You are Grishka Otrepief the thief, we know you of old." But they confined themselves to saying: "We do not know who you are but you are not Dimitry Ivanovitch."

The Dimitry did not hide himself during his campaigning. The monks must have seen him and have been aware of the trick that was being worked on them. There is no evidence that they did actually identify him as Grishka. They had been instructed by the Patriarch Job as well as by Boris Godunof and their special line of persuasion with the people of Putivl had been to remind them of the anathema and the danger to which they were exposing their immortal souls. It seems probable that they were chosen for the task by the Patriarch who believed firmly that the Pretender was Grishka Otrepief. If Job truly had a hand in this that would account for their dual mission. It was more like the Patriarch to make an appeal to the soul and more like Boris to think of poison.

That was Boris' last weak card. The arrest of the monks took place about the middle of March. Dimitry wrote a further pious remonstrance to the Tsar. Within a month Boris Godunof was dead and the prophecy of Alina was fulfilled.

XXVIII.

DEATH OF BORIS GODUNOF

ON the 13th of April, 1605, in the early afternoon, the Tsar died suddenly. He had been eating promiscuously at guest tables which had been spread in the reception hall of the palace. He went across to the look-out window to gaze for a last time over Moscow, and then suddenly he was crying with pain. Someone helped him to a chair but before the court doctor could get to him blood was gushing from his eyes, ears and nose. He was writhing and shrieking. Someone asked him his will regarding Russia. It was clear that he would die there and then. "I leave Russia to God's will and to the Council," said he. It was almost as if he had renounced the throne for his son. Not a word of Fedor! Boris fell unconscious. The old Patriarch came hurrying in with the Holy Elements. The dying man received the last sacrament and was at once shorn as a monk. Before the breath had gone from his body he was made Father Bogolep that he might not come before the Judgment Seat weighed down by a crown.

The physician who attended Boris did not make any official announcement of the cause of death, but he may have been responsible for the story that the Tsar when he went over to the little window, turning his back on his guests, took poison. The popular verdict was that he committed suicide. One version (Margeret) is that he died of apoplexy. Some say his death was caused by the weight of grief upon him. He had been ailing for some years though chiefly from gout. But poison seems the more probable agency. His face was black a few minutes after death and his corpse was hideous to look upon.

The death was kept secret or at least was unannounced for twenty-four hours. The Patriarch and Semyon Godunof took precautions against a popular disturbance. They discovered with relief that the position of the Godunofs in Moscow still seemed to be sound. Peter Basmanof undertook to quell the insurrection of the Pretender. Mstislavsky and Sheremetief were to be recalled to Moscow. It was decided that Boris' son, Fedor, now sixteen years of age should be proclaimed Tsar. An oath of allegiance to mother and son would be taken from everyone. It was important, in framing the terms of that oath, that express denial of the claims of the Pretender should be made. There was a consultation between Job and the Council of Boyars and it was decided to omit the name Grishka Otrepief. That the Pretender was the runaway monk must have become generally doubtful, if not demonstrably absurd. The phrase "the thief who calls himself Dimitry Ivanovitch" was used. Some of the boyars were in favour of bringing the ex-Tsaritsa Marya, the mother of Dimitry, back to Moscow and giving her complete liberty. If the Pretender were not her son, her denial of him must be the most convincing evidence available. It is curious, but about the same time the Dimitry had written to Mstislavsky a friendly letter, asking him to confront him with his mother, and if she did not accept him as her own let him be cut to pieces! But the Patriarch did not think that Sister Martha was sufficiently dispassionate. One could not rely on the testimony of a woman who nursed such wrongs as she did.

On the evening of the 14th of April, the Patriarch announced that Boris Godunof had died and in death had renounced to him his throne. That probably referred to the renunciation which the dying man was allowed to have made when he became the monk, Bogolep. In any case Job only held the throne to give it to Fedor with Fedor's mother as Regent. A constitutional difficulty had arisen. Boris Godunof had been elected to the throne. What right he had was based solely on election. But it could hardly be argued that he and his heirs in perpetuity had been elected. The throne had become elective and not hereditary. Another election was necessary but at such a time of disaffection an election could not be risked. Therefore in the proclamation which the Patriarch Job caused to be sent far and wide over Russia, it was said that, all, everyone with tears in their eyes, had beseeched Fedor to become Tsar. This was a falsification and although the boyars as a whole gave their tacit consent to its publication, yet Fedor and his mother had little standing with them and they waited the course of events and especially the action of the commanders in the field against the Pretender.

The body of Boris Godunof was immured in the resting place of Tsars and Grand Dukes of Muscovy, the Cathedral of the Archangel Michael. In death as in life it seemed he would have the place of a Tsar. But the body was like a man without means in a fine hotel. The Patriarch told the mourners that Boris' sinless and righteous soul had gone peacefully to God, but there was no assured peace for his body in the great cathedral. That was destined to be moved quite soon to a humbler hotel.

Fedor was nominally Tsar, but the Council of Boyars took the control of Moscow into their own hands. One of the first acts was to pardon and recall Bogdan Bielsky. Semyon Godunof must have begun to tremble in his shoes as the first of the enemies of the Godunof family was restored to power and influence. Bielsky was not likely to forgive having had his beard torn out by the order of the late Tsar.

Fedor Mstislavsky, Vasilly and Dimitry Shuisky were recalled from the army, but not to give an account of their inefficient soldiering. They should rather form a committee of safety for the protection and guidance of the young Tsar. Peter Basmanof was sent to the front to take over the command. With him was associated Prince Katyref-Rostovsky. Isidor, Metropolitan of Novgorod the Great, was sent to swear in the troops to the new Tsar.

If the recorded dates are correct, Basmanof galloped to Kromy as fast as horse could carry him. Boris had died on the 13th of April; Basmanof arrived at the front on the 17th. Basmanof could not have remained long in conference with the Patriarch and the boyars in Moscow. It is related that the young Fedor said to him at parting: "Serve us as you did our father before us, faithfully and well!" But it is not certain that he took formal oath of allegiance. Basmanof may have hastened away to avoid that ceremony. Basmanof was secretly of the opinion that the Dimitry was the true heir to the throne but had kept his counsel and had revealed his mind to none. He had such a reputation for loyalty to the Godunofs that his taking the oath was not urgent.

When he arrived at Kromy he did not tell of his secret conviction but allowed the army to be sworn in duly by the Metropolitan of Novgorod. Mstislavsky and the Shuiskies left at once for Moscow without staying to parley with the new commander. The swearing in of the army did not pass without incident. Many soldiers avoided the oath and were not punished. Others openly insulted the Metropolitan. There was no discipline in camp. The army which had been playing at besieging the little fortress of Kromy for months was out of hand. Basmanof took no steps to support the clergy. Nor did he order a more vigorous onslaught upon the fortress.

It might have seemed to the Dimitry at Putivl that the appointment of Basmanof cast a shadow on his prospects. The intrepid defender of Novgorod-Seversk was not forgotten. In him the Pretender seemed to have a much more serious enemy than in the wavering and incapable Fedor Mstislavsky. He wrote optimistically to Poland demanding reinforcements and telling George Mniszech that he would do well to return to the seat of action. Russian towns continued to declare for him, but with the advent of Basmanof the issue must again have been cast into doubt. With his Tartar and German troops alone Basmanof might have dealt effectively with the Pretender's forces at Putivl. On the other hand, some think that if he had moved an inch against the Dimitry he would have been liable to have been lynched by his own army. One defence of

Basmanof's action is that he had no other course open. Still this man was no coward. He had demonstrated that at Novgorod-Seversk. We believe that he went over to the Dimitry through inner conviction.

He appears to have sounded some of the princes and personalities in the army first. He found abundant confirmation of his own secret belief. He told Saltikof and Golitsin that Semyon Godunof had practically confessed to him that the Pretender was indeed the son of Ivan the Terrible. About the end of April he wrote to Dimitry, acknowledging him as the true Tsar and asking pardon for having resisted him in ignorance at Novgorod-Seversk. "I was never a traitor. I do not wish ruin for my country but happiness. Now almighty Providence has revealed much; amongst other things Semyon Nikititch Godunof confessed to me that you were the Tsarevitch. Now I see that God punished us with the plagues, first the misery of the rule of Godunof as Tsar; then confusion in the counsels of the boyars; then the great famine. He visited us thus because Boris took the throne while there was a righteous heir alive. . . ."

On the 7th of May, mounted on his war horse, Basmanof proclaimed to his army that the Pretender against whom they had been fighting was Dimitry Ivanovitch, the true heir to the throne. The announcement caused no surprise. It was received with acclamation. Some of the army leaders such as Katyref-Rostovsky, Andrew Teliatevsky and Ivan Godunof fled at once with the news of the betrayal. Basmanof sincerely wished a bloodless victory for Dimitry and may have been confident that his adherence to the cause of the Tsarevitch would be followed by a *coup d'état* in Moscow. It is probable that he would not have hindered the flight of those who remained partisans of the old *régime*, but the rabble of the army fell upon the fugitives and beat them almost to death.

Then the people of Kromy came out and fraternised openly instead of clandestinely with the besiegers. The army leaders went to Putivl. Dimitry sat on a throne and received them as Tsar. The civil war was over.

Dimitry had done much to strengthen his position. Although nominally a Catholic he worshipped according to the Orthodox rite. He even had a famous wonder-working Madonna set up in Putivl and did homage to the ikon daily. The Jesuits permitted him to do this and there was no religious strife or rivalry among his supporters. Then he dealt finally with the legend that he was Grishka Otriepief. The real Grishka was found and shown to the people of Putivl. He stood up and told of all his adventures since he had been a boy in the household of the Romanofs, his stay at Chudof Monastery, his personal contact with the Patriarch Job, how he had met the Tsarevitch at Kief and become his supporter. The testimony which he gave added to the prestige of the Dimitry and perhaps convinced some who had secret doubts.

Dimitry, taking advantage of the new situation, exercised his clemency and liberated all prisoners. That was clever: they were free to confess their error and most of them incontinently did so. If Peter Basmanof had confessed that he had been mistaken it was easy for lesser persons to do so. Basmanof came personally to make submission and came at once under the influence of the personal charm of the Dimitry. You had but to see him to become his follower. In a previous letter to Basmanof, Dimitry had deceived him by pretending that very large Polish reinforcements were on the way, but Basmanof forgave him this chicane. It pleased him better to serve a heroic young man than it had done to serve the craven Boris Godunof. Basmanof was confirmed in the command of the army under the Tsar Dimitry and was sent to swear it in to the new allegiance. On the 24th of May Dimitry began his advance to Moscow.

XXIX.

THE DESTRUCTION OF THE GODUNOFS

IN Moscow, in April and May, there were sympathetic risings. With all the rest of Russia swaying to the cause of the Dimitry, that is not surprising. The people were moved in the depths. The silence which Boris Godunof had enforced so long was broken. Whispering began again and, unchecked, soon grew to clamour. Menacing crowds of men and women invaded the Kremlin shouting: "Down with the Godunofs!" The people demanded the return of the mother of Dimitry from the convent. They believed that she would recognise her son and that would be the end of the power of the hated Godunofs. The boyars, unaware of Basmanof's intentions at Kromy, were afraid to countenance the popular demands. Vasilly Shuisky went to the people and swore on the cross that the Tsarevitch Dimitry was dead: "I with my own hands laid his body in the grave at Uglitch. The man who calls himself by the Tsarevitch's name is an unfrocked runaway monk in league with Satan and sentenced to death for his abominable practices. You people would be better employed praying almighty God that He visit us not again with His wrath."

But the arrival of Katyref-Rostovsky and Teliatevsky put a different complexion on affairs. When it was learned that Basmanof had gone over to Dimitry with

THE DESTRUCTION OF THE GODUNOFS 253

almost the whole of the army, it was impossible to suppress the popular movement. There were renewed scenes of disorder on the 30th of May. It was rumoured that the advance guard of Dimitry's army had been sighted from church towers. This was false news; there was as yet no sign of any army on the horizon. But the masses did not stop to argue or be convinced. When Dimitry came they would rise to greet him. There was no division of feeling. The boyars, especially Vasilly Shuisky, did not plan to deliver the Tsardom to the Dimitry. When Fedor's position proved untenable it would be Shuisky's opportunity to seize the throne. How otherwise account for the dangerous caution of the boyars? The mob was not without a ringleader. Bogdan Bielsky, since his return to Moscow, had devoted himself to revenge upon the Godunofs. As has been seen before, he was a highly capable organiser and leader. He at once made himself the hero of the crowd. Ivan the Terrible had made him the guardian of the young Dimitry and he now appeared as the champion of the wronged child whom Boris had wished to murder. Apparently Bielsky accepted the claim of the Pretender without question. It may be assumed that he knew something about him when he was building Tsaref-Borisof and was arrested. Now he had planned a spontaneous rising in Moscow as soon as the Dimitry showed himself. The people were so eager for the fray that they beat the signal. The populace turned out all shouting for Dimitry. The Kremlin was in a state of panic all day, but no Dimitry came. Toward evening the crowds dispersed.

Next day the boyars ordered the manning of the guns for the defence of the city should the Pretender appear, but they were very ill obeyed.

On the 1st of June messengers arrived from Dimitry but waited to know what sort of reception they would get. Pleshcheyef and Pushkin bore the Tsarevitch's proclamation to the boyars, the officials and the people of Moscow. They stopped in a suburb of the capital and had the church bells rung to announce their arrival. They had not long to wait: the common people shouldered them or led their horses by the bridle, and they were taken to the Red Square by an ever-increasing vast concourse of supporters. There were so many of them, and the defence of the Kremlin was so ill-organised that no one said them nay. No shot was fired; no force applied. Some of the Kremlin guards remarked that if the envoys had a message they had better be allowed to take it into the palace and present it peacefully to Tsar Fedor. But the revolutionary crowd would have none of that. The envoys, standing at the *lobnoye miesto* were told to break the seal of Dimitry's message and read it there and then.

"Demetrius now sent messengers with letters which entered the suburbs, where the Commons in infinite numbers brought them safe into the spacious plain before the Castle gate. There (the messengers) made demand for many of the Council, especially for the Godunofs, to come to hear their right King Demetrius Ivanovitch speaking unto them by letters: who yet after refusal, and I cannot condemn all, many came. The Commons being resolved else to fetch them out. Then

THE DESTRUCTION OF THE GODUNOFS 255

by the (envoys) aloud was read the Emperor's letter."*

The message announced pardon for the boyars and others who had acted against Dimitry in ignorance of the truth that he was the true son of Ivan to whom and to whose children many of them had, years back, taken oath of loyalty and service. It warned them that he had all Russia behind him and was advancing with a great army. It called Tsar Fedor and his mother traitors; recounted the wrongs done by the Godunof family to all classes and promised redress. Finally, it summoned the boyars, *dyaks* and commanders to Dimitry's presence at Tula.

In the hubbub which accompanied the reading of the message little was heard. The mob leaders, probably instructed by Bielsky, called for Vasilly Shuisky. "Let Vasilly Shuisky tell us the truth about the Tsarevitch and give answer for himself and for the others!"

Vasilly Shuisky, in the face of the tumult, was not likely to say again that he had seen with his own eyes the Tsarevitch dead and laid him in the tomb with his own hands. He stood at the place of execution and decided to save his own head. The hour was come when he could with safety settle his account with the Godunofs. No one would argue with him if he said the acceptable thing.

"*Boris sent to Uglitch to murder the Tsarevitch but the Tsarevitch was saved,*" said he. "*The child we buried was a priest's son.*"

Shuisky denied himself. He was yet to deny himself

* Sir Thomas Smith: *Voyage and Entertainment in Russia*, 1605.

again. The cock was to crow and he would be Tsar—but that is to anticipate history. His words were like torches handed to the crowd and with them, they went shouting mightily, to pillage and destruction.

Sir Thomas Smith appears to have been a witness of the scene and had some gift in the use of words. . . . "All confusedly like fettered and chained horses stamping . . . all as one running violently into the Castle."

The Kremlin guards were rushed; the mob entered the palaces and houses, looting and destroying as they went. "Down with Fedka! Down with the sons of bitches!" they cried. Their fury was increased by the discovery of previous messengers of Dimitry in a torture chamber of Semyon Godunof. These victims told them,

"as sufficiently as their insufficiency would permit them, the wild manner of their torturing, whipping and roasting, which was indeed a whip and spur to drive them without wit or humanity, as if they had been fired like gunpowder with the very sparks of heat, such barbarous cruelty, beastly actions and inhuman spectacles, as without the great Devil had been their general, no particular could have acted."

The Patriarch Job failed at the supreme moment, shut himself in a cell and wept hysterically. The young Tsar Fedor mounted the throne in the throne-room of the palace and sat there unattended with the diadem on his head, believing that the mob dare not lay its hands on Majesty. The mother and Xenia came out on to the Kremlin Square holding ikons in front of themselves like breastplates. The ikons were knocked out of their hands. They wept. The mother beseeched and

THE DESTRUCTION OF THE GODUNOFS

implored: spare her children. They stripped the jewels from their persons and threw them to the rabble. The Tsar sat there on his throne like an arranged *tableau vivant* and said nothing. But it was not for long. The hooligans invaded the throne and dashing up the steps pulled the young man headlong down. But there was as yet no murder. Mother, son and daughter were rushed to the packhorse stables of Boris' old house which he had occupied before he was Tsar and they were imprisoned there.

The mob wished to enter the wine cellars of the palace but Bielsky dissuaded them. "What, shall we drink all the wine? And when our Lord and Master comes back there will be nothing on the table. Let's go rather to the houses of the foreign doctors. They have plenty of good wine."

Bielsky did not forget that it was a Scotch doctor who at the command of Boris Godunof had pulled out his black beard by the roots. He had his revenge. The doctors' houses were sacked. The barrels were burst open and the populace filled their boots with mead and wine and drank from them as from tankards. But robbery was not confined to wine cellars. The very clothes were stripped from the backs of the servants of the Godunofs and by evening there were many naked, destitute people wandering about. It was a day of great pillage, but not of great bloodshed. Not more than a hundred people lost their lives in the riot.

Next day Moscow was more calm. The people stayed in their homes counting their ill-gotten gains. Boris' old house, *dom Skuratova*, was closely guarded, but the rooms were opened for the Tsar and his sister and mother, and they had more comfortable quarters than the stables. Nevertheless, they were consumed with anxiety as to their fate. There was no movement on their behalf. The boyars were preparing to go to Tula and make their submission to Dimitry. The Patriarch seemed to have bowed to the inevitable and instead of rousing the Church against the heretic seems to have been disposed to make his peace with Dimitry and to accept him as Tsar. But that was not to be. Dimitry gave orders that he was to be stripped of his rank. Job appeared in the Cathedral of the Assumption to give his last blessing as Patriarch. And there indeed he denounced the heretic, though without vigour. He was seized and thrown into a cart and driven away to a simple monkery at the Staritsky Monastery.

The kindred of the Tsar, including the Saburofs and the Veliaminofs, were seized and deported, some of them meeting violent deaths. Semyon Godunof was taken to Pereyaslavl and put in a cell underground and starved to death. When he asked for bread he was always given a stone. Dimitry had sent plenipotentiaries to Moscow, Princes Vasilly Golitsin and Mosalsky, to remove all dangerous persons and especially the Godunofs. Whether on his express orders the Tsar and his mother were murdered is not known. It seems probable that he did not command that they should be spared. On the 10th of June, Golitsin and Mosalsky gave orders for the murders. Ruffians broke into the Godunof house and placing a rope about the Tsaritsa's neck, strangled her. They went for Fedor in another room and he defended himself to the last. They seized and crushed his sexual parts so that he screamed in agony, and then they strangled him between cushions. The unfortunate Xenia, offered to so many men but still a virgin, feared something worse than death. While the murderers were attacking mother and brother she took poison, falling to the ground, seemingly dead. A purge was at once administered and she vomited the poison and recovered. No violence was done her, but her ultimate fate is unknown. Some say she was taken into Dimitry's household and there debauched. Others aver that she was forced to take the veil and banished to a convent. The death of the Tsar and his mother was announced to the people of Moscow as suicide.

It was rumoured then that Boris Godunof had never died but had worked a trick on the Court, having a metal figure of himself buried in the Cathedral of the Archangel Michael. Some said he had fled to England. The notion of the metal figure probably derived from the black, mask-like countenance of Boris in death. However, his remains were soon disinterred and laid in a poverty-stricken chapel far from the Kremlin. His wife and son were buried with him there. At a later date the bodies were removed to Sergey-Troitsky Monastery. A chronicler of the time thus commented on the end of Boris Godunof and his family: "With what measure ye measure it shall be measured unto you, and the cup ye fill for others ye shall yourself drink. He thirsted for worldly vanities such as thrones and wealth, affeared neither of oath nor perjury. Behold the fruits of his actions! Where is now his sagacity, where his consort and beloved children, where his gilded halls and magnificent feasts? Where are the slaves who ran to do his will, where his magnificent attire and golden plate? Who in the fateful hour could save wife and children when they looked hither and thither for someone to protect them from the executioner?"*

* Quoted by Kostomarof: *Smutnoye Vremya.*

XXX.

DIMITRY CROWNED, MARRIED, MURDERED

I

ALL power was in Dimitry's hands. He commanded that his mother be set free and sent a party of nobles to escort her from the wilderness of Vyksa, where she was immured, to Moscow. Supposing, as most Russian historians have assumed, that he was not her son, Dimitry, this was a gesture of unusual audacity. But it was more than a gesture. The mother came; the Dimitry met her. There is no need to describe in detail the jubilation of the people of Moscow over the arrival of the new Tsar. There was a great Restoration movement which might be compared to the time when England had shaken Cromwell off and welcomed the Stuart back. Dimitry swept in glory to the throne. But he would not be crowned Tsar until his mother arrived. He wished to share his triumph with her.

On the 18th of July, Sister Martha, the ex-Tsaritsa Marya, widow of Ivan the Terrible and mother of the Tsarevitch Dimitry, arrived at Troitsky Monastery and was brought thence in festival parade to Moscow. Dimitry rode out to meet her. At his approach the carriage with the mother stopped. Dimitry alighted from his horse and flung himself into Sister Martha's arms. There was no doubt or uncertainty. Mother and son embraced and kissed and cried. A vast crowd of people were witnesses of the scene. After a quarter of an hour of excited conversation, Dimitry mounted his charger once more, the curtains of the carriage were drawn and Sister Martha was escorted to the palace. After fourteen years in narrowing nunnery walls, Marya Nagy returned in honour to the Kremlin. Dimitry provided her with every comfort, visited her every day, asked her blessing for each thing that he undertook.

Afterward it was said that Sister Martha was forced to play the part of mother to the Pretender and that she was told she would be murdered if she did not. But that is not credible. One cannot believe that a woman confined in cells for fourteen years could come out and act a great scene of maternal joy and transport to the satisfaction of a crowd of witnesses. On the other hand, it might have been urged that between Dimitry, aged seven, and the same person aged twenty-one there must have been a great difference. Therein lies a possibility of doubt. But first it must be admitted that she did not believe her son had been killed at Uglitch. She did not believe him dead. When Boris Godunof had asked her in the previous year, 1604, whether her son was dead, she had told him her belief that Dimitry had been saved. In later years it was given out by Vasilly Shuisky that Sister Martha had denied that the grown Dimitry was her son, but that can be discounted because Shuisky was capable of any lie which could be of advantage to him. On the evidence available there seems to be at least circumstantial proof that the claim of the Dimitry was genuine.

It was important for him to convince everybody that he was no interloper but indeed of the blood royal. Before his mother came to Moscow he exhibited once more the man who confessed to being Grishka Otrepief. His enemies of course were not slow to say that this man was not Otrepief at all. But they could not produce kindred of Grishka Otrepief to lay bare the supposed imposture.

II

Those victims of Godunof's rule who were still alive were recalled from banishment, the Nagy, the Romanofs. The remains of the dead Romanofs were brought with honour to Moscow and buried there. Fedor Romanof did not wish to renounce his forced monastic vows, although his wife and his son Michael were restored to him in Moscow. He was still Father Philaret. Dimitry advanced him to be Metropolitan of Rostof. Ivan Romanof was promoted to the Council of Boyars. Those who had helped Dimitry to the throne received advancement, and especially Basmanof was held in high honour. Ignatius was made Patriarch in the place of Job, but a synod of metropolitans and bishops was placed over him to regulate his actions.

Vasilly Shuisky, annoyed by the recall of the Romanofs and the high favour which lesser gentry were obtaining, went back on his words given to the Moscow populace, and again began to spread the story that the Tsar was Grishka Otrepief and predicted calamities for his country if it should continue to be governed by a man who was under the anathema of the Church. He began belatedly to do what the Patriarch Job might have done earlier, foment suspicion of the Jesuitical contingent which accompanied Dimitry and warn the people of the menace to Orthodoxy. At the same time, he conducted himself in his own quarters as if he were the dictator of Russia. His ambition was the throne. Mstislavsky had a stronger claim to the throne after Dimitry, but he renounced all ambition to attain it. The returning Romanofs were, however, a source of danger to the pretensions of Shuisky, and because of them he felt he must act quickly. He planned a palace revolution for the 25th of August. But the conspiracy was betrayed. Shuisky was arrested, tried, condemned to death. Dimitry, however, pursued his policy of clemency. Shuisky was standing bound with his head on the block. Basmanof read the sentence. The headsman was ready to do his work, when a messenger came post haste from the palace with a reprieve. Shuisky was allowed to live under banishment to Viatka. Mercy in this case was foolish and out of place. Shuisky had been and he remained a mortal enemy.

On the 30th of July, 1605, Dimitry was crowned Tsar of Russia. The ceremony took place in the Cathedral of the Assumption under Orthodox rites, but the congregation was astonished when after the service the Jesuit Chernikovsky came forward and made a long speech in Latin. But as no one understood this the impression was short lived. The crown had been embellished and was more magnificent than any worn by previous monarchs of Russia. The fine carpets and silks spread on the floor of the cathedral were torn into pieces by the people and taken away as mementoes. All went well: Dimitry was exceedingly popular. The day ended with national feasting and rejoicing and Bogdan Bielsky felt he had done well in saving the Kremlin wine vaults.

III

Had Dimitry been less honourable it is likely he would have lasted longer. He felt he must fulfil the promises he had made in Poland and that led to his ruin. The national antipathy of Poles and Russians is such that they cannot in large numbers be socially united. Byzantinism is as distasteful to Catholics as the Latin rite is to the Orthodox. Dimitry, as an instalment of what he had promised, gave freedom of worship to the Catholics. Passport formalities on the Polish-Lithuanian frontier were abolished and Catholic missionaries came in. The new Pope, Paul V, prepared to use the "God-given" opportunity to unite Eastern and Western Churches under the rule of Rome. It may be admitted however that Dimitry once Tsar was a less zealous Catholic. He was a Liberal. He said Protestants, Catholics and Greek Orthodox all believed in the same Saviour and God and there seemed no reason why they should not be tolerant of one another. His project to build a Roman Catholic cathedral in Moscow met with strong opposition but he did not press it. He allowed Jesuits to conduct services in the Kremlin and we have the curious phenomenon of Chirzhovsky and Savitsky putting on false beards and vestments of Orthodox priests to disguise their Latinism. This sounds ludicrous but it is actually interesting and significant. Had Russia become Catholic in the sixteenth or seventeenth centuries she must have had a strong influence on Romanism and made it more mystical and less legalistic. Jesuits putting on beards was a symbol.

The new Tsar went about dressed as a Pole. He sat down to dinner with a Polish orchestra playing. He had a new silver throne made with six silver lions on each side of it. That new throne displeased the boyars and was one of the indictments of him made after his death. He considered Russia uncivilised and out of date. The Poles were superior in culture; they had poetry and music. They were even superior in horsemanship. Dimitry himself was a superb horseman and knew all the tricks of Polish equestrianism. He rode a fine mettlesome horse and was not averse to showing off before his subjects. He was also somewhat of a gladiator and would enter the Moscow bear-pits sword in hand to fight with the bear, a sport in which he excelled. He knew no fear. It was his practice also to go out at night like some Haroun-al-Raschid and talk with his subjects as man to man. He had a premature instinct for democracy. He never despised his Russians; he liked them but he wished they had been less barbarous. He had a stronger wish to put Russia to school and educate her than to convert her to Catholicism. He remained true in thought to his Polish bride, Marina, and felt he required her aid to civilise his country. He sent her rich presents from the treasure of the Kremlin, pearls of great price, diamonds, illuminated breviaries, silks and brocades, curios and did not forget her father, though seeing that George Mniszech had deserted him in the field he withheld the large indemnity he had promised to defray the cost of mobilisation. The new *dyak*, Vlassyef, was sent to Cracow to gain the

DIMITRY CROWNED, MURDERED

consent of King Sigizmund to the marriage of Dimitry and Marina.

This asking the King's consent was a formality. King Sigizmund was only too anxious to have some proof that the Dimitry was going to fulfil the promises he had made to him. But the formality was important because it made the marriage a national occasion. It was as if the Tsar were marrying the King's ward and not merely some local Galician lady. The Polish Diet and gentry who had been opposed to the entanglement of Poland with the cause of the Pretender were repentant or made it appear that they had always been in secret, partisans and wellwishers of the Tsar. The murmurs against the chicane of George Mniszech were all hushed and when the father came to Cracow he was congratulated on all hands. Dimitry had asked permission that the marriage ceremony in Russia be conducted in the Orthodox rite. That was disappointing but it was not stressed as an obstacle to union. The piety of Marina was sufficient pledge for the future of her husband's conscience. A Catholic marriage was solemnised by Cardinal Maciejowsky without the presence of the bridegroom. There were present the King himself, Princess Anne of Sweden, the Prince Royal Vladislas, the papal nuncio and representatives of foreign powers. Marina in white robes decked with magnificent sapphires and pearls appeared supported by her father's arm and won all hearts by her dignity and beauty.

After the ceremony there was a splendid banquet, not without incidents caused by Vlassyef who did not think his master the Tsar was done sufficient honour.

There were toasts. There was a rivalry of poets praising the delights of Hymen. There was a ball. Thus the 12th of November, 1605. On the 22nd Marina left Cracow for Promnik. There was an unexpected delay in her being allowed to depart for Moscow. The great gifts which Dimitry had sent were not considered enough. His bride was held to ransom. The Tsar sent 250,000 zloti as indemnity for military aid and still more gifts for Marina. This was in January, 1606; negotiations dragged on for three months more before the Tsar's bride was allowed to leave Poland. It was the 2nd of May when she arrived in Moscow.

It is difficult to see good reason why Marina was not allowed to go to Dimitry earlier. Too much reliance might easily have been placed on the constancy of Dimitry's passion. It must have been realised that Dimitry was not secure upon the throne. Vasilly Shuisky had received complete pardon from the Tsar and was allowed to return to Moscow. He at once began a secret conspiracy against Dimitry and went so far as to send an agent to King Sigizmund to assure him that Sister Martha, the ex-Tsaritsa Marya, had only recognised Dimitry upon compulsion and had given him secret assurance that the Dimitry was not her son. It was also rumoured that Dimitry had plotted to aid and abet revolutionaries in Poland with the object of dethroning Sigizmund. It was said with truth that the Poles in Moscow were not adequately protected from insult and assault in the Moscow streets. The policy of Mniszech and of Sigizmund was to get from Dimitry in advance all that they could and then await eventualities. The Pope alone pressed for a more vigorous opportunism.

At last George Mniszech and his daughter, accompanied by Adam and Constantine Wisniowiecki and a numerous retinue, set off for Russia. They made a very slow progress but were received lavishly at every point. Dimitry wept for joy when he received his bride and the triumph of his passion was expressed in unheard of prodigality. He was an amazing spendthrift and during the few months up to the time of his marriage ran through six times the annual income of the Tsardom. The Poles had reason to be gratified by the liberality of their royal host.

On the 8th of May Marina was crowned Tsaritsa of all Russia and after that was married with Orthodox rites to Dimitry. The Catholics demanded seats in the cathedral. But the Tsar upheld Orthodox custom; no one may sit down in the House of God. But the ceremonies went on for many hours and the Poles who understood nothing kept expecting them to come to an end. But no; they went on. The Catholics lounged against the holy ikons and some of them became so weary and restless that they sat down on the floor of the cathedral. Many at last lost patience, pushed their way out of the massed congregation and went to their quarters.

IV

Vasilly Shuisky and George Mniszech led the bridal pair to the bedchamber. Beyond that bedchamber the hymeneal night rolled on in unbroken festivity. Moscow got joyously drunk. The next day was much the same; Moscow was bestial. On the third and fourth days the Russians were sleeping it off. On the fifth day the Russians were morose but the Poles were still noisy. It was Monday, the Muscovites wished to return to the humdrum routine of ordinary life but the roistering Polish guests, riding the streets, shouting and singing, would not let them. On the Sunday night there had been a great banquet in the Granovity palace. All was in the Polish style. Dimitry and Marina, clad as Poles, sat in silver chairs and wore their crowns on their heads. The Polish ambassador, Olesnitsky, sat on the Tsar's right hand. George Mniszech did not sit at table but stood, hat in hand, facing the Tsar and Tsaritsa, serving them. But the Russian guests were displeased because it was so arranged that they all sat with their backs to the Tsar while the Poles sat facing them. It was a stupendous feast. There were thirteen different meat courses, roast woodcock garnished with lemon, hares' heads on mince, mutton in beetroot soup, chicken in sour white sauce, chicken in yellow sauce, mutton pies, ham pies, honey pies stuffed with minced lamb, egg pies, curd pies. The sweets and the wines were on the same scale. But the Russians cooked without salt and the Poles said the food nearly made them vomit. Nevertheless, they allowed an enormous supper to be sent to their houses so that they could continue the feast after they departed from the palace.

On the Monday there was another banquet even more in the Polish style but very few Russian guests were bidden. Veal had been ordered to be served. At that time there was in Russia a strong prejudice against

DIMITRY CROWNED, MURDERED

veal and many thought it to be forbidden by the Church. Dimitry had introduced it directly he became Tsar but its appearance at table had caused repeated protests. So violent was the prejudice that Shuisky could use it for his ends and whisper repeatedly: "He eats veal!" On this occasion the palace cooks who had probably been suborned by Shuisky came out on strike and told the morose Muscovites who were getting tired of the wedding festivities all about it. But, nevertheless, veal was served and Dimitry did not cause the cooks to be strangled. He and his Polish guests merely laughed at the incident. He and his Poles and Marina made merry and danced till a late hour.

The Tuesday was like the Monday; the Poles were bidden to another great banquet and dance. Most of the boyars had taken umbrage at the favour shown to the Poles. The populace of the city followed the doings of the Poles with black looks. The dress of the new-fangled halberdiers evoked malice. Sixty drummers and trumpeters on a platform set up within the Kremlin kept up a deafening hubbub for many hours of the day. Tipsy Polish revellers in broad day rolled along the Moscow streets, singing Polish songs, firing their muskets at random into air, interfering with the Russian women, dancing or trying to dance with them in foreign steps.

Shuisky's agents were busy stirring up sedition, encouraging brawls, trying to start street fighting with the Poles, whispering again that the Tsar was Grishka Otrepief, a forsworn monk who intended to use his power to destroy the Church and the traditions of Russia. One of these agents was caught and brought before the Tsar but Dimitry, drunk with love and happiness, was in a foolish state of mind. "Let the drunkard go!" said he. "Why should I bother my head about tittle-tattle of this kind?" The Poles saw the danger before the monarch did and warned him against leniency but it was to no avail. Dimitry was not going to spoil his festivities with tortures and executions. No fear of treason was allowed to intrude upon the gaiety of the Tuesday banquet. It carried the Polonisation of the Kremlin a stage further. The guest chamber and dining hall had been arranged by Polish servants to be an exact replica of the same room in King Sigizmund's palace at Cracow and the ikons had been taken away.

That night Vasilly Shuisky called the chief conspirators to his house to make plans for the murder of Dimitry. Besides a number of gentry there were present representatives of the army and of the merchants. Shuisky harangued his midnight meeting unnecessarily. The individuals he had brought together were all trusty adherents. There were no doubtful people in the Shuisky house that night. All they asked was the plan. They were ready to make an end of the Polish revellers and of Dimitry. Shuisky was the leader; he should be made Tsar. He promised his fellow conspirators much in the case of his success. Dimitry was so lenient with traitors that none were apprehensive as to what might happen to them in case of failure.

Shuisky sent them forth to recruit armed bands to be in readiness for a rising on the following Saturday. Let the houses where the Poles have their quarters all be marked on the Friday night! On the Saturday morning an alarm would be sounded and it would be noised over

DIMITRY CROWNED, MURDERED

the city that the Poles were conspiring to kill the Tsar and the chief members of the Council and make themselves masters of Moscow. They would rush in to the Kremlin ostensibly to save the Tsar. Dimitry would be killed and then the armed bands reinforced by all the rabble would turn in vengeance on the Poles and accounts would be cleared with them.

On the Wednesday the Tsaritsa Marina gave a banquet in honour of her Russian subjects and several of the conspirators including Shuisky himself were present. Marina was so charming in her treatment of her guests that some who had given ear to the murderous plot resolved to have no further part in it. But the pious resolution faded when the festivity was over. Shuisky was a plausible talker and knew how to deal with waverers. Incidentally something of the conspiracy was already known. The Poles making merry in another place while Marina was regaling the boyars in the Kremlin heard that there was a plot to attack the Wisniowieckis. Mniszech mobilised the whole of his retinue to be on the defensive. Word of the danger was sent to Dimitry who laughed at it and assured the Poles that there was no danger of any kind.

Thursday was the Catholic feast of Corpus Christi. The Poles forgot their fears of the day before and continued their celebrations in the Moscow streets, interfering with the women, dancing and singing and firing in air. There were numerous allegations of rape. One Pole accused of committing rape was brought before Dimitry this day but was proved to be innocent. Whom the Gods wish to destroy they first make drunk with wine. By pestering the women in the streets they made it possible for Shuisky's agents to talk of rapes in the market place. By firing so much in air they gave the impression that they were vaunting their weapons. All went armed and in their drunken state it seemed quite possible they might commit murders as well as rapes, that they might seize the Kremlin and murder the Tsar, the Patriarch and the chief officers of the state.

That day also the Jesuit, Savitsky, arrived from Rome bearing gifts from the Society of Jesus and desiring to know when the conversion of Russia would take place. Dimitry was agitated by the question. "You have but to order conversion and it is done," said the Jesuit father. But the Tsar knew there was more in it than that and that it would be impossible to bring Russia to Rome. He was evasive. "I am mobilising an army against the heathen; that comes first. . . . I must have schools and universities in Russia and educate the people. . . . The Polish King does not give me my full title. . . ." Dimitry's excuses sounded lame and Savitsky was not pleased.

On the Thursday night the Kremlin guards tried to seize six men whom they found in hiding in the palace yard and evidently for no good purpose. Three escaped. The other three were put to the torture and questioned but they gave no information to their capturers. On the morrow the conspiracy was denounced. An anonymous letter was handed to the Tsar giving full details. He dismissed it as rubbish. But the Poles were alarmed and especially George Mniszech who implored his son-in-law to take adequate measures for his safety. Basmanof also had an inkling of what was going on and thought that certain people should be arrested forthwith and examined. Dimitry was at last persuaded that he ought to deal with the question of a possible conspiracy. He promised Basmanof that he would start an investigation but he put it off till the Saturday as there was to be festivity again on the Friday afternoon and evening.

That evening the last dance took place. Forty musicians played merrily till midnight. Shuisky, whose authority without personal reference to the Tsar could not be gainsaid, went the round of the guards and told most of them that they could dismiss. The two hundred halberdiers, most of them Scotsmen and *strieltsi*, were reduced to some twenty or thirty, and the Tsar was completely unaware that his protection had been withdrawn. After the dance he retired with Marina to sleep. But Shuisky and his fellow conspirators spent the night making their final arrangements. Among other things he opened the city prison and armed the prisoners, telling them the work he had in hand for them to do. At dawn the national alarm was sounded from the belfries of many churches. As previously arranged the various armed bands rushed to the Kremlin. There was some delay because the crowds started looting outside the citadel. Shuisky himself was caught up in the confusion. The Tsar himself had time to start from his bed and rush forth and take some measures for his personal safety.

The little, fat, bald-headed Shuisky, with a cross in one hand and a naked sword in the other, managed to break through the frenzied throngs and enter the Kremlin, followed by Tatishchef and the Golitsins. Dimitry met him in a corridor of the palace. "What's toward?" he asked. "The city is on fire," answered Shuisky.

Basmanof was roused and quickly learned the truth, that Shuisky's armed followers in a great mass were coming to destroy the Tsar. "You're to blame. I told you yesterday," said Basmanof to Dimitry.

One of Shuisky's partisans, the *dyak* Osipof, got ahead of the howling mob and rushed in to insult the Tsar and call him thief and Grishka. Basmanof struck him down with his sword and his dead body was hurled through the window.

Dimitry called for his brave halberdiers but there were only thirty of them. They fired on the mob but their volleys were ineffectual. There was firing from the crowd. Basmanof endeavoured to lead the Tsar to safety, giving him the shelter of his body against musket fire. Tatishchef rushed up and knifed Basmanof to the heart and his body followed that of Osipof over the battlements. Dimitry flung a door in Tatishchef's face and fled to rouse the rest of the halberdiers. Then he changed his mind and rushed back to protect his wife but could not get to her. He fled to a bath-house, locked the door and then got through a little window, dropping thirty feet to a closed yard at the back of the place. He broke a leg or sprained an ankle. He could not get to the common people at the back of the conspirators. Had he done so he would have been saved for they were inflamed against the Poles and wanted to save him. But Fate was against Dimitry that day.

In the palace Shuisky's plans went momentarily wrong. The Tsar could not be found. The mob instead of seeking him turned to snatching the gold and precious stones, turning all the apartments upside down. Marina, fleeing from room to room, got mixed up in the crowd and was not recognised. She got to the women's quarters and, being very small, hid behind her ladies in waiting. The guard at the door of the terem was hacked to small pieces. The crowd burst in and demanded the *Polka*, demanded to know where the Tsar was. They did not see Marina there. The boyars intervened and prevented the rape of the whole party.

The mob then murdered all the Polish musicians they could find. Suddenly they got on the track of Dimitry. He had been found by some *strieltsi* and halberdiers, under a Scotch captain, and they formed in a fighting square for his protection. They fired repeatedly on the conspirators and drove them off several times. Had it not been that Shuisky came up and rallied his supporters, the *strieltsi* might have got the Tsar to safety. But it was in truth an uneven battle. The Tsar's guards were broken down by sheer force of numbers. Curiously enough, when the mob had Dimitry at its mercy, it did not kill him at once. Possibly some thought they had come out to save Dimitry from the Poles. There was a parley and Dimitry asked why they wished to kill their true Tsar and again asserted with his last words that he was Dimitry of Uglitch, the son of Ivan Vasillievitch and called his mother to witness. Someone shouted out that Sister Martha had denounced him. A noble with a short gun fired and shot him dead.

Then Sister Martha was brought in terror from the cathedral hostelry where she was lodged and confronted with the body of the dead Dimitry. "Now," commanded Shuisky, "say who he is."

There are several versions of what the mother answered, but one may take the most original as least likely to have been invented: "Did you not ask me when he was alive, but now that he is dead he is already not mine."

The bodies of Dimitry and Basmanof were trussed up with the legs over the shoulders and placed on a little table in the Red Square. The kindred of Basmanof obtained permission to take his body away and give it Christian burial. But Dimitry's corpse lay in the open for many days. Then it was burned, then cut to pieces and burned again; then the ash was fired from the mouths of cannons. It was feared, that being a sorcerer, so his bits, his ash, might re-assemble: therefore the ash was fired from the mouths of cannon.*

The Moscow mob settled their account with the Poles, but there was not such a slaughter of foreigners as might have been expected. Mniszech and the rest, when they heard the alarm and realised what was afoot, mobilised their followers and kept the rabble of Moscow at bay. Some three hundred Poles perished and perhaps double the number of Russians. The gentry mostly escaped with their lives but their apartments were pillaged. George Mniszech lost all that he had gained. But his daughter was saved. The tumult in the streets died down very rapidly. The Polish survivors were given protection. Vasilly Shuisky became Tsar.

* *Vide* also Appendix: "The Tragedy of Dimitry Viewed by English Eyes."

APPENDIX

I

THE TSARITSA MARINA

GEORGE MNISZECH and his daughter were not allowed to return to Poland after the murder of Dimitry. In 1607 a new Pretender arose saying he was the Tsar Dimitry who had never been slain. He wrote affectionate letters to Marina as to his wife. Seeing that he was obtaining a strong following, George Mniszech decided to recognise him. He made his daughter pretend that this adventurer was her husband whom they had thought to be dead. "And this Demetrius," wrote Purchas, "acted the other so nearly and could so cunningly and confidently relate particular passages of past occurrents that the Lady of Demetrius was by him bedded."

Marina then followed the fortunes of the False Dimitry till he was murdered on the 10th of December, 1610. A few days after his death Marina gave birth to a son, Ivan. In 1613 her father died. In June, 1614, the child Ivan, aged only four, was taken from her and hanged. At that point Marina disappears from the page of history.

II

THE TRAGEDY OF DIMITRY VIEWED BY ENGLISH EYES

"The late Pretender was of stature low, but well set, hard favoured and of no presence; howsoever otherwise of a princely disposition, executing justice without partialities and not remitting the insolency even of the Poles; well seen in martial practices and training his nobility to the discipline of war; not given either to women or drink but very liberal and bountiful, which occasioned some grievous exactions to maintain the same. . . . A man not unworthy of a better gotten and longer continued empire, which he lost chiefly through the greatness of his mind, supposing that none of his subjects durst attempt any such matter against his person. . . . It is reported by some of ours that he was rather inclinable to our nation. . . . He is said to have been a resolute man of his hands, to have delighted in fighting with the bear, active and strong. I have likewise heard that he gave the command of his guard consisting of strangers, to one Captain Gilbert, a Scot."

The writer goes on to say that the grandees of the conspiracy slew the Dimitry like another Cæsar, shouting "Liberty!" and that Captain Gilbert led his halberdiers out of Moscow in safety to Kaluga.

Vide posthumous papers of Hakluyt: Purchas, *His Pilgrims*, Vol. XIV.

III

FEDOR ROMANOF (PHILARET)

Born in 1558, he was twenty-six at the death of Ivan the Terrible, a dandy and accomplished courtier during the reign of Fedor. He was forty at the time of Fedor's death, banished to Siisk and became a monk, Father Philaret, at the age of forty-three. He was made Archbishop of Rostof by Dimitry. In 1619 he became Patriarch of Russia. He lived to be seventy-five years of age. His son Michael became Tsar in 1613; Michael's son Alexis became Tsar in 1645. Peter the Great was a son of the Tsar Alexis.

BIBLIOGRAPHICAL NOTES

BORIS GODUNOF by Alexander Pushkin. The book of the famous opera composed by Mussorgsky. This fine drama, conceived in the grand style or Shakespearean manner, is marred by historical errors. It is based largely on the assumptions of the historian Karamzin. Of course, doubt as to identity is a handicap to stage drama and Pushkin had to decide definitely that the Pretender Dimitry was the runagate monk, Grishka Otrepief. He goes so far as to make the Pretender confess to his Marina that he is in fact that monk and not the son of Ivan the Terrible. Marina, after a short-lived inward struggle, forgives him the initial deceit and resolves to keep his secret and to follow his fortunes in any case. The scene of the death of Boris Godunof which is so effective in the opera hardly corresponds to the historical picture. He takes a long farewell of his beloved son Fedor and makes the boyars swear allegiance to him, but actually in his frightful death agony he was almost bereft of speech and could only mumble a few words about God and the Council. He had been morose and apathetic for a long while and seemed incapable of protecting either himself or his succession.

Pushkin's drama was first published in 1825. The opera was composed in 1872.

Estat de l'empire Russe par le Capitaine Jacques Margeret. Margeret was a French soldier of fortune who in 1600 obtained from Boris Godunof the command of a squadron of cavalry. He distinguished himself at the battle of Sievsk against the Dimitry in January, 1605, but it would appear went over with the rest of the army to Dimitry a few months later. The Dimitry, when he became Tsar, gave him the command of the foreign contingent of the Kremlin guards. He was ill on the day of Shuisky's rising and took no part in the defence of Dimitry. He remained in hiding for some time after that, but eventually obtained a *laissez-passer* from Shuisky and returned to France. He was brought before Henri Quatre and greatly entertained that monarch by the recital of his adventures. On the King's advice he wrote his book on Russia, *Estat de l'empire Russe*. This valuable little volume has much in common with Fletcher's *Of the Russe Commonwealth*. Margeret was intelligent; his book is restrained and was written to instruct rather than to amuse. He must have had much personal contact with Dimitry and it is interesting that he came to the conclusion that Dimitry was indeed the long-lost son of Ivan the Terrible. The last words of the book are: "*Je conclus qu' il estoit le vray Demetrius Johannes, fils de l'empereur Johannes Basileus, surnommé le Tiran.*" The book was published in 1607.

Of the Russe Commonwealth by Dr. Giles Fletcher. Fletcher was sent ambassador by Queen Elizabeth to Moscow in 1588, and he wrote this valuable descriptive treatise which has been much used by Russian historians.

The Travels of Sir Jerome Horsey. Horsey visited Russia in 1571 as an agent of the Russia Company. Subsequently, he was held in high favour both by Ivan the Terrible and Boris Godunof. He was employed by both on their secret affairs and wrote afterward vivid accounts of his adventures.

Voyage and Entertainment in Russia by Sir Thomas Smith. Smith was ambassador of James I to the Court

BIBLIOGRAPHICAL NOTES 283

of Boris Godunof, eye-witness of many stirring events which he described graphically.

Occurents in Russia, etc. Purchas, *His Pilgrims*, 4th book of second part; Vol. XIV of standard edition.

Akti Siiskago Monastirya: Archangel, 1913.

Boris Godunof by C. F. Platonof: Petrograd, 1921. This short biographical work is in the nature of an apologia for the career of Godunof. Emphasis is laid on the fact that there is no definite proof that Godunof ordered the murder of the Tsarevitch Dimitry.

Ocherki po Istorii Smuti by C. F. Platonof: St. Petersburg, 1910.

La crise révolutionnaire by K. Waliszewski: Paris, 1906.

Smutnoye Vremya by N. I. Kostomarof: St. Petersburg, 1904. The most orderly and detailed history of the "confused times" in Russian history.

Earlier Russian histories such as those of Karamzin and Shcherbatof have too strong a bias against Godunof to be valuable in a study of this character. Solovief is a little better but not inspired. Kliutchevsky's lectures on Russian History are also of little help. The main facts were in doubt and Kliutchevsky was disinclined to discuss them critically.

Other important sources are:

Hakluyt, *Principal Navigations*, Vol. III.
Purchas, *His Pilgrims*, Vol. XIV.
Polish Affairs, Nos. 26, 27, 30: *Moscow Archives.*
Chronicle of Pskof: 1848.
Chronicle of Nikon.
Chronicle of Bussof.
Chronicle of Palitsin.
Peer Persson in *Rerum Rossicarum Scriptores Exteri.*
Sapieha, J., *Diary.*

Borsza, S., *Historya Dmitra Falszywego.*
Letter of Supposed False Dimitry to Clement VIII,
 published by P. Pierling.
The dramatic trilogy of Count Alexey Konstantinovich Tolstoy:
 The Death of Ivan the Terrible, 1866 (Eng. tr. by I. Henry Harrison: London, 1869).
 Tsar Fyodor Ivanovitch, 1868 (Eng. tr. by Jenny Covan: Brentano's, 1922).
 Tsar Boris, 1870.

INDEX

Abbas, Shah of Persia, hostile to Turkey, 99; seeks Russian support, 99–100; described, 100
Adashef, Alexey, 4, 9
Alexandra, Sister, 109, *see also* Irina, Tsaritsa
Alina, religious clairvoyant, 241, 243
Amurath, Sultan, 94–99
Anne, Princess of Sweden, 267
Arabian Nights, 240, 266
Arianism, 175
Astrakhan, Russian territory, 94; return of, demanded by Sultan, 97; rising at, 181
Autocracy, 106, 126

Baku, 102
Banditry, 172
Basmanof, Peter, heroic defence of Novgorod-Seversk, 229–231; received by Godunof, 239; takes command against Dimitry, 245; goes over to Dimitry, 247–249; slain by mob, 276; body exposed, 278
Bielsky, Bogdan, 15; objects to banishment of Tsaritsa Marya, 19; rebellion of, 18–19; banished to Nijni Novgorod, 21, 155; returns to Moscow, 112; claim to throne, 112; protector of Nagy family, 155, 253; sent to build Tsaref-Borisof, 157; arrested and tortured, 159; pardoned, 247; mob leader, 253, 257
Bitiagovsky, Michael, 63, 65
Bokhara, 101, 102
Boris-Tsaref, *see* Tsaref-Borisof
Borzha, Stanislas, 227, 237
Bowes, Sir James, 17

Cannibalism, 146

Catholicism, project of union with Orthodoxy, 34–35; militancy of, 133; project of conversion of Russia, 193–194, 215–216, 220–221, 265, 269, 274
Charles IX, King of Sweden, 134, 137
Chernigof, 225–228
Chess, game of, 1, 16
Chodkiewicz, 190
Christian IV, King of Denmark, 137
Chudof Monastery, 88, 113, 203, 221, 250
Clement VIII, Pope, 196, 211
Cossacks, as colonisers, 95; relationship to Boris Godunof, 158–159; partisans of Dimitry, 181–182, 191, 210; loot Chernigof, 227
Council of Boyars, 35, 114, 125, 165, 223, 245, 247
Council of Five, 15, 23 *seq.*, 112
Cracow, 35, 179, 180, 190 *seq.*, 198, 268
Cromwell, Thomas, 7
Cruelty, 1, 2, 236, 256–257

Denmark, 137
Derbent, 102
Dimitry, the Tsarevitch, born, 11, 16; sent to Uglitch, 18–19; referred to by Godunof as heir-presumptive, 28; seemingly murdered by Godunof's agents, 63 *seq.*; name of, omitted from Church prayers, 65; considered an epileptic, 68–69; supposed to have killed himself, 68; his double said to be held in reserve by Boris Godunof, 112–113; supposed not dead, 150, 152, 155, 159, 163, 169–170; reappears, 171; sought by Boris'

agents, 170; announces himself in Lithuania, 175 *seq.;* religious doubts of, 175–176; in love with Marina Mniszech, 186, 198; received by King of Poland, 191–192; converted to Rome, 195; appeals to the Pope, 196; affianced to Marina, 208; recruits his army, 209–210; letter to Godunof, 214–215; promises to uphold Orthodoxy, 215; excommunicated, 220–221; invades Russia, 225; first successes, 225 *seq.;* defeated by Mstislavsky, 234–235; character of, 236, 250–251, 264–265, 266; plot to assassinate him, 242; asks to be confronted with his mother, 245; advances on Moscow, 251; Moscow rises in his favour, 253; embraces supposed mother, 261–262; crowned Tsar, 264; married, 269; murdered, 277; ashes fired from cannon, 278

Dionysy, Metropolitan, 27, 28–29

Eavesdropping, 171
Elizabeth, Queen of England, 17, 22, 31, 39, 43; letter to Tsaritsa Irina, 45; opinion of Boris Godunof, 128; death of, 218
Epileptics, regarded as holy, 72
Eric XIV, King of Sweden, 130
Evdokia, 41

Famine, 145 *seq.*, 173
Fawkes, Guy, 218
Fedor, son of Boris Godunof, 89, 127, 218; proclaimed Tsar, 245; faith in Basmanof, 247; murdered, 258
Fedor, Tsar of Russia, character of, 11, 17, 28, 47, 106; crowned, 17; religiosity of, 47; informally elected King of Poland, 56; illness and death, 104 *seq.*
Fletcher, Dr. Giles, 46, 85, 282

Gabriel, Doctor, 159
Garaburda, 34
Georgia seeks Russian protection, 98
Ghosts, 153, 169–170
Gilbert, Captain, 280
Godunof, Boris Fedorovitch, born, 3; character of, 1, 3, 4–5, 48, 85, 86, 126, 148–149, 168–169, 217; described, 5, 38, 119–120, 219, 220; made boyar, 11; family of, 1, 3–4; illiterate, 4, 132, 153; married to Marya Skuratof, 6; Master of the Horse, 21; "Lord Protector," 22; *Sluga*, 85; Tsar, 120; wealth of, 21–22, 85–86, 125; wisdom of early rule, 22; his court, 37, 93, 131–132, 139–140, 218–219; may have suggested murder of Tsarevitch Dimitry, 62; his character assailed, 75, 79, 88, 149–150, 215, 217, 259; organises military defence of Moscow, 80–81; dealings with sorcerers, magicians, soothsayers, 85, 132, 240–241; receives Persian envoy, 99; behaviour after the death of Tsar Fedor, 108, 110 *seq.;* offered throne by Patriarch, 115; exacts oath of allegiance, 116, 124; feasts the army, 117–118; coronation, 120–123; promises abolition of capital punishment, 122; protects Protestants, 133; punishes Bielsky, 159–160; disperses the Romanof family, 161 *seq.;* secrecy of, 169; suffers from gout, 174, 219, 244; declares the Pretender an impostor, 203; his despair, 241 *seq.;* death, 244; burial, 246, 259; an epitaph, 259–260
———, Dimitry Ivanovitch, 127
———, Gregory, 85
———, Ivan, 249

INDEX

[Godunof], Semyon, 127, 136, 162, 166; considered a new Skuratof, 168; attacked by Cossacks, 181, 239; dreams that Pretender is the authentic Dimitry, 240; starved to death, 258
Golitsin, Vasilly, 249, 258, 275
Golovin, 24; flees to Lithuania, 25; a traitor, 34; pardoned, 87
Gregory XIII, Pope, 193
Gustavus of Sweden, 128, 130–136

Helena, Regent, 105
Henri Quatre, of Navarre, 47, 185, 282
Horsey, Sir Jerome, quoted, 29–30, 71, 119–120; visits Marya, "Queen of Livonia," 40–43; missions to Queen Elizabeth, 42–46; brings English musical instruments to Russia, 46; has news of the murder of the Tsarevitch, 71
Hoscki, Gabriel, 175

Ignatius, Patriarch, 263
India, 100
Irina, Tsaritsa, 17; plot to divorce her, 27; childlessness of, 43–44; birth of a daughter, 46, 88; her husband dies, 107; allegiance sworn to, 108; retires to convent, 108–109; asks brother to take throne, 114; death, 173–174
Ivan the Terrible, character, 1–4, 8 seq., 105; death of, 1, 16; marriage with Marya Nagy, 10; murders his son, 12, 105; chastisement of Novgorod, 73; responsible for the destruction of his own dynasty, 105

Jacob, Doctor, 45, 46
James I, King of England, 217
Jelladin, 100

Jeremiah, Patriarch of Constantinople, 51–52
Jesuits, 193, 194, 196, 210, 216, 220, 250, 274
Job of Rostof, Metropolitan of Moscow, Patriarch of Russia, 29, 49; made Patriarch, 52–53; exonerates Boris Godunof, 70; his enhanced authority, 110; offers throne to Godunof, 114–115; explains Boris' title to the throne, 120; demands arrest of Otrepief, 213; anathematises the Pretender, 220–222; position after death of Boris, 245–246, 256; ceases to be Patriarch, 258
John III, King of Sweden, 57, 130
John, Prince of Denmark, 138 seq.

Kachalof, 63
Katyref-Rostovsky, Prince, 247, 249, 252
Khiva, 101
Khlopko, 172–173
Khorassan, 101
Khozrov, Azi, 99
Khrushchof, 204
Khvorostinin, Prince Dimitry, 58, 79
Kief, 175, 213
Kirghiz, 102
Kleshnin, 62, 68
Kromy, surrenders to Dimitry, 230; siege of, 238, 247, 248
Kursk, 95, 230

Livonia, lost conquests in, 31, 133; "Queen" of, 37 seq.; Boris' designs upon, 133–134
Loyola, 192

Maciejowsky, Cardinal, 267
Magnus, Duke, 39, 135; widow of, 39 seq.
Mahomet III, 98

Margeret, Captain Jacques, 75, 235, 244, 281–282

Maximilian, Emperor, 56

Mniszech, George, Palatine of Sandomir, 180, 183, 184; brings Pretender to Cracow, 190; price of his support, 207–208; blamed, 212; venality of, 268; arrives in Moscow, 269; at court, 270

——, Marina, 184, 206–207; marriage pact, 207–208; receives gifts from Tsar Dimitry, 266; Catholic ceremony of marriage, 267; Orthodox wedding, 269; subsequent adventures, 279

Moravsk, 225–226

More, Sir Thomas, 121

Mosalsky, 258

Moscow, destroyed by Tartars, 7, 76; scene of popular uprisings, 19–20, 255–256, 278; embellished by Godunof, 48; proclaimed the Third Rome, 50; fire of 1591, 75–76; defence against the Tartars, 78–79; fire of 1595, 93; history of, identified with that of Rurik dynasty, 104, 109; famine of 1601–1602, 145 *seq.*; cannibalism in, 146; the rising for Dimitry, 252 *seq.*; jubilation at Restoration, 261

Mstislavsky, Prince Fedor, commands against Sweden, 58; against Tartars, 79; against Dimitry, 230; at coronation of Boris Godunof, 122; forbidden to marry, 168; defeated by Dimitry, 232; victory of, near Sievsk, 234–235; besieges Kromy, 237–238; incurs displeasure of Boris, 238; recalled to Moscow, 245

——, Prince Ivan, 15; sent to appease insurrectionaries, 20–21; pact of friendship with Boris Godunof, 23; shorn as a monk and banished, 25; death, 27

Murmansk, 137

Musical instruments, 46

Nagy, Marya, seventh wife of Ivan the Terrible, marriage, 10; banished to Uglitch, 18–19, 60 *seq.*; persecution of family of, 29, 62, 63, 73, 84; cross-examination of, 69; made a nun, 74; brought before Boris Godunof, 199 *seq.*; refuses to admit son is dead, 201; embraces the Pretender, 161–162; words spoken at sight of murdered Dimitry, 277–278

——, family, at Uglitch, 60 *seq.*; condemned, 70; persecution of, 84; survivors recalled to Moscow, 268

Nashchokin, 96–97

Nijni Novgorod, 21, 112

Novgorod-Seversk, siege of, 228–234

Novodevitchy Convent, 109, 173, 199

—— Monastery, 111, 113

Olesnitsky, 270

Opritchina, 4, 8–9, 15, 158; suggested revival of, 18

Orthodox Church, project of union with Rome, 35; Patriarchate instituted, 47 *seq.*; and Latinism, 265

Ostrog, Prince of, 175

Ostrozhsky, Prince, 213

Otrepief, Grishka, story of, 113, 202–204, 213, 215; excommunicated, 220–222; sought at Putivl, 242; exhibited to people, 250, 263

——, Smirnoi, 204

Patriarchate, instituted, 47 *seq.*

Persia, seeks friendship of Russia, 94 *seq.*

INDEX

Petitioners, 142, 149
Philip, Metropolitan, 3, 5
Pleshcheyef, 254
Poland, peace with, 31 seq., 54 seq.; project of union with Russia, 34–35, 54; election of King of, 56; not responsible for the conspiracy of the Tsarevitch Dimitry, 179; receives the Pretender, 183 seq.; threatened by Godunof, 223; reply to Boris, 242; compared with Russia, 266
Possevin, Anthony, 193
Postnik-Ogarof, 204, 242
Pushkin, Alexander, the poet, 3, 152, 281
Putivl, surrenders to Dimitry, 229; headquarters of rebels, 236, 243

Rangoni, 191
Romanof, Alexander, 107; strangled, 165; Moscow burial, 263
——, Fedor Nikititch, Father Philaret, at deathbed of Tsar Fedor, 106–107; right to throne, 111; origin of family, 161; described, 161; quarrel with Boris, 163; banished and made a monk, 165–166; supposed to have sheltered the Pretender Dimitry, 170; made Metropolitan of Rostof, 263; Patriarch of Russia, 280
——, Ivan, 107, 165, 167; made a boyar, 263
——, Michael, 107, 165
——, Vasilly, 165
Rudolph II, 90
Rurik, dynasty of, 104–105, 109
Rylsk, surrenders to Dimitry, 230; besieged, 236–237

Saltikof, Michael, 138, 229, 249
Sambor, 180, 184, 198, 205, 233
Sapieha, Leon, 32, 33, 177, 212, 242
Savitsky, confessor, 212, 265, 274

Semigradsky, 56
Sergey, St., 46, 142
Shakespeare, quoted, 37, 87, 210; references to, 6, 62, 87
Shchelkalof, Andrew, 90, 91
——, Vasilly, 91, 114, 170
Shchepin, Prince Vasilly, 93
Sheremetief, Fedor, 238, 245
Shuisky, Andrey Ivanovitch, 29
——, Dimitry Ivanovitch, brother-in-law of Boris Godunof, 66; commander of the Kremlin, 80; sent against the Pretender, 237; recalled, 247
——, Ivan Petrovitch, defender of Pskof, 15, 25; conspiracy of, 23–24, 26 seq.; death, 29
——, Vasilly, sent to investigate the supposed murder of Tsarevitch Dimitry, 66 seq.; his position at court, 66; character of, 67; forbidden to marry, 67, 168; claim to throne, 107, 111; questioned regarding Tsarevitch Dimitry, 152; sent to fight Dimitry, 234; recalled to Moscow, 247; declares against Dimitry, 252, 262, 268; declares for Dimitry, 255; condemned to death but reprieved, 263–264; at wedding of Dimitry and Marina, 269; conspiracy of, 268, 272, 275–278; becomes Tsar, 278
Siberia, 22, offered to Mstislavsky in fief, 231
Sievsk, surrenders to Dimitry, 229; battle near, 234–235
Sigizmund II, King of Poland, 8
—— III, King of Poland, 56; King of Sweden, 130; abdicates Swedish throne, 134; character of, 184; hostile to Boris Godunof, 184, 188–189; receives Pretender, 191–192; names price of his support, 197; accused of setting on Pretender,

220–221; allows wedding of Dimitry and Marina, 267
Siisk, Monastery of, 166–167
Simeon, the Tartar, 91; career of, 91–92; blinded, 92; boyars decide to invite to become Tsar, 117; feared by Boris Godunof, 124
Skuratof, Maliuta, 3, 5, 169
——, Marya, Tsaritsa, 6, 66; described, 126; regent, 246; seized by mob, 256; murdered, 258
Smith, Sir Thomas, quoted, 217, 218, 254–255, 256; reference to, 282–283
Smolensk, Polish designs upon, 34, 197, 208–209; fortified, 93
Sorcery, 87, 162, 170, 222, 240
Spies, 91, 113, 126, 238
Stephen, King of Poland, 23, 31, 32, 33, 34, 35; death, 36
Sutupof, Bogdan, 229
Sweden, war with, 57; intrigue against, 130; Dimitry promises Sigizmund III aid to recover, 197

Tamerlane, 101
Tarnowski, 190
Tartars, 76, 77, 78; slave trading by, 78; invasion by, 78 *seq.*, 96; defeated by Godunof, 83; propose to lay waste Lithuania, 96; bogus news of invasion by, 117, 220
Tatef, 226
Teliatevsky, Andrew, 249, 252
Theodosia, Tsarevna, birth of, 46, 88–89
Tiufiakin, Vasilly, 102
Tolstoy, Count Alexey Konstantinovich, dramatic triology of, 284
Tretiakof, 63
Troekurof, Prince Fedor, 33–34
Troitsky Monastery, pilgrimages to, 46, 75, 142–143

Tsaref-Borisof, 158, 160; declares for Pretender, 237
Tula, besieged by Tartars, 79
Turks, 77; Russian overtures to the, 96–98

Uglitch, described, 60; insurrection at, 63; investigation of murders at, 68 *seq.;* chastisement of, 72–73; residence of Gustavus of Sweden, 136

Vasilly III, 105
Veal, 271
Viasemsky, 3
Vladislas, Prince, 267
Vlassyef, 266
Volokhof, Osip, 63
Voronezh, 95; declares for Dimitry, 237
Vyluzgin, 68

Warkotch, 90
Wisniowiecki, Adam, 175 *seq.*, 210, 222, 269
——, Constantine, 179, 183, 185, 210, 269
——, Ursula, 180, 185

Xenia (Godunof), education of, 127; offered in marriage to Duke Gustavus, 128, 134; to Duke John of Denmark, 128, 137; to another Danish prince, 151; to Fedor Mstislavsky, 231; to Peter Basmanof, 239; described, 136–137; fate of, 259

Yelets, 240
Yurief, 15, 22

Zamoyski, John, 179, 180, 188, 189, 190, 209, 212
Zaporozhians, 234, 237
Zinovief, Afanasy, 160
Zvenigorodsky, Prince Andrew, 100–102